T0311674

Contests

Contest theory is an important part of game theory used to analyze different types of contests and conflicts. Traditional microeconomic models focus on situations where property rights are well defined, and agents voluntarily trade rights over goods or produce rights for new goods. However, much less focus has been given to other situations where agents do not trade property rights, but rather fight over them. *Contests: Theory and Applications* presents a state-of-the-art discussion of the economics of contests from the perspective of both core theory and applications. It provides a new approach to standard topics in labor, education, welfare, and development, and introduces areas like voting, industrial organization, mechanism design, sport, and military conflict. Using elementary mathematics, this book provides a versatile framework for navigating this growing area of study and serves as an essential resource for its wide variety of applications in economics and political science.

Carmen Beviá is Full Professor at Universidad de Alicante. Her work appeared in the *Journal of Economic Theory, Economic Theory, Games and Economic Behavior, RAND, International Journal of Industrial Organization,* and *Mathematical Social Sciences.* She is coeditor of the volume *The Political Economy of Democracy* (2008). She has served as associate editor for *Mathematical Social Sciences* and advised four PhD students. She is currently a coeditor of the *Journal of Mathematical Economics.*

Luis Corchón is Emeritus Professor at Universidad Carlos III de Madrid. He is the author of *Theories of Imperfectly Competitive Markets* (1996) and *The Theory of Implementation of Socially Optimal Decisions in Economics* (1996), and coeditor of *Handbook of Game Theory and Industrial Organization* (2018). His work appeared in the *Quarterly Journal of Economics, Journal of Economic Theory, Games and Economic Behavior, RAND, International Journal of Industrial Organization,* and *Economic Theory.* He has served as associate editor for the *Journal of Public Economic Theory, Review of Economic Design, Mathematical Social Sciences,* and *Journal of Dynamics and Games,* and has advised fifteen PhD students.

Contests

Theory and Applications

CARMEN BEVIÁ
Universidad de Alicante

LUIS CORCHÓN
Universidad Carlos III de Madrid

Shaftesbury Road, Cambridge CB2 8EA, United Kingdom

One Liberty Plaza, 20th Floor, New York, NY 10006, USA

477 Williamstown Road, Port Melbourne, VIC 3207, Australia

314–321, 3rd Floor, Plot 3, Splendor Forum, Jasola District Centre, New Delhi – 110025, India

103 Penang Road, #05–06/07, Visioncrest Commercial, Singapore 238467

Cambridge University Press is part of Cambridge University Press & Assessment, a department of the University of Cambridge.

We share the University's mission to contribute to society through the pursuit of education, learning and research at the highest international levels of excellence.

www.cambridge.org
Information on this title: www.cambridge.org/9781009504423
DOI: 10.1017/9781009504409

First published 2024

A catalogue record for this publication is available from the British Library.

A Cataloging-in-Publication data record for this book is available from the Library of Congress.

ISBN 978-1-009-50442-3 Hardback
ISBN 978-1-009-50439-3 Paperback

Contents

Illustrations

Tables

Preface

This book represents the work of eight years and compiles several PhD and advanced undergraduate courses given by us in various institutions around the world, including the Institute for Advanced Studies (Vienna), Centre d'Etudes et de Recherches sur le Développement International (CERDI), University Clermont Auvergne, CNRS, Universidad de Alicante, and Universidad Carlos III, Madrid.

Its short-term goal is to provide a platform for a course in contests suitable for advanced undergraduates and graduate students studying economics, political science, or applied mathematics. Additionally, it can serve as a seminar book for third-year PhD students, providing them an opportunity to present chapters and engage in discussions with faculty on new research ideas. Its long-term goal is to contribute to a larger endeavor, namely to consolidate the candidacy of contests as a field of economics on an equal footing with other recently emerged fields. The role of conflict has been neglected by mainstream economics, and, in our view, it is high time to bring it to the forefront. We acknowledge other excellent earlier books that can complement our efforts, such as the ones by Gil S. Epstein and Shmuel Nitzan (2007), Kai Konrad (2009), and Milan Vojnovic (2015). These three books provide basic coverage of contest theory. The first book focuses on applications of contest theory to public policy, the second on dynamics, and the third on online services applications.

Over the last decade, we have been indebted to many people for comments on our work and for having written wonderful papers that we attempted to summarize in this book the best we can. Among them (in random order), we have interacted frequently with Matthias Dahm, Atsu Amegashie, Sandeep Baliga, Subhasish M. Chowdhury, María Cubel, Christian Ewerhart, Humberto Llavador, Ron Siegel, Qiang Fu, Jingfeng Lu, Magnus Hoffmann, Kai Konrad, Dan Kovenock, Orestis Troumpounis, Matt Jackson, Wolfgang Leininger, Iryna Topolyan, Eric Maskin, Shmuel Nitzan, Tomas Sjöström, Stergios Skaperdas, Santiago Sanchez-Pages, Massimo Morelli, and Karl Wärneryd. Not forgetting our university colleagues Mikhail Drugov, Leandro Prados, David Pérez-Castrillo, Joan María Esteban-Marquillas, Diego Moreno, Philip Denter, Marc Möller, and Boris Ginzburg, to whom we owe so much.

Our debt extends to the authors of the papers summarized in this book and beyond. Unfortunately, they are too numerous to be individually acknowledged here.

We received constructive feedback from five anonymous referees, which made us reconsider certain aspects of the book.

Special thanks are extended to Ratul Lahkar and Ignacio Ortuño-Ortín for their significant contributions to Sections 9.2 and 12.4.2, respectively.

Finally, we are also grateful to our former PhD students Jörg Franke, Ramon Torregrosa, Alexis Vázquez-Sedano, Marco Serena, Anil Yildizparlak, Federico Masera, Michele Rosenberg, and Galina Zudenkova, who also provided us with very good comments and the stimulus that only young people can offer.

Last but not least, we are grateful to the team at Cambridge University Press, including Philip Good, Sable Gravesandy, Chris Hudson, and Dhivyabharathi Elavazhayan, for their guidance and exceptional work in editing this book. Our thanks also extend to Sanjv Kumar Sinha, who compiled the index efficiently.

We also thank the Agencia Estatal de Investigación for their financial support through grants PID2019-108193-100 and PID2020-118022GB-I00/AEI/10.13039/501100011033, and Generalitat Valenciana through grant PROMETEO2021/073.

Book Outline

This book is divided into three parts. Part I serves as an introduction to the field of contests and establishes the fundamental concepts and tools necessary for the subsequent applications.

In Chapter 1, the concept of a contest is introduced, with examples such as political competition, litigation, wars, lobbying, awarding a prize or contract, sports, and patent races. These examples demonstrate the wide range of applications of contests, and prepare the reader for the consideration of contests as a field of study in their own right. Additionally, the main game theoretical concepts and the primary tool of this field, the Contest Success Function (CSF), are presented. The CSF, given the expenses/efforts/investments of the contestants, yields the probabilities that the contestants will win the contest or, in the case of a shared prize, the shares of the prize.

In Chapter 2, the main CSFs used in the literature are reviewed and their basic properties are explored. Different CSFs yield different games and outcomes, so it is essential to understand the differences between what is embedded in each CSF. In some cases, a little extra effort wins the field, as in racing, while in others, no matter the expense, all contestants receive a positive probability of getting a positive share, as in voting with captive voters. In others, like soccer and some armed conflicts, the probability of winning is proportional to the relative expenses. This chapter also begins an analysis of the existence and properties of a Nash equilibrium in contest games, either with identical contestants or, in the context of a couple of CSFs, with two contestants.

Chapter 3 presents the main results and properties of equilibria in contests with heterogeneous contestants. This heterogeneity may be caused by different valuations of the prize, different costs of effort, or efforts being asymmetrically treated in the CSF. In the presence of such heterogeneities, it is shown that some contestants may remain inactive in equilibrium. The chapter concludes with an overview of the empirical estimations of CSFs that can be found in the literature, drawing data from various sources such as real or virtual battlefields and laboratory-generated data.

In Chapters 2 and 3, the CSF is presented as a "black box" that encapsulates the rules and workings of the contest. Chapter 4 explains the mechanisms behind this black box. This could include how efforts may translate, with some uncertainty, into performance, or a planner with given objectives such as designing a contest on television or procuring inputs for a firm. Additionally, the outcome of a conflict may be negotiated or decided by a jury once claims have been presented. Finally, the chapter explores the basic properties that a contest must have, such as the relationship between effort and probability of winning, and how these properties translate into different CSFs. This is known as the axiomatic approach. These different approaches are able to recover some of the main CSFs already presented in the previous chapter.

Part II expands upon in several directions the basic model presented in Part I.

Chapter 5 explores the concept of contests among groups and addresses the issue of free riding within each group as well as the relative effectiveness of large and small groups. Additionally, it addresses the question of how groups divide the spoils of victory and the impact of such divisions on the behavior of contestants. The literature on group contests is influenced by the seminal work of Mancur Olson in his book *The Logic of Collective Action: Public Goods and the Theory of Groups*, published in 1965. Olson posits that politically stable societies tend to accumulate interest groups over time, which infiltrate governments and shape policies to serve their interests, hindering economic growth. The defeat of Germany and Japan in World War II resulted in the devastation of the interest groups surrounding the Nazi party and the Japanese Emperor. Conversely, the interest groups in the United Kingdom and the United States not only survived but also gained prestige for their contribution to victory. This led to the proliferation of crony capitalism in Anglo-Saxon democracies. The question is how these small interest groups can exert such decisive influence. Olson posits that the key factor is the concept of "free riding of effort" in large decentralized groups. He conjectures that small decentralized groups exert more aggregate effort than large groups, which explains their success. However, as discussed within this chapter, the validity of this assumption is contingent upon the nature of the prize, whether it is a private or public good, and the nature of the costs associated with exerting effort.

Chapter 6 examines an alternative strategy for increasing the chances of winning in contests, namely sabotage. The chapter provides examples of sabotage in various contexts such as the Luddite movement, the workplace, and political campaigns. It delves into the rational motives for sabotage and studies the determinants of such actions and the individuals or groups that are more likely to be targeted. Contests highly responsive to efforts may create a significant incentive for sabotage, leading to a trade-off between meritocracy and sabotage.

Chapter 7 explores contests that occur in stages, as opposed to the one-shot contests analyzed in previous chapters. Examples of one-shot contests include decisive battles in war and final matches in sports. However, some contests are inherently dynamic, such as lengthy wars, electoral competitions, patent races, sports leagues, and advertising campaigns. Dynamic contest theory is still a developing field, and this chapter focuses on analyzing specific examples of dynamic contests, including Endogenous Timing Contests (where contestants choose when to compete), Elimination Contests (where contestants compete and the winner advances to the next stage), Races (where the first contestant to achieve a certain number of victories wins), Contests with Investments (where current efforts impact future outcomes), and Repeated Contests (where contestants compete repeatedly in the same contest).

Chapter 8 delves into the complexities introduced by asymmetric information, where some contestants possess more information than others, or neither of the contestants has complete information about the characteristics of the others. The chapter examines contests in which the true common value of the prize may be unknown to certain contestants, such as an incumbent having a better understanding of the value of office than a challenger, or a current resource owner having more information about its true value than potential entrants. It also examines situations where no contestant has complete information about the value assigned for each contestant to the prize, such as companies competing to develop a new product or technology. Each company knows its own valuation of the potential market but does not know the competitor's valuation. The chapter also analyzes the existence and properties of equilibrium and other related questions, such as the following: How do outcomes in complete and incomplete information scenarios compare? Should a well-informed planner disclose information to maximize total effort in a contest involving both informed and uninformed contestants?

Part III applies the models and frameworks presented in previous chapters to various scenarios. This part aims to demonstrate the applicability and usefulness of the models in understanding and analyzing a range of different contests. The chapters in this part present specific examples, highlighting the key insights and findings that can be derived from the application of the contest models to these examples.

In Chapter 9, we explore extensions to the basic model, focusing on Draws, Large Contests, and Entry. Previous chapters assumed contests had one winner, with all others classified as losers. However, alternative outcomes like draws are possible. Draws occur when contestants have equal points or the outcome is inconclusive, as in certain soccer matches, chess games, or wars without a clear winner. They can also happen when prizes are shared or not awarded, like some Nobel Prizes or R&D contests. The chapter examines these extensions, along with equilibrium existence. We display an estimation of a CSF with draws with data from European soccer leagues, which is close to one maximizing aggregate effort. In the section on Large Contests, we study scenarios where each contestant feels insignificant in a mass of contestants, such as in official exams, and address the contest as an individual decision problem. Lastly, we discuss complications when contestants can choose among alternative contests. Here, equilibrium existence is not always guaranteed but can occur in specific instances.

In Chapter 10, contest models are utilized to illuminate crucial elements of traditional economic problems. These include competition for surplus within divisionalized firms, where inefficient divisions often dominate efficient ones; the significant expenses required to attain a monopoly position, including potentially bribing public officials for the allocation of monopoly rights; and the expenses incurred in obtaining property rights that, once secured (sometimes by violent and costly means), will be efficiently exchanged in the marketplace. In the last two cases, these expenses are so substantial that they might leave no social surplus. Additionally, the cost of political campaigns, in which factions compete for the vote to control a portion or entirety of the public sector through convincing voters of the correct choice, is also examined. Overall, it is shown that contests introduce a substantial and previously unnoticed welfare cost to the traditional issues studied, thereby complementing the existing literature on the subject.

Chapter 11 examines the role of institutions. Specifically, it explores how institutions can be undermined by rent-seeking activities that bias decision-making toward suboptimal alternatives and consume valuable resources. Furthermore, this erosion of institutions leads to a decline, or at best stagnation, in the standard of living of society by diverting a significant portion of productive forces. The chapter presents two models of war in which the armed conflict is produced by resource inequality (the book also acknowledges other types of causes of war like ethnic, religious, etc.) and offers recommendations on how to prevent them. Specifically, a one-sided transfer of resources from wealthy to less developed countries may provide incentives for peace even in the absence of enforceable agreements.

In the final chapter of the book, Chapter 12, the optimal properties of contests from a social perspective are outlined. It presents three main criteria for evaluating contests from a social welfare standpoint by considering the total effort, average effort, and effort of the contest winner. Additionally, the chapter delves into the discussion of how to organize different simultaneous contests and how free entry in several exclusive contests leads to social welfare maximization. Furthermore, the chapter examines the social optimality of aggregating local contests – limited to participants from specific areas, like EU countries – into a larger, open contest, such as one based in Brussels. Finally, the chapter provides a new perspective on two significant issues, compulsory education and affirmative action, by illustrating how active public policies can improve social welfare.

The book ends with a summary of the main takeaways delivered by the 12 chapters.

How to Use This Book

The reading of this book assumes knowledge of basic concepts of intermediate microeconomics and game theory, such as normal and extensive form games, Nash equilibrium, subgame perfection, infinitely repeated games, and Bayesian equilibrium. These topics are typically covered in an introductory game theory course at a level that is appropriate for reading this book.

The contents of this book are mostly self-referential. This has both positive and negative consequences. On the positive side, the reader will find most of the main results in the field of contests in the same volume with the same notation. On the negative side, since we did not want to repeat what was already written, some topics may not be fully understood without knowledge from previous chapters. In this sense, we recommend that the reader not skip the following sections of Chapters 1, 2, and 3.

Chapter 1: Sections 1.1 to 1.5.

Chapter 2: Sections 2.1 to 2.5.

Chapter 3: Sections 3.1 to 3.5.

These sections constitute the backbone of the book. It would be difficult to fully benefit from the chapters that follow without a good understanding of the material there. Curious readers may also read Chapter 4 if they want to know the inner workings of the machine. To be familiar with the workings of the machine, the sections mentioned above would suffice.

At the end of every chapter, a list of exercises is included to assist readers in comprehending the key concepts and references of the subject matter. When reading a book, it is common to become engrossed in the details and lose sight of the overall context. Exercises are beneficial in consolidating readers' comprehension of the material and demonstrating how the different concepts interconnect.

Exercises also serve as a training tool for readers to apply the concepts and references they have learned to real-world situations. By working through exercises, readers can practice problem-solving and critical thinking skills, which are essential for success in any field.

In addition, exercises help readers to work out the main references in the field. By requiring readers to consult the primary literature, exercises encourage readers to explore the original sources and gain a deeper understanding of the concepts and theories presented in the book.

Part I

Foundations

1 An Introduction to Contests

Contests are a prevalent aspect of everyday life, where multiple agents compete against each other by investing valuable resources, such as effort, time, or money, to win a prize. Examples of contests can be seen in various scenarios such as securing a taxi by occupying a favorable location, making an informed decision in choosing a university, publishing a scholarly article, or vying for a Michelin star as a chef. And, sporting teams participate in contests to win major events like the Super Bowl in American football, the Champions League in soccer, the World Series in baseball, or the NBA Finals in basketball. Furthermore, nations also engage in contests, either through legal or through illegal means, to attain control over territory or resources.

But contests not only intrude in our daily lives. They are essential to understanding how the world looks. Why is China communist? And Cuba? Why have countries like Germany and Japan, which previously lacked a strong democratic tradition, transitioned into functioning democracies? Why are most countries close to Russia democracies but Russia is not? And why was Russia communist? Why is English the predominant language north of El Paso, while Spanish and Portuguese are commonly spoken to the south of El Paso? Why do so many countries in America, Africa, and Asia resent their recent past?

The answers to these questions stem from historical conflicts – be they violent or more "cold" in nature – invasions, battles, or contests that ultimately terminated previous regimes and instituted new ones. Contests are the blood and the sap going across history.

Standard economic theory has overlooked the role of contests as an allocation mechanism. This is evident, e.g., in the absence of contests in the conventional analysis of natural resources, which focuses on intertemporal optimal allocation, perfect competition, monopoly, and externalities, among other important topics. It is important to note that standard economic theory provides valuable insights into the efficiency and limitations of markets and central planning. However, it is limited in scope, as it does not account for the importance of contests, especially in the context of natural resource allocation, which is often of interest to powerful nations, leading to contests that can be peaceful or violent. Broadly speaking, standard economic theory takes initial endowments as given while contest theory focuses on how these endowments are obtained and or preserved.

In this chapter, we introduce the concept of a contest. We provide examples of contests such as political competition, litigation, wars, lobbying, awarding a prize or contract, sports, and patent races. Despite their apparent differences, these examples share the same structure. We present our primary tool, the Contest Success Function (CSF). The CSF, given the expenses/efforts/investments of the contestants, yields the probabilities that the contestants will win the contest or, in the case of a shared prize, the shares of the prize. With this concept in hand, we define strategies (efforts/investments) and payoffs, the latter being the expected return of effort minus the cost of effort. Then, we arrive at our main game theoretical tool, namely Nash equilibrium. The chapter ends by discussing some extensions that will and some that will not be pursued in the main text.

1.1   Contests in the Early Economic Literature

Karl Marx (1818–1883) was one of the early thinkers who recognized the significance of contests in economic analysis.[1] He believed that conflict was a crucial factor in understanding both history and the economy, and he developed his system around the notion that the struggle for the appropriation of the surplus was the driving force behind the succession of different modes of production. Marx made substantial efforts to support his claims with both empirical evidence and theoretical models, famously stating in Capital (1867) that "[i]n actual history, it is notorious that conquest, enslavement, robbery, murder, briefly force, play the great part" (p. 507). However, by the time he published his seminal work, his methods, particularly his labor value theory, had become outdated.

Mikhail Pavlovich Osipov (1859–?), a Russian general and topographer, and the engineer Frederik Lanchester (1868–1946) published in 1915–1916 the first mathematical model of war between two armies. The model postulates that the losses suffered by an army during a specific period of time are proportional to the strength of its adversary.

In 1967, Gordon Tullock (1922–2014) published a seminal paper which challenged the conventional analysis of the welfare losses caused by monopolies. Tullock argued that this analysis (see, e.g., Tirole, 1988, chapter 1) underestimated the losses by failing to account for the ways in which monopolies were established, such as through patent litigation (like Alexander Graham Bell, who faced 600 lawsuits in securing his telephone patent), through bribery, or by forcing favorable legislation. Tullock posited that the competitive struggle to secure a monopoly position leads to the dilapidation of most monopoly profits, thus rendering monopoly profits a form of welfare loss. Unfortunately, the lack of publication in a prominent journal limited Tullock's impact and recognition for this contribution (Tullock, 2003).

The next contribution was by Anne Krueger (1934–) in 1974. She found that the explanation of foreign trade policies, in particular tariffs, is not in the standard reasons

---

[1] Marx was the first prominent economist for whom the conflict was key to understanding history. But before him many writers, beginning, at least in classical Greece, studied the causes and consequences of war and conflicts; see Vela Tejada, 2004. In the Renaissance, these studies were revitalized following in the footsteps of Machiavelli (1532).

found in International Trade manuals, but in what she called rent-seeking, i.e., the effort of domestic producers to limit foreign competition by pushing for laws and regulations that protect the domestic market.[2]

Edward Lazear (1948–) and Sherwin Rosen (1938–2001) in 1981 analyzed a ranking-based payment scheme, which awards prizes to both the winners and the losers of labor market contests. In this scheme, earnings are determined by the relative ranking of contestants rather than by the level of output produced during a particular contest. As a result, salaries are not tied to individual performance, as prizes are predetermined. This approach has been applied in the design of executive compensation packages as a means of providing performance-based incentives.

Finally, Gary Becker (1930–2014) studied lobbying in his 1983 paper. Until then, the impact of lobbies on resource allocation was ignored. Income redistribution was seen as a result of marginal productivity and government intervention, which transfers wealth from the rich to the poor. While government intervention does result in a more equal distribution of income, as indicated by the Gini coefficient before and after taxes,[3] lobbying also plays a role in redistributing income, often benefiting organized groups over unorganized ones.

With this background knowledge, we are now equipped to further examine contests in-depth.

1.2 Examples

At the outset of this chapter, we presented several examples to illustrate the reasons behind our interest in contests. It is now time to be more systematic and clearly define the scope and focus of our study.

(1) **Political competition**: This refers to the competition between political parties to attain political office through various means such as political campaigns, vote buying, etc.

(2) **Litigation/War**: This refers to the situation where two individuals or nations engage in a competition for resources, land, or similar assets. This competition often involves the allocation of significant resources toward the hiring of lawyers, building armies, etc.[4]

(3) **Lobbying**: This refers to the competition for a specific public policy outcome, such as the allocation of subsidies, regulations, or laws. Contestants in this competition often employ strategies such as bribery, advertising, and similar efforts to influence the outcome.

---

[2] In their book *Interest Groups and Trade Policy*, Grossman and Helpman (2002) examine the role of lobbying and rent-seeking in shaping international trade flows and trade agreements.

[3] See, e.g., https://ourworldindata.org/grapher/inequality-of-incomes-before-and-after-taxes-and-transfers-scatter

[4] For contests on property rights, see Ekelund, Street, and Tollinson (1997). And for legal contests, see Farmer and Pecorino (1999).

Table 1.1 Table of contest examples: prizes and required efforts or investments

Contest	Prize	Effort/Investment	Example
Politics	Office	Political campaigns/Vote buying	Elections
Litigation	Stake	Lawyers	Inheritance/Resource
War	Resources	Military expenses	Civil/World Wars
Lobby	Law, contract	Ads/Bribes	Regulation/Trade policy
Beauty C	Prize	Build-up	TV/Civil servants
Sports	League, Cup	Hiring expenses/Training	Soccer/Basket
R&D	Patent/Grant	R&D expenses	Drugs/Technology

(4) **Awarding a prize/contract**: This refers to the competition for a prize or contract, such as the Nobel Prize or the awarding of a procurement contract. Contestants in these competitions often invest effort, incur expenses related to bribery, or incur costs associated with training, such as hiring personal coaches, etc.

(5) **Sports**: This refers to athletic competitions such as tennis, the Olympic games, soccer, basketball, etc. Participants – whether individuals, teams, or nations – compete to win a contest and expenses include team budgets.[5]

(6) **Patent race**: This refers to a competition among multiple firms or researchers to secure a patent or grant for an invention. Competition can lead to significant investment in research and development (R&D).[6]

See Table 1.1 for more details.

To conclude this section, it is worth mentioning that animals also engage in contests for resources such as territory, food, and mating. This interesting topic will not be covered in this book, but those interested can consult Hardy and Briffa (2013) for more information.

1.3   The Main Concept

We are ready to offer a more synthetic definition of our field of study.

DEFINITION 1.1   *A contest refers to a scenario where multiple agents compete to attain a prize or prizes, through the expenditure of costly actions such as effort or investments.*

In other words, a contest is the allocation of scarce resources through a fight!

It is time to delve into the distinction between contests and standard microeconomics. Standard microeconomics examines scenarios where property rights are clearly defined and agents voluntarily exchange rights over goods or produce rights for new goods. This approach has produced significant insights into market and planning processes, including the proof of the existence and efficiency of

---

[5] See Szymanski (2003) for a comprehensive overview of the economic design in sports contests.

[6] For the relationship of innovation and contests, see Baye and Hoppe (2003).

perfect competition, the study of the causes and consequences of international trade, the role of prices as information providers, the design of incentive-compatible mechanisms, and the understanding of imperfectly competitive markets. However, standard microeconomics does not encompass situations in which agents do not trade property rights but instead compete for property rights. These scenarios are referred to as contests. As noted by Jack Hirshleifer (1925–2005), a prominent early contributor to contest theory, contests are *The Dark Side of the Force* (1994).

Given its strategic nature, contest theory is a branch of the expansive field of game theory, along with industrial organization, political economy, and mechanism design, among others. It is a distinct mechanism for resource allocation, separate from market and authority mechanisms.

1.4 Contest as a Normal Form Game

Let n be the number of contestants. Each contestant exerts effort, $g_i \in \mathbb{R}_+$, to win a prize. In some applications, like sports or wars, g_i is the monetary investment made by contestant i. We will refer to g_i as the effort or investment of contestant i indistinctly. The value of the prize for each contestant is V_i. There are two possible interpretations of a contest, either the prize is indivisible and is awarded to contestant i with probability p_i or the prize is divisible and each contestant, say i, receives a share p_i of the prize.[7] The function that determines p_i as a function of efforts, $\mathbf{g} = (g_1, \ldots, g_n)$, is called the Contest Success Function (CSF from now on).[8] Mathematically,

$$p_i : \mathbb{R}_+^n \to [0, 1]$$

with $\sum_i p_i(\mathbf{g}) = 1$ in most of the contests studied in this book.[9] This concept is due to Tullock (1980). It is the tool that allows a unified treatment of the various examples of contests that we have seen so far. The CSF is increasing in g_i and decreasing in g_j for all $j \neq i$. Additionally, sometimes CSFs are assumed quasiconcave or concave in g_i and continuous in $\mathbf{g}$ whenever $\mathbf{g} > 0$.

In most of this book, we will assume that payoffs for each contestant i are additively separable in expected revenue, $p_i(\mathbf{g})V_i$, and cost, $c_i(g_i)$,

$$\pi_i(\mathbf{g}) = p_i(\mathbf{g})V_i - c_i(g_i). \tag{1.1}$$

A payoff function like (1.1) is the building block of a **Contest Game** in which efforts are the strategies. For simplicity, we will refer to a contest game as a contest. We usually assume that costs are linear in effort, $c_i(g_i) = g_i$.

Given that no rational contestant will make a costly effort greater than the value of the prize, we assume that $c_i(g_i) \in [0, V_i]$.

---

[7] These two interpretations can be applied generally and interchangeably without impacting the strategic behavior of agents or payoffs. However, there are cases where differences arise, especially in dynamic games with the possibility of bankruptcy. For more details, refer to Exercise 7.20.

[8] We write vectors in bold letters.

[9] Notable exceptions include contests with draws, which are examined in Chapter 9.

Our equilibrium concept was defined by John Nash (1928–2015) in a seminal paper (Nash, 1950a). It is a generalization of a previous idea due to Agustin A. Cournot (1801–1877) in a book published in 1838.

DEFINITION 1.2   *A vector of efforts,* $\mathbf{g} = (g_1^*, ..., g_i^*, ..., g_n^*)$, *is a Nash equilibrium if*

$$\pi_i(g_i^*, \mathbf{g}_{-i}^*) \geq \pi_i(g_i, \mathbf{g}_{-i}^*) \; \forall g_i \in \mathbb{R}_+, \; i \in \{1, ..., n\},$$

where $\mathbf{g}_{-i}$ is a list of efforts of all contestants minus i.

Standard arguments showing the existence of a Nash equilibrium in pure strategies cannot be applied here because the CSF in some cases is discontinuous in $\mathbf{g}$, or payoffs are not quasiconcave. In Chapters 2 and 3, we will present several approaches to the existence of equilibrium.

Assuming differentiability, the first-order condition of payoff maximization for contestant i is

$$\frac{\partial p_i(\mathbf{g})}{\partial g_i} V_i - \frac{\partial c_i(g_i)}{\partial g_i} = 0.$$

This equation is valuable as, in many cases, a candidate equilibrium can be calculated directly from the first-order condition by assuming a specific form for the costs and the CSF. The final step is to verify that this candidate indeed maximizes payoffs for each contestant.

1.5   Extensions

In this book, the basic model introduced in this chapter will be expanded to incorporate intergroup contests (Chapter 5), sabotage (Chapter 6), dynamic contests (Chapter 7), asymmetric information (Chapter 8), and contests with draws large contests and entry in contests (Chapter 9).

There are numerous other extensions to the basic model that are not covered in this book but are nonetheless significant. For example:

(1) **Several prizes**

In many contests, there are prizes for contestants other than the winner. For instance, in the Olympic games, the three best athletes in a competition receive medals and those who compete in the final receive diplomas. In soccer finals, there is a monetary prize for the runner-up, and so on. The basic model presented in this book can be understood as considering two prizes, with the second prize normalized to zero. Chapter 9 explores contests that may end in a draw, such as some wars, trials, or sports matches, with the draw representing a distinct prize. Nevertheless, the literature on contests with multiple prizes is extensive. Readers interested in further knowledge can consult the comprehensive reviews by Sisak (2009) and Fu and Wu (2019).

(2) **Multidimensional effort**

In professional sports, effort encompasses not only the physical exertion of the athletes on the field but also the investments made by clubs to recruit talented players, construct facilities, and so forth. Additionally, firms engage in various forms of effort such as funding R&D and incurring legal expenses for rent-seeking and patent protection. The design of contests with multidimensional effort is explored by Clark and Konrad (2007) and by Arbatskaya and Mialon (2010), among others. Faria et al. (2014) provides an application of this concept in the context of the US telephone market.

(3) **Variable prize**

The value of a prize may fluctuate in response to the level of effort exerted during the contest. This is due to contestants' subjective valuation of the prize, which may be affected by the difficulty of winning, as well as the monetization of substantial effort by the contest organizer through higher admission fees. Furthermore, investments made by contestants can increase the value of the prize, thereby enhancing its quality. This phenomenon has been studied by Chung (1996) and Amegashie (1999a). When the prize is a function that increases with effort, it can be viewed as output, and the corresponding problem is referred to as "Cooperative Production." This term was first coined by Sen (1966) and was inspired by an early paper by Ward (1958). A comprehensive review of this subject can be found in Beviá and Corchón (2018).

(4) **The role of contests in the philanthropic industry**

Philanthropists and governments have used prizes to drive the best possible philanthropic project. These prizes are meant to correct some market or societal failures. Prizes may be educational (Fulbright, Rhodes), artistic (literary, musical, painting), scientific (Nobel, Abel, Fields), or just aimed to foster human values (justice, fraternity, peace, freedom, equality, etc.). The directory of awards, honors, and prizes lists about 30,000 worldwide, but they are only the tip of the iceberg since there are literally millions of small prizes and awards that are important for both donors and recipients like Doctor Honoris Causae for some department or university. The interested reader may consult the data and the analysis offered by McKinsey & Company (2009).

2   Contest Success Functions

As discussed in Chapter 1, Contest Theory heavily relies on Game Theory, for the time being on Nash equilibrium, to make predictions. In determining the properties of the equilibrium and ultimately the expected outcomes of a contest, the form of the contest success function (CSF) plays a crucial role. As a result, it is imperative to be cautious in selecting an appropriate CSF to model a contest.

This chapter presents a comprehensive review of the primary CSFs utilized in the literature and investigates their fundamental properties. Additionally, we provide a preliminary analysis of the existence and properties of the Nash equilibrium with various CSFs in a contest game. A more thorough examination of the existence of equilibrium in technically demanding cases is reserved for Chapter 3.

The origin of the functional forms defining the CSFs is not always clear, as tractability is not the sole consideration. In Chapter 4, we aim to address the question of understanding the microfoundations of the CSFs used in the literature. We will see that these microfoundations, sometimes, suggest new CSFs!

Throughout this chapter and most of the book, we assume that $c_i(g_i) = g_i$, and thus the payoff for each contestant i is given by

$$\pi_i(\mathbf{g}) = p_i(\mathbf{g})V_i - g_i.$$

2.1   All Pay Auction (Hillman and Riley, 1989)

We begin by assuming that the prize is awarded through an auction in which the highest bid wins. In other words, the contestant who exerts the greatest effort wins the prize with a probability one. In the event of a tie between the largest efforts, a lottery is held to determine the winner. Formally, the following rules for allocating the prize apply. Let K be the set of agents with maximal effort, i.e., if $i, j \in K$, $g_i = g_j$ and $g_i > g_l$ for all $l \notin K$. Then

(i) If $g_i \in K$, $p_i = 1/\#K$, where $\#K$ denotes the cardinality of the set K.
(ii) If $g_l \notin K$, $p_l = 0$.

The All Pay Auction yields a contest in which the prize is awarded through an auction process, but unlike traditional auctions, all participants are required to pay regardless of whether they win or not, hence the term "all pay." This type of auction represents a reverse form of Bertrand competition, where instead of the firm offering the lowest price winning the entire demand, the prize is awarded to the participant with the highest bid.

All Pay Auction models are characterized by intense competition, where even a small increase in effort can make a significant difference. Examples of the latter are the final sprint in an athletic competition or the Tour de France, where the time difference between the winner and the 10th place finisher may be as little as 0.4%.[1]

The All Pay Auction has no equilibrium in pure strategies. Suppose that $\mathbf{g}$ is such that g_i is the unique largest effort. Then $g_i - \varepsilon$ with ε sufficiently small also wins the prize and reduces costs, so there is a profitable deviation and no equilibrium in pure strategies with this characteristic is possible. Suppose now that $\mathbf{g}$ is such that there are, at least, two contestants i and j with the largest effort. Clearly $g_i < V_i$. By playing $g_i + \epsilon$ she wins the prize for sure with, almost, the same cost. So, again, we have a profitable deviation.

When there is no equilibrium in pure strategies, Game Theory recommends looking for an equilibrium in mixed strategies.[2] Here we just prove that such equilibrium exists in the case of two contestants.

PROPOSITION 2.1 *Suppose an All Pay Auction with $n = 2$ and $V_1 \geq V_2$. An equilibrium in mixed strategies exists where both contestants randomize on $[0, V_2]$ according to the following distribution functions:*

$$F_1(g_1) = \frac{g_1}{V_2}, \tag{2.1}$$

$$F_2(g_2) = \frac{g_2}{V_1} + 1 - \frac{V_2}{V_1}. \tag{2.2}$$

Proof First note that no contestant would expend more than the value of the prize. Consequently, there is no gain for contestant 1 to expend more than V_2. For each contestant, any g_i in the support has to be optimal. If g_i is in the support of contestant i, the probability of winning, given the mixed strategy of contestant j, is the probability that $g_j < g_i$, i.e., $F_j(g_i)$. The payoff for contestant i is $F_j(g_i)V_i - g_i$. So, g_i is optimal if $V_i dF_j(g_i)/dg_i = 1$. Integrating both sides of this equation, we obtain $F_j(g_i) = g_i/V_i + K_j$, where K_j is a constant. For contestant 1, $F_1(V_2) = 1$, thus $K_1 = 0$. For contestant 2, $F_2(V_2) = 1 = V_2/V_1 + K_2$, thus $K_2 = 1 - V_2/V_1$. $\qquad\square$

In equilibrium, the expected effort for contestants are

$$Eg_1 = \int_0^{V_2} g_1 \frac{1}{V_2} dg_1 = \left[\frac{g_1^2}{2V_2} \right]_0^{V_2} = \frac{V_2^2}{2V_2} = \frac{V_2}{2},$$

---

[1] In the 2021 Tour de France, the winner Tadej Pogačar spent a total of 83 hours on the road. The difference between his time and that of the runner-up was 5 minutes, representing a difference of 0.1% of the winner's time. Meanwhile, the difference between his time and that of the 10th place finisher was approximately 18 minutes, equating to a difference of 0.36%.

[2] For a discussion on this equilibrium concept, the reader may refer to textbooks on Game Theory, such as Fudenberg and Tirole (1991) or Binmore (1991).

$$Eg_2 = \int_0^{V_2} g_2 \frac{1}{V_1} dg_2 = \left[\frac{g_2^2}{2V_1}\right]_0^{V_2} = \frac{V_2^2}{2V_1}.$$

Each contestant expends a fraction $V_2/2V_1$ of their valuation. The ranking of efforts is the same as the ranking of valuations. Moreover, the ratio between expected efforts matches exactly the ratio of valuations. Effort for contestant 2 is increasing in her valuation (the more you like the prize, the harder you fight for it) and decreasing in the valuation of contestant 1. However, the effort of contestant 1 depends only on the valuation of contestant 2 and it is increasing. This is because contestant 1 expects a tougher fight with contestants whose valuations are closer to hers and adjusts her effort accordingly. Total expected effort is given by

$$Eg_1 + Eg_2 = \frac{V_2}{2}\left(1 + \frac{V_2}{V_1}\right).$$

Note that when both contestants have identical valuations, the sum of expected expenses equals the value of the prize. In the parlance of Tullock (1980), rents are completely dissipated.

In equilibrium, all efforts in the support of the mixed strategy should give the same payoff. Hence, given $g_1^* \in [0, V_2]$, payoff for contestant 1 is

$$\pi_1(g_1^*) = F_2(g_1^*)V_1 - g_1^* = \left(\frac{g_1^*}{V_1} + 1 - \frac{V_2}{V_1}\right)V_1 - g_1^* = V_1 - V_2.$$

And similarly for contestant 2, given $g_2^* \in [0, V_2]$,

$$\pi_2(g_2^*) = F_1(g_2^*)V_2 - g_2^* = \frac{g_2^*}{V_2}V_2 - g_2^* = 0.$$

Note that contestant 1 can obtain the prize for sure by making an effort infinitesimally above V_2. Thus, the payoff for contestant 1 in equilibrium is $\pi_1(g^*) = V_1 - V_2$. Given this, contestant 2 cannot expect to obtain more than zero. Continuing the comparison between this model and Bertrand's, it becomes evident that in both models, the weaker competitor (in this case, the contestant with a lower valuation, and in Bertrand's model, the firm with higher costs) earns no profit. If both competitors are identical, both earn zero profit. This intense competition, where even a small difference can have a significant impact, undermines the profits of underdogs.

The All Pay Auction with more than two contestants is analyzed in Chapter 3, Section 3.5.

2.2   Difference CSF (Hirshleifer, 1989)

In the Difference CSF, the probability of winning is based on the difference between efforts. As stated by its originator, "this CSF captures the tremendous advantage of being slightly stronger than one's opponent" (Hirshleifer, 1991, p. 131).

Assuming $n = 2$, the difference CSF is written as

$$p_1(\mathbf{g}) = F_1(g_1 - g_2), \ p_2(\mathbf{g}) = 1 - F_1(g_1 - g_2), \tag{2.3}$$

where F_1 is a strictly increasing function with a range in $[0, 1]$. Notice that this CSF is akin to the All Pay Auction. In fact, when $n = 2$, it can be regarded as a generalization of the All Pay Auction where $F_i(a) = 1$ if $a > 0$, $F_i(a) = 0$ if $a < 0$, and $F_i(a) = 0.5$ if $a = 0$.

In contests with more than two contestants, the previous definition is easily generalized. Let $M(\mathbf{g}_{-i})$ be a measure of the average of the efforts made by all contestants but i. This measure can be the arithmetic average (i.e., the sum of efforts divided by $n - 1$), the geometric average (the $n - 1$ root of the multiplication of efforts), the maximum effort made by competitors, etc. Then

$$p_i(\mathbf{g}) = F_i(g_i - M(\mathbf{g}_{-i})), \ i \in \{1, 2, \ldots, n\}.$$

When $n = 2$ and $M(g_j) = g_j$, we have (2.3).

Variations of this CSF were proposed by Baik (1998) and Che and Gale (2000). The first author assumes the following:

$$p_1(\mathbf{g}) = F_1(g_1 - \sigma g_2) \text{ and } p_2(\mathbf{g}) = 1 - p_1(\mathbf{g}), \text{ with } \sigma > 0,$$

which, for $\sigma = 1$, collapses (2.3).

Che and Gale (2000) proposed a special non-smooth form of (2.3):

$$p_1(\mathbf{g}) = \max \left\{ \min \left\{ \frac{1}{2} + s(g_1 - g_2), 1 \right\}, 0 \right\} \text{ and } p_2(\mathbf{g}) = 1 - p_1(\mathbf{g}). \tag{2.4}$$

The number s measures how responsive the probability of winning is to the difference of efforts. When $s = 0$, this CSF is a pure lottery. When $s \to \infty$, the difference of efforts is paramount and the CSF becomes the All Pay Auction in which the highest bidder takes it all.

A defining feature of the Difference CSF, when F is differentiable, is that, in any equilibrium in pure strategies, only the contestant with the highest valuation exerts a positive effort. To see this in a very simple way, let $F'(g_1 - g_2)$ be the derivative of $F(g_1 - g_2)$. Let $V_1 > V_2$. Suppose both contestants exert positive effort. Since $p_2(\mathbf{g}) = 1 - p_1(\mathbf{g})$, and the first-order conditions of payoff maximization hold with equality for both contestants, we have that

$$F_1'(g_1 - g_2)V_1 - 1 = 0 \text{ and } - F_1'(g_1 - g_2)V_2 - 1 = 0,$$

which is a contradiction.

In other cases, such as with the CSF outlined in (2.4), a pure strategy equilibrium does not exist, and instead, the equilibrium is in mixed strategies (see Che and Gale, 2000).

A drawback of the Difference CSF is that it is not unit-independent. As a result, in the Che and Gale CSF, the parameter s must be adjusted to the units used to measure the difference $g_1 - g_2$, to keep the impact of the difference constant.

A comprehensive analysis with heterogeneous contestants for the following alternative difference CSF

$$p_i(\mathbf{g}) = \frac{1}{\sum_{j=1}^{n} \exp(\alpha(g_j - g_i))} = \frac{\exp(\alpha g_i)}{\sum_{j=1}^{n} \exp(\alpha g_j)}$$

can be found in Ewerhart and Sun (2022). They found that when α is small (a high level of noise) two types of equilibria in pure strategies exist, one in which all contestants exert zero effort, and another with at most one active contestant. In all other cases, there are mixed-strategy equilibria.

2.3   Ratio Form CSF (Tullock, 1980)

In the Ratio CSF, the probability that a contestant wins equals the ratio of her effort to the aggregate effort, namely

$$p_i(\mathbf{g}) = \frac{g_i}{\sum_{j=i}^{n} g_j}. \tag{2.5}$$

The Ratio Form CSF can be interpreted as saying that the probability that contestant i obtains the prize when she holds g_i tickets and there are $\sum_{j=i}^{n} g_j$ tickets is just the proportion of tickets in i's hand. Hence, this CSF is also known as the "Tullock lottery."

It's noteworthy that the probability in Equation (2.5) is a homogeneous function of degree zero, meaning it does not change with the units used to measure expenses. This makes the Ratio Form CSF unit invariant.

To fully define the CSF, we need to explain how the prize is allocated when no contestant makes an effort. The standard convention is to assume that when $\mathbf{g} = \mathbf{0}$, $p_i(\mathbf{g}) = 1/n$, meaning that the prize is awarded through a fair lottery. Note that this CSF is discontinuous at $\mathbf{g} = \mathbf{0}$. This means that when all contestants minus, say i, make zero effort, an infinitesimal effort by i yields the full prize. But, an even smaller effort yields the prize too, so the best reply of i when $\mathbf{g}_{-i} = \mathbf{0}$ does not exist. Fortunately, this does not cause much trouble from the point of view of the existence of equilibrium. It just implies that the standard procedure of showing the existence of a Nash equilibrium cannot be applied here because payoffs are not continuous.

The next proposition illustrates how to handle existence issues in the specific scenario where $V_1 = V_2 = \cdots = V_n = V$.

PROPOSITION 2.2   *There is a unique Nash equilibrium of the contest game in which the CSF is the Ratio Form and all valuations are identical.*

Proof   The strategy of the proof is that, first, we look for a candidate equilibrium. Once we have identified it, we show that this candidate is indeed an equilibrium.

How to find the candidate? The equilibrium candidate must fulfill the first-order condition of payoff maximization. Thus for each i,

$$\frac{\sum_{j=i}^{n} g_j - g_i}{\left(\sum_{j=i}^{n} g_j\right)^2} V \le 1, i \in \{1, 2, \ldots, n\} \tag{2.6}$$

with strict inequality if $g_i = 0$. We first see that if an inequality is strict, say for contestant j, it must be strict for all contestants. Suppose not, so there are two contestants, say i and k such that

$$\frac{\sum_{j=i}^{n} g_j - g_i}{(\sum_{j=i}^{n} g_j)^2} V < 1 \; ; \quad \frac{\sum_{j=i}^{n} g_j - g_k}{(\sum_{j=i}^{n} g_j)^2} V = 1.$$

In this case $g_i = 0$. But this implies that $g_k < g_i$ which is a contradiction. And $\mathbf{g} = \mathbf{0}$ is not an equilibrium because if a contestant makes an infinitesimal effort, he will obtain the full prize. So we are left with the case in which, for all contestants, (2.6) holds with equality. Next, note that any solution to this system of equations must be symmetric, i.e., $g_i = g_j$ for all i, j since the term $\sum_{j=i}^{n} g_j$ appears in the same way in all of them. We have found a candidate, namely

$$g_i^* = \frac{n-1}{n^2} V. \tag{2.7}$$

It is only left to show that this candidate is indeed a Nash equilibrium. Given $\mathbf{g}_{-i}^*$, payoff for i looks like

$$\pi_i(g_i, \mathbf{g}_{-i}^*) = \frac{g_i}{g_i + (\frac{n-1}{n})^2 V} V - g_i.$$

Clearly, (2.7) is a solution to the first-order conditions of payoff maximization, and, given that payoffs are strictly concave in g_i, it is the only solution, so the candidate is indeed the unique Nash equilibrium. □

From (2.7), probabilities of winning, total effort, and payoffs in equilibrium are given by

$$p_i(\mathbf{g}^*) = \frac{1}{n}, \quad \sum_{j=i}^{n} g_j^* = \frac{n-1}{n} V, \quad \pi_i(\mathbf{g}^*) = \frac{V}{n^2}. \tag{2.8}$$

The symmetry of equilibrium actions translates into equal probabilities (shares) of obtaining the prize. But this could have been achieved by making no effort at all! In this sense, symmetric contests can be seen as a rat race in which participants invest substantial effort in vain.

Other comparative statics results are as follows:

(a) Individual and aggregate equilibrium efforts increase with V. Individual effort decreases with n, but aggregate effort increases with n.

Contestants respond to incentives, and when expected reward decreases – either because the prize is less valuable or there is more competition – individual efforts decrease as well.[3]

---

[3] The impact of prizes motivating effort is well-documented. For example, Ehrenberg and Bognanno (1990a,b) studied the relationship between the magnitude of prizes and the performance of participants in major golf tournaments. Their findings revealed a negative association between larger prizes and lower scores, which was interpreted as an indicator of effort. These results can be refined by including the composition of the contestants (higher prizes attract better athletes) and gender (men and women seem to react differently to prizes); see Matthews, Sommers, and Peschiera (2007).

(b) When $n \to \infty$, aggregate efforts tend to V, and individual payoff tends to 0. This result was named by Tullock as *Rent Dissipation* because the value of efforts (almost) equals the value of the rent in contests with a large number of contestants.[4] In very competitive contests, contestants should expect very little reward. In other words, the candy (rent) dissipates into too many mouths. We recall that similar results can be found in oligopolist markets with a large number of firms.[5] In fact, a contest with the Ratio Form CSF is formally identical to a Cournot model with inverse demand $V / \sum_{j=i}^{n} g_j$ (so the elasticity of demand is one) and marginal costs are constant and equal to one (in this interpretation g_i stands for the output of firm i).

The last observation leads us to inquire if the methods developed in Industrial Organization can be applied to our field. Despite the similarity noted above, there is a serious problem. In Industrial Organization, at least since the work of Bulow, Geanakoplos, and Klemperer (1985), the models are divided into two subfields: Those in which strategies are strategic substitutes, i.e., the best reply of any player is decreasing in the actions of the competitors (typically the Cournot model), and those in which strategies are strategic complements, i.e., the best reply of any player is increasing in the actions of competitors (typically Bertrand models). These two cases use different methods of analysis.[6] Thus, we are led to ask what the best replies look like in a contest in which the CSF is the Ratio. The answer is that they do not fall into the category of strategic substitutes or complements. Let us see why.[7]

From the first-order conditions of payoff maximization and letting $g_{-i} = \sum_{j \neq i} g_j$ (note that now g_{-i} is a number and not a vector as when we write $\mathbf{g}_{-i}$), the best reply function for contestant i with valuation V_i is given by

$$BR_i(g_{-i}) = \sqrt{V_i g_{-i}} - g_{-i}.$$

We see that

$$\frac{dg_i}{dg_{-i}} = \frac{\sqrt{V_i}}{2\sqrt{g_{-i}}} - 1.$$

For $g_{-i} = V_i/4$, it is zero. For $g_{-i} < V_i/4$, it is positive. For $g_{-i} > V_i/4$, it is negative. Thus, strategies are neither strategic substitutes nor strategic complements. In Figure 2.1, the best replies for two contestants in a contest with $V_1 = V_2 = 1$ are depicted.

Note that equilibrium in Figure 2.1 occurs at $g_i^* = 0.25$, exactly where $dg_i/dg_{-i} = 0$. With more contestants, since equilibrium is symmetric, it is located in the intersection of the best reply and a straight line of slope $1/(n-1)$. In Figure 2.2, the case for $n = 7$ and $V_i = 1$ for all i is plotted.

---

[4] We have seen another example of Rent Dissipation in the section when the CSF is the All Pay Auction.
[5] An exposition of these results can be found in Corchón (2001), propositions 2.2, 2.3, and 3.5.
[6] For an exposition of these methods, see the books by Corchón (2001) and Vives (2001).
[7] The careful reader will have noticed that the Cournot model with an isoelastic demand curve mentioned in the previous paragraph yields a best reply that is neither a strategic substitute nor a complement. This is why we said that "typically" Cournot models yield strategic substitution.

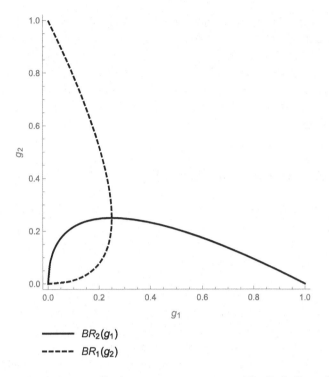

Figure 2.1 Best replies in a two-contestant case with a Ratio Form CSF and $V_1 = V_2 = 1$

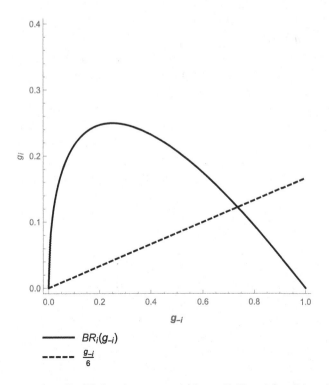

Figure 2.2 Equilibrium in a contest with $n = 7$, $V_i = 1$ for all i, and a Ratio Form CSF

When $n > 2$, equilibrium occurs in the decreasing part of best replies, so, locally, strategies are strategic substitutes. When n is very large, the straight line representing symmetry is really close to the horizontal axis so g_i^* is close to 0 and total expenses tend to 1, which is the value of the prize (Rent Dissipation).

The study of the heterogeneous contestants brings a new issue, namely, that some contestants may opt to spend no effort in equilibrium. The analysis of this scenario is deferred to Chapter 3.

2.4   Extensions of Ratio: Logit CSF (Dixit, 1987)

In the Logit CSF, the linear terms g_i in the Ratio Form CSF are substituted by a more general function ϕ of g_i. When $\mathbf{g} \neq \mathbf{0}$,

$$p_i(\mathbf{g}) = \frac{\phi(g_i)}{\sum_{j=1}^{n} \phi(g_j)}.$$

The function ϕ measures the impact (or the merit) of g_i in the contest, and $\phi(g_i)/\sum_{j=1}^{n} \phi(g_j)$ measures the relative impact (merit) of i. The probability (share) of contestant i winning the contest equals her relative merit. For instance, the *generalized Ratio Form* is $\phi(g_i) = g_i^\epsilon$, as originally written by Tullock (1980). When $\epsilon = 1$, this form yields our old friend (2.5). When $\epsilon = 0$, it yields a pure lottery. You can check in Exercise 2.1 that if $\epsilon \in [0, 1]$, the CSF is concave in g_i and the unique symmetric Nash equilibrium is

$$p_i(\mathbf{g}^*) = \frac{1}{n}, \quad g_i^* = \frac{\epsilon(n-1)V}{n^2}, \quad \text{and} \quad \pi_i^*(\mathbf{g}^*) = \frac{V(n - \epsilon(n-1))}{n^2}.$$

These expressions generalize those in (2.8). But now there is no rent dissipation when n is very large, which should serve as a warning about the generality of this result. See Exercise 2.11 for further properties of this CSF.

Another example is given by $\phi(g_i) = g_i + k$ (Amegashie, 2006). The parameter k can be interpreted as noise or as a head start (Kirkegaard, 2012). See Exercise 2.2 for the calculation of the unique Nash equilibrium in this case. Another special case of $\phi(g_i)$ in which this function is not everywhere increasing is presented in Exercise 2.19. See Cornes and Hartley (2005) for a general discussion of the importance of the form of ϕ.

Finally, note that if ϕ is strictly increasing, defining G_i as $G_i = \phi(g_i)$ payoffs can be written as

$$\pi_i(\mathbf{G}) = \frac{G_i}{\sum_{j=1}^{n} G_j} V - \phi^{-1}(G_i).$$

In this case, the contest with a Logit CSF is strategically equivalent to a contest with a Ratio Form CSF in which costs are not necessarily linear.

We will see that the main insights obtained with the Ratio CSF hold when the CSF is Logit. We assume that ϕ is differentiable, strictly increasing and concave to make sure that the first-order conditions of payoff maximization yield a maximum. Indeed, the first-order conditions are

$$\frac{\phi'(g_i)\sum_{j\neq i}\phi(g_j)}{(\sum_{j=1}^n \phi(g_j))^2}V - 1 = 0, \ i \in \{1, \ldots, n\}, \tag{2.9}$$

where ϕ' is the derivative of ϕ. Since ϕ is concave, ϕ' is nonincreasing in g_i, and so the numerator inherits this property. And the denominator is increasing in g_i. Thus, since all these magnitudes are nonnegative, the ratio is decreasing in g_i. In other words, the second derivative of the payoff is nonpositive. Therefore, the first-order conditions are also sufficient conditions for payoff maximization.

To derive the best reply, we write the left-hand side of (2.9) as $F(g_i, \mathbf{g}_{-i})$. Totally differentiating this function with respect to g_i and g_j, we obtain

$$\frac{dg_i}{dg_j} = \frac{\frac{\partial F(g_i, \mathbf{g}_{-i})}{\partial g_j}}{-\frac{\partial F(g_i, \mathbf{g}_{-i})}{\partial g_i}}.$$

Note that in the Ratio case, payoffs are aggregative, i.e., depend on the sum of efforts.[8] Assuming that in the maximum, the second-order conditions of payoff maximization hold with strict inequality, we see that $sign(dg_i/dg_j) = sign(\partial F(g_i, \mathbf{g}_{-i})/\partial g_j)$. In our case

$$sign\frac{\partial F(g_i, \mathbf{g}_{-i})}{\partial g_j} = sign\left(\phi(g_i) - \sum_{j\neq i}\phi(g_j)\right).$$

As in the Ratio Form case, given the efforts of all other contestants, there is a unique effort of i at which $dg_i/dg_j = 0$, namely $\phi(g_i) = \sum_{j\neq i}\phi(g_j)$, which for $n = 2$ implies $g_1 = g_2$. If for $\sum_{j\neq i}\phi(g_j)$ large enough the best reply of i is 0 (as it happens when $\phi(g_k) = g_k^\epsilon$ and $k \in \{1, 2, \ldots, n\}$), the best reply in this case has the same form as in the Ratio CSF, namely hump-shaped. It can be proved that an increase of the prize increases efforts but an increase in the number of contestants decreases efforts; see Exercise 2.11.

2.5 Extensions of Ratio: Ratio Plus Luck and Relative Difference CSFs

The Ratio CSF does not account for the influence of pure luck on the contest result. As mentioned in Section 2.4, Amegashie proposed a CSF that specifically considers this factor. Nitzan (1991a) introduced another CSF to model the impact of luck, specifically

---

[8] See Corchón (2021) for a survey on aggregative games.

$$p_i(\mathbf{g}) = a\frac{1}{n} + (1-a)\frac{g_i}{\sum_{j=1}^{n} g_j}, \, a \in [0,1]. \tag{2.10}$$

Here, success is driven by two factors: merit (as in the Ratio CSF) and luck (as in the Che and Gale CSF), which is assumed to be evenly distributed among all contestants. If the CSF is imposed by a planner, it reflects her preference for equality. In Nitzan's CSF, luck does not affect merit directly (as in Amegashie), but it does impact the outcome. In the context of elections, this fixed effect means that some voters are firmly committed to one political party (e.g., Democrats or Republicans) and will never change their vote. As a result, even if a party makes minimal effort in an election, it will still receive a significant number of votes and have a nonnegligible chance of winning. In Amegashie's CSF, merit is perceived with a degree of noise.

Note that the sum of probabilities in (2.10) is one, as it should be. It is left to the reader to show that, in the unique Nash equilibrium,

$$g_i^* = \frac{(n-1)(1-a)V}{n^2}$$

(see Exercise 2.3). When the contest is decided by pure luck (i.e., $a = 1$), equilibrium efforts are zero, and when it is decided by relative merit (i.e., $a = 1$), they equal those obtained with the Ratio Form CSF.

Beviá and Corchón (2015) proposed an extension which adds, to the luck factor, the relative difference between contestants. This extension considers that a difference of, say, one battalion in a battle (or a million dollars in an R&D contest) is very different when the absolute number of soldiers is in the tens (or the R&D expenditure is in a few million dollars) than when it is in the thousands (or when R&D expenditure is in the billion dollars). Differences count, but they should be weighted by the expenses incurred by contestants. Sun Tzu's *The Art of War* counsels that how to arrange an army depends on ratios: "It is the rule in war, if our forces are ten to the enemy's one, to surround him; if five to one, to attack him; if twice as numerous, to divide our army into two" (p. 9).

The formal definition of this idea is not straightforward. A preliminary concept is needed. A *notional* CSF, denoted by f, is defined ignoring the requirement that probabilities are nonnegative and must sum up to one.

With two contestants and $\sum_{k=1}^{2} g_k \neq 0$,

$$f(g_i, g_j) = \alpha + \beta\frac{g_i - sg_j}{\sum_{k=1}^{2} g_k}, \, i, j \in \{1, 2\}, \, i \neq j \tag{2.11}$$

with α, β, and s being nonnegative numbers. On top of the luck term α, the relative difference between expenses, where the competitor's expense is weighted by a factor s, is introduced. This is made to recover, as a special case, the Ratio Form CSF ($s = 0$ and $\alpha = 0$). The parameter s can be interpreted as how the probability of winning reacts to differences in efforts and β as how this probability reacts to relative differential efforts. Both parameters reflect how competitive a contest is.

To convert a notional CSF into a CSF, first we have to guarantee that the functions f defined in (2.11) add up to one, which is the case if and only if $2\alpha + \beta(1 - s) = 1$.

So from the three parameters of this CSF, only two are truly independent. If $s = 0$ and $\alpha = 0.5a$, $a + \beta = 1$, and the Nitzan's CSF defined in (2.10) is recovered. Finally, we have to make sure that the values coming from the notional CSF are between zero and one. With all these ingredients in hand, the probability of winning is defined using the notional CSF,

$$p_i(\mathbf{g}) = \min(\max(f_i(g_i, g_j), 0), 1), \ i, j \in \{1, 2\}, i \neq j.$$

This is the Relative Difference CSF. To find a Nash equilibrium in this setting, we disregard the nonnegativity constraint and go to the first-order condition of payoff maximization of the notional CSF. In the case of identical valuations, the first-order condition for contestant 1 is

$$\beta V \frac{(1+s)g_2}{(g_1 + g_2)^2} - 1 = 0.$$

By the same reasonings made in Proposition 2.2, a candidate equilibrium is symmetric and is given by

$$g_1^* = g_2^* = \beta V \frac{1+s}{4},$$

which coincides with the Ratio case when $\beta = 1$ and $s = 0$. Note that the probability of obtaining the prize, if contestants exercise these efforts, is $\alpha + \beta(1 - s)/2 = 0.5$.

Now consider the maximization of payoffs of contestant 1 when $g_2 = g_2^*$, namely

$$\min\left(\max\left(\alpha + \beta \frac{g_1 - sg_2^*}{g_1 + g_2^*}, 0\right), 1\right) V - g_1.$$

Since $g_1 \in [0, V]$ and payoffs are continuous in g_1 by a theorem by Weierstrass the maximum exists. It could be only located either in the extremes of $[0, V]$ or when the first-order conditions are met. Clearly, $g_1 = V$ is worse than $g_1 = 0$ because in the former the best outcome would be to obtain the prize with a probability 1, payoffs are going to be nonpositive. Therefore, if we show that in the candidate equilibrium profits are nonnegative, this candidate is indeed an equilibrium. Indeed,

$$\pi_i(\mathbf{g}^*) = \frac{V}{2} - \beta V \frac{1+s}{4} = \frac{V}{4}(2 - \beta(1+s)) \geq 0 \quad \text{if and only if } 2 \geq \beta(1+s).$$

What to take home from this argument is that when using the relative difference CSF, you can disregard the constraints imposed by nonnegativity and use the notional CSF (2.11). And the first-order conditions of payoff maximization when these constraints are ignored yield indeed the Nash equilibrium we are looking for, provided that $2 \geq \beta(1+s)$. The latter indicates that the contest cannot be very competitive (recall the interpretation of s and β given above) so we stay away from the All Pay Auction.[9]

The same procedure can be applied when $n > 2$. In this case, the notional CSF can be written as

---

[9] Note that the inequality $2 \geq \beta(1+s)$ always holds for the Ratio Form CSF since $s = 0$ and $\beta = 1$.

$$f(g_i, \mathbf{g}_{-i}) = \alpha + \beta \frac{\left(g_i - \frac{s}{n-1} \sum_{j \neq i} g_j \right)}{\sum_{k=1}^{n} g_k}.$$

In this case, the condition for the first-order condition to be an equilibrium is $n \geq \beta(n - 1 + s)$, and equilibrium effort for each contestant i is

$$g_i^* = \beta V \frac{n - 1 + s}{n^2}.$$

See Exercise 2.4 for the calculations leading to the above formula.[10]

2.6   Additive Separable CSF

In the Additive Separable CSF, success in a contest is represented by

$$p_i(\mathbf{g}) = \frac{1}{n} + \varphi(g_i) - \frac{1}{n-1} \sum_{j \neq i} \varphi(g_j) \qquad (2.12)$$

with $\varphi(0) = 0$ and φ increasing. Clearly, the sum of the terms in (2.12) is 1. To make each term nonnegative, we add that $\varphi(V) \leq 1/n$, and thus

$$p_i(\mathbf{g}) = \frac{1}{n} + \varphi(g_i) - \frac{1}{n-1} \sum_{j \neq i} \varphi(g_j) \geq \frac{1}{n} - \frac{1}{n} = 0$$

for the relevant range of efforts, namely for those in $[0, V]$. The success in a contest depends on luck $(1/n)$ and the difference between your impact on the contest $(\varphi(g_i))$ and the average impact of the others, $\sum_{j \neq i} \varphi(g_j)/(n - 1)$. The difference with the Che and Gale CSF is that we do not need the max operator to guarantee that p_i's are nonnegative. In this case, the trick is provided by the boundedness assumption $\varphi(V) \leq 1/n$. The reader can check that when $n = 2$, (2.12) looks similar to what is inside the minmax operator in (2.4) when $s = 1$. But this would hold if $\varphi(g_i) = g_i$ and this form violates the boundedness assumption.

An advantage of this CSF is that Nash equilibrium strategies are dominant strategies, i.e., they are not only the best reply to what others do, but they are the best reply to anything the others might do! Contestants do not have to wonder about what the others are going to do. To prove this, we see that the terms that do not depend on g_i enter additively in payoffs. Thus, when other contestant actions increase, payoffs are just smaller, but the relationship between expected revenue $(p_i V)$ and costs is the same. In other words, payoffs are transformed monotonically by the strategies of other contestants and, as consumer theory teaches us, this transformation does not affect the maximum. Mathematically this is seen by looking at the first-order condition of payoff maximization, $\varphi'(g_i)V = 1$, and realize that it only depends on g_i.

---

[10] Hwang (2012) presented another generalization of the Difference and the Ratio Form CSF; see Section 3.6.

Particular forms of this family of CSF were proposed by Skaperdas and Vaidya (2012) and Polishchuk and Tonis (2013) and axiomatized by Cubel and Sanchez-Pages (2016).

There are other CSF that yield dominant strategies. Consider a CSF like the following one: Given a cutoff $g \in [0, V/n)$, define

$$p_i(\boldsymbol{g}) = \frac{1}{\#C(\boldsymbol{g})} \text{ for all } i \in C(\boldsymbol{g}),$$

$$p_i(\boldsymbol{g}) = 0 \text{ for all } i \notin C(\boldsymbol{g}), \text{ and}$$

$$p_i(\boldsymbol{g}) = \frac{1}{n} \text{ for all } i \text{ if } C(\boldsymbol{g}) = \varnothing,$$

where $C(\boldsymbol{g}) = \{i \in \{1, \ldots, n\} \mid g_i \geq \underline{g}\}$.

In this CSF, contestants are requested to make a minimum effort $\underline{g}$ to qualify for a pure lottery of the prize unless no one makes this minimum effort in which case all qualify for this lottery. It is easy to see that $g_i = \underline{g}$ is a dominant strategy for all contestants. But, this CSF is not additively separable. If this CSF were additively separable, it should satisfy the following property: For all $(g_i, \boldsymbol{g}_{-i})$, $(g_i', \boldsymbol{g}_{-i}')$, $p_i(g_i, \boldsymbol{g}_{-i}) + p_i(g_i', \boldsymbol{g}_{-i}') = p_i(g_i, \boldsymbol{g}_{-i}') + p_i(g_i', \boldsymbol{g}_{-i})$. Suppose that $g_i \geq \underline{g}$, $\boldsymbol{g}_{-i}$ is such that $C(\boldsymbol{g})\backslash\{i\} = k$, $g_i' < \underline{g}$ and $\boldsymbol{g}_{-i}'$ is such that $C(\boldsymbol{g})\backslash\{i\} = m$. Then, $p_i(g_i, \boldsymbol{g}_{-i}) + p_i(g_i', \boldsymbol{g}_{-i}') = 1/(k+1)$ but $p_i(g_i, \boldsymbol{g}_{-i}') + p_i(g_i', \boldsymbol{g}_{-i}) = 1/(m+1)$.

However, it is possible to construct an additive separable CSF that gives the same equilibrium efforts, probabilities, and payoffs than the contest described above. Let $p_i(\boldsymbol{g})$ be such that

$$p_i(\boldsymbol{g}) = \frac{1}{n} + \varphi(g_i) - \frac{1}{n-1} \sum_{j \neq i} \varphi(g_j), \text{ with}$$

$$\varphi(g_i) = 1/n \text{ if } g_i \geq \underline{g} \text{ and } \varphi(g_i) = 0 \text{ otherwise.}$$

This CSF is additively separable with $g_i = \underline{g}$ being a dominant strategy for all contestants. Beviá and Corchón (2022) prove that given any CSF yielding a contest with dominant strategies, there is an additively separable CSF yielding a contest with the same efforts and probabilities in equilibrium. This implies that additively separable CSFs, somehow, characterize those CSFs yielding dominant strategies.

2.7   Advanced Material: The Existence of a Symmetric Equilibrium with General CSF

At this point, the reader may wonder that given the variety of CSFs presented so far, we would need idiosyncratic arguments to show the existence of a Nash equilibrium in symmetric contests. Recall a general theorem showing the existence of a Nash equilibrium in general games (see Fudenberg and Tirole, 1991, p. 34). But this proof is of no avail here since we have seen that, at least, for CSF homogeneous of degree zero, payoffs are not continuous at $\boldsymbol{g} = \boldsymbol{0}$.

In this section, we present two approaches to the existence of a symmetric equilibrium that will cover many of the cases seen before. The strategy of the proof in both cases is identical to the one used in Proposition 2.2. First, we look for a candidate equilibrium found by solving the first-order conditions, and later we show that this candidate is indeed an equilibrium. Throughout this section, we will assume that the CSF is symmetric, twice differentiable whenever there is, at least, a positive effort and $\partial p_i(\mathbf{g})/\partial g_i > 0$. We will refer to these assumptions as $\mathbf{D}$.

The first approach is taken from Malueg and Yates (2006), and it works for contestants with identical valuations and CSF homogeneous of degree zero. We have seen that there are plenty of CSFs satisfying this assumption.

Again, let us start by looking at the first-order conditions of payoff maximization. Since the CSF is homogeneous of degree zero, $\partial p_i(\mathbf{g}^*)/\partial g_i$ is homogeneous of degree -1. (See Sydsæter and Hammond, 2012, chapter 12, p. 432.) This implies that we can write

$$\frac{\partial p_i(\mathbf{g})}{\partial g_i} = \frac{1}{g_i} \frac{\partial p_i\left(\frac{g_1}{g_i}, \frac{g_2}{g_i}, \ldots, \frac{g_n}{g_i}\right)}{\partial g_i}.$$

Since we are looking for a symmetric equilibrium, all ratios g_j/g_i are 1. The first-order condition is written as

$$\frac{\partial p_i(1, 1, \ldots, 1)}{\partial g_i} V = g^*. \tag{2.13}$$

Now g^*, which is strictly positive because $\partial p_i(\mathbf{g})/\partial g_i > 0$, is our candidate equilibrium. Exercise 2.5 asks the reader to prove that $(0, 0, \ldots, 0)$ cannot be an equilibrium; therefore our candidate is the only candidate. Thus, if a symmetric equilibrium exists, it is given by (2.13). Malueg and Yates gave sufficient conditions that guarantee the existence of such an equilibrium, mainly:

(1) There exist $\bar{g}$ such that $\partial^2 p_i(g, 1, \ldots, 1)/\partial g_i^2 \begin{cases} < 0 & \forall g > \bar{g} \\ > 0 & \forall g < \bar{g} \end{cases}$.

   Condition (1) allows for nonconcave CSF as long as at some point concavity is recovered.

(2) $1/n - \partial p_i(1, \ldots, 1)/\partial g_i > p_i(0, 1, \ldots, 1)$.

   Condition (2) guarantees that choosing zero effort is not a profitable deviation.

PROPOSITION 2.3 *Under conditions (1)–(2) above, there is a unique symmetric equilibrium for any contest with identical valuations and a CSF homogeneous of degree zero satisfying* $\mathbf{D}$.

Proof The interested reader can see the complete proof in Malueg and Yates (2006); we just give here a guide to the proof's steps.

From the analysis above, it is only left to prove that when all contestants but i choose g^*, g^* is the best reply of i to $\mathbf{g}^*_{-i}$.

(1) When all other contestants are choosing g^*, payoff functions are continuous.
   Since $g_i \in [0, V]$, a payoff-maximizing effort, call it $\tilde{g}$, exists. This maximum

can be located only in three places: at the first-order condition if the maximum is interior or at the bounds, namely, 0 or V, the latter clearly not an optimal choice.

(2) Condition (2) implies that 0 cannot be a maximum because
$$\pi_i(\mathbf{g}^*) = V(1/n - \partial p_i(1, 1, \ldots, 1)/\partial g_i) > p_i(0, 1, \ldots, 1)V = \pi_i(0, \mathbf{g}^*_{-i}).$$

(3) Condition (1), implies that there are at most two strategies that satisfy the first-order condition; we already know that g^* is one of them; let $\hat{g}$ be the other possible one.

(4) Finally, the proof ends by showing that if $\hat{g}$ exist, $\pi_i(\hat{g}, \mathbf{g}^*_{-i}) < \pi_i(g^*, \mathbf{g}^*_{-i})$.

□

As an example, let $n = 2$ and consider the generalized Ratio Form CSF

$$p_i(g_i, g_j) = \frac{g_i^\epsilon}{g_i^\epsilon + g_j^\epsilon}; \ p_j(g_j, g_i) = 1 - p_i(g_i, g_j)$$

then our candidate is

$$g_1^* = g_2^* = \frac{\epsilon}{4}V.$$

For this particular case, condition (1) holds whenever $\epsilon \leq 2$ and condition (2) also holds (see Exercise 2.6).

What about CSFs that are not homogeneous of degree zero? Let us follow the footsteps of the previous proof. First, let us find a symmetric candidate. Let $\alpha(y)$ be the elasticity of p_i when $g_i = y > 0$ for all $i \in \{1, \ldots, n\}$.

$$\alpha(y) = \frac{\partial p_i(y, y, \ldots, y, \ldots, y)}{\partial g_i} ny.$$

When all contestants choose the same effort y, the first-order condition can be written as

$$\frac{\alpha(y)}{n}V = y. \tag{2.14}$$

From now on, and without loss of generality, we will take $y \in [0, V]$ because, as we said earlier, no rational contestant will spend more in the contest than the value of the prize. Now we assume the following:

(I) α is continuous for all $y > 0$.
(II) $\lim_{y \to 0} \alpha(y)$ is well defined. Call it $\alpha(0)$.
(III) $p_i(0, \mathbf{g}_{-i}) = \beta$ a constant for $\mathbf{g}_{-i} = (y, y, \ldots, y)$ with $\beta < 1/n$.
(IV) $\alpha(0) > 0$ and $\alpha(y) < 1 - n\beta$ for all $y \in [0, V]$.

How does this assumption look like when CSF is Logit? Defining $\epsilon(g_i)$ as the elasticity of ϕ, i.e.,

$$\epsilon(g_i) = \frac{g_i \phi'(g_i)}{\phi(g_i)},$$

we see that $\alpha(y) = \epsilon(y)(n - 1)/n$ and, given that $\beta = 0$, part (IV) of the previous assumption says that $\epsilon(0) > 0$ and $\epsilon(g_i) \leq n/(n - 1)$. This is the assumption used by

Pérez-Castrillo and Verdier (1992). A constant elasticity $\phi(g_i)$ with $\epsilon \leq 1$ (e.g., the Ratio CSF) fulfills this assumption. When $\beta \neq 0$ like in the CSF proposed by Nitzan, we have that if a is the constant multiplying $1/n$ in the CSF, $\beta = a/n$ and the second part of (IV) above says that $\alpha(y) < 1 - n\beta = 1 - a$. And similarly with the CSF of Beviá and Corchón.

With these assumptions in hand, we focus on (2.14). We see that for $y = 0$, $\alpha(0)V/n > 0$ and for $y = V$, $\alpha(V)V < nV$ since $\alpha(y) < 1 - n\beta$. Thus, the intermediate value theorem applied to (2.14) says that there is a positive number $y^* \in (0, V)$ such that

$$\frac{\alpha(y^*)}{n}V = y^*.$$

The last assumption imposed is:

(V) $\partial\pi_i(\varepsilon, \mathbf{y}_{-i})/\partial g_i > 0$ for ε sufficiently close to zero, $\partial\pi_i(\varepsilon, \mathbf{y}_{-i})/\partial g_i < 0$ when ε is large enough. And there is at most a unique g_i such that $\partial^2\pi_i(g_i, \mathbf{y}_{-i})/\partial g_i^2 = 0$.

This assumption is similar to condition (2) above of Malueg and Yates. The Ratio Form CSF indeed fulfills these five properties (see Exercise 2.8).

PROPOSITION 2.4 *There is a symmetric equilibrium for any contest with identical valuations and a CSF satisfying (I)–(V) above and* **D**.

Proof It is only left to prove that when all contestants but i choose y^*, y^* is the best reply of i. The key fact is that when all other contestants are choosing y^*, payoff functions are continuous. Since $g_i \in [0, V]$, a payoff-maximizing effort, call it $\bar{g}$, exists. This maximum can be located only in three places: at the first-order condition if the maximum is interior or at the bounds, namely, 0 or V, the latter clearly not an optimal choice. Setting $\bar{g} = y^*$, the payoffs when contestant i plays y are

$$\frac{V}{n} - \frac{\alpha(y^*)}{n}V > \beta V \text{ if and only if } 1 - n\beta > \alpha(y^*).$$

It is only left to prove that there is only one strategy that satisfies the first-order condition. For this, it is enough to invoke condition (V) above. Thus, when all contestants but i choose y^*, y^* is the unique best reply for i and we have found a Nash equilibrium. □

In some cases, we can prove that the equilibrium is unique. For instance, when the CSF is Logit with concave and strictly increasing ϕ, the first-order conditions are

$$V\frac{\phi'(y)(n - 1)}{\phi(y)n^2} = 1, i \in \{1, 2, \ldots, n\}. \tag{2.15}$$

Since the left-hand side of (2.15) is strictly decreasing in y, the symmetric equilibrium is unique. More generally, if the function α is decreasing, the solution to (2.14) is unique so the symmetric equilibrium is unique too.

The map of the conditions under which an equilibrium exists is still incomplete, even if we assume the generalized Ratio Form CSF. It seems intuitively obvious that when the elasticity of efforts, ϵ, is very large, this CSF tends to the All Pay Auction, so only equilibria in mixed strategies exist. When $n = 2$, Baye, Kovenock, and de

Vries (1994) showed that the symmetric two-player contest with $\epsilon \in (2, \infty)$ allows a mixed-strategy Nash equilibrium. Further characterization of these mixed equilibria is given by Alcalde and Dahm (2010) and Ewerhart (2015, 2017). See Exercise 2.12 for the case of an additively separable utility function.

2.8   Exercises

2.1 Compute the Nash equilibrium of a contest with n contestants, linear cost, $V_i = V$ for all i, and the Logit CSF when $\phi(g_i) = g_i^\epsilon$, $\epsilon \in (0, 1]$.

2.2 Compute the Nash equilibrium of a contest with n contestants, linear cost, $V_i = V$ for all i, and the Logit CSF when $\phi(g_i) = g_i + k$.

2.3 Compute the Nash equilibrium of a contest with n contestants, linear cost, $V_i = V$ for all i, and the CSF proposed by Nitzan (1991a).

2.4 Compute the Nash equilibrium of a contest with n contestants, linear cost, $V_i = V$ for all i, and the CSF proposed by Beviá and Corchón (2015).

2.5 Show that in a symmetric contest with a CSF homogeneous of degree zero and strictly increasing in g_i, $(0, , 0)$ cannot be an equilibrium.

2.6 Show that if $p_i(\mathbf{g}) = g_i^\epsilon / \sum_{j=1}^n g_j^\epsilon$, the sufficient conditions of Malueg and Yates (2006) hold if $\epsilon \leq n/(n-1)$.

2.7 Suppose that the best reply of a symmetric game, denoted by B, is continuous in $\mathbb{R}_+$. Let $R(y) = B(y, \ldots, y, \ldots, y)$ be the best response when all contestants except i choose y. Suppose that R is such that
(a) $\exists \underline{x}$ such that $\forall y \in (0, \underline{x})$, $R(y)(n-1) > y$
(b) $\exists \bar{x}$ such that $\forall y \in (\bar{x}, \infty)$, $R(y) = 0$.
(1) Show that under (a) and (b) above, a symmetric Nash equilibrium exists (equilibrium is not necessarily unique). (Hint: Use the intermediate value theorem.)
(2) Give a micro foundation to (a) and (b) (hint for a) find the slope of B differentiating the first-order condition).

2.8 Show that the Ratio Form CSF fulfills assumptions (I)–(V) in the main text.

2.9 Compute the symmetric Nash equilibrium of a Possibly Indecisive Contest (a contest where the probability that no one receives the prize is not zero) in which cost is linear and the CSF is $p_i(\mathbf{g}) = g_i/(\sum_{j=1}^n g_j + a)$, $a > 0$.

2.10 There are n identical firms that can acquire each other prior to a contest. Let $\pi(m)$ be payoffs from the contests when there are m firms. Acquisition price is $P = a\pi(n) + (1-a)\pi(n-1)$ with $a \in [0, 1]$, i.e., the acquisition price is a linear convex combination of payoffs with n firms (status quo) and $n-1$ firms (when the acquisition takes place). If acquisition takes place, total payoffs for a firm are the payoffs from the contests with $n - 1$ firms minus the price paid by the acquisition. Study conditions on π and a under which acquisition does not take place.

2.11 Prove that, with the Logit CSF with a differentiable, strictly increasing and concave ϕ, an increase of the prize increases efforts but an increase in the number of contestants decreases efforts (see Nti, 1997 and Corchón, 2007).

2.12 Show the existence of equilibrium when contestants have an additively separable utility function $u(p_i V) - c(g_i)$, where p_i is the Ratio CSF, u is concave, and c is convex. See Dickson, MacKenzie, and Sekeris (2022).

2.13 Consider a two-person contest with payoff functions $\pi_1(\mathbf{g}) = p(g_1, g_2)V - g_1$, and $\pi_2(\mathbf{g}) = (1 - p(g_1, g_2))V - g_2$. Assume differentiability as much as you need. From the first-order condition, compute the infinitesimal effect of a change in V on total effort and find conditions under which this effect is positive.

2.14 A contest with a variable prize: Consider a contest with n individuals and a variable prize, $V = \sum_{i=1}^{n} g_i^{\gamma}$, with $\gamma \in (0, 1)$. Assuming a Ratio Form CSF and a linear cost of effort, find the Nash equilibrium. Give an interpretation of this game.

2.15 Consider n experts, with $n \geq 2$, making predictions about the outcome of a random variable that can take on m different values with probabilities $p_1, p_2, \ldots, p_m$ (common knowledge among experts). Assume that $p_1 \geq p_2 \geq \cdots \geq p_m$. Experts get a reward from the public (prestige, money, etc.). In particular, assume that if n_I experts announce I and I occurs, the reward for each of these experts is V/n_I. The rest of the experts get zero. An equilibrium in the prediction market is a list of natural numbers $(n_1^*, n_2^*, \ldots, n_m^*)$ such that $\sum_{I=1}^{m} n_I^* = n$ and for all $I \in \{1, 2, \ldots, m\}$, if $n_I^* > 0$,

$$\frac{V}{n_I^*} p_I \geq \frac{V}{n_J^* + 1} p_J, \forall J \in \{1, 2, \ldots, m\}, J \neq I$$

so no expert announcing I has an incentive to switch and announce any other prediction. Show that there is an equilibrium in which experts announce different predictions.

2.16 Consider a piece of land with a value of V that may be invaded by a large number of identical potential invaders. The number of actual invaders is denoted as n. The probability of a successful invasion is given by

$$\frac{g(n)}{g(n) + kg(n)},$$

where $g(n)$ measures the strength of the invaders, and $kg(n)$ represents the strength of those opposing the invasion (such as police, armed forces, or current owners) which is assumed to be proportional to the strength of the invaders. If the land is successfully conquered, it will be divided equally among the invaders.

(1) Determine the payoffs for a potential invader in this scenario.

(2) Let R be the opportunity cost of an invader, which is assumed to be independent of the number of invaders. Determine the equilibrium number of invaders by taking into account the opportunity cost R.

(3) Give historical examples of land invasions, see Falcone and Rosenberg (2023).

2.17 Suppose a contest where the objective function of each contestant is to maximize the difference in payoffs (where payoffs are defined as has been assumed throughout this book). Assume two contestants and a Logit CSF with $\phi(g_i) = g_i^\epsilon$ with $\epsilon \in (0, 1]$.

(1) Find the Nash equilibrium of such a game.

(2) Suppose now that the contestant's objective is to maximize the ratio of the payoffs. Find the Nash equilibrium of such a game.

For a motivation of the assumption on the objective function of contestants, see the natural selection model of Schaffer (1989).

2.18 Suppose rent-seeking activities can be taxed with a constant unit tax rate of t on expenses. The CSF is a generalized Ratio Form. All contestants value the prize at V.

(1) Write the payoff of a typical contestant.

(2) Use the first-order condition and symmetry to find the unique symmetric equilibrium.

(3) Find the equilibrium payoffs. Comment on how payoffs depend on t. Interpret this relationship.

(4) Calculate the total revenue raised by taxes. Determine the value of t that maximizes total revenue. Compute the sum of payoffs and total revenue.

2.19 Suppose a Logit CSF in which $\phi(g_i) = \max(ag_i - \frac{b}{2}g_i^2, 0)$. This function is increasing if and only if $g_i \le a/b$.

(1) Find reasons why an increase in expenses might decrease the probability of winning the prize.

(2) Find the unique symmetric equilibrium. (Hint: Disregard the nonnegativity constraint in $\phi(g_i)$ and show that a symmetric solution to the first-order condition satisfies this constraint.)

2.20 An organization with n identical individuals is going to be "purged." In particular, $k \le n - 2$ individuals are selected at random and expelled from the organization with probability $1 - q$. They enjoy zero utility. The remaining individuals enter into a contest with a prize V and a Ratio Form CSF.

(1) Assuming that q is given, find the k for which all individuals support the purge. Comment on the solution

(2) Now assume that $q = (n - k)/n$ (favorable cases divided by total cases). Find the k such that all individuals support the purge.

2.21 Suppose that the CSF is Ratio Form, agents are identical and have constant absolute risk aversion. Write the payoff functions and the first-order condition of payoff maximization of a typical contestant. Give an example in which a symmetric division of the prize will not increase the aggregate investment when the players are risk neutral but it is possible for a symmetric division to increase the aggregate investment when the players are risk averse. (See example 4 in Brookins and Jindapon, 2022.)

3 Equilibrium with Heterogeneous Agents

The assumption that all contestants are identical is a first cut to deal with the problem of the existence of an equilibrium: Once we have solved the maximization program for one contestant, we assume that all contestants display identical behavior and the equilibrium candidate emerges as a solution of this equation. There are several problems with this approach. First, asymmetric solutions may arise from symmetric games, e.g., the "chicken game." Second, the case of identical contestants is really special. We would like a theory that is independent of this extreme assumption. In the analysis of all pay auctions and difference CSFs (Sections 2.1 and 2.2 of Chapter 2), we ventured into the case of two, possibly different, contestants. But this is not enough. The reader is asked to return to Table 1.1 in Chapter 1 and to realize that outside war and two-party politics, real-life examples of contests involve in a fundamental way three or more contestants that may have different characteristics. This chapter will provide an approach to the study of equilibrium that does not depend on the number or the symmetry of contestants.

3.1 Introduction

Asymmetries among contestants can have a significant impact on the outcome of a contest. In Chapter 2, outside the case where there are two contestants, we simplified the analysis by assuming that all contestants were identical. However, in reality, there can be several sources of heterogeneity:

(1) Different valuations: Agents may have different valuations for the prize, due to sentimental reasons or to differential efficiency exploiting the prize.
(2) Different costs of effort: The cost of effort or money may have a different value for different contestants.
(3) Different weights in the CSF: The same effort may translate into different winning probabilities, due to home bias or the bias of decision-making committees.

Under certain conditions, these three sources of heterogeneity can be represented by just one of them. This will be further discussed in what follows.

Consider a contest in which the three sources of heterogeneity are present simultaneously. Suppose that the CSF can be written as

$$p_i(\mathbf{g}) = p_i(\alpha_1 g_1, \ldots, \alpha_i g_i, \ldots, \alpha_n g_n).$$

The weighting factor, α_i, reflects the quality of effort or the production of influence by i through effort (g_i) and capital (α_i). This factor can also represent the sympathies of the jury toward a specific candidate. An example of such a CSF is

$$p_i(\mathbf{g}) = \frac{\alpha_i g_i}{\alpha_1 g_1 + \alpha_2 g_2 + \cdots + \alpha_n g_n},$$

where $\alpha_1 g_1$ represents the influence of candidate 1 in the contest. The winning probability is determined by the relative influence of each candidate.

The cost of effort for contestant i is given by $c_i g_i$ with $c_i \in \mathbb{R}_+$. The marginal cost of effort represents the level of enthusiasm for work or the source of financing for each contestant. If there is a difference between the interest rates of lenders and borrowers, those with their own funds will face lower financing costs compared to those relying on external sources.

Additionally, each contestant may have a different value for the prize, represented by $V_1, V_2, \ldots, V_n$.

These three sources of heterogeneity determine the payoffs of each contestant $i \in \{1, \ldots, n\}$,

$$\pi_i(\mathbf{g}) = p_i(\alpha_1 g_1, \ldots, \alpha_i g_i, \ldots, \alpha_n g_n) V_i - c_i g_i.$$

By defining $G_i \equiv \alpha_i g_i$, payoffs can be expressed as

$$\begin{aligned}
\pi_i(\mathbf{G}) &= p_i(G_1, \ldots, G_i, \ldots, G_n) V_i - c_i \frac{G_i}{\alpha_i} \\
&= \frac{c_i}{\alpha_i} \left(p_i(G_1, \ldots, G_i, \ldots, G_n) V_i \frac{\alpha_i}{c_i} - G_i \right) \\
&= \frac{c_i}{\alpha_i} (p_i(G_1, \ldots, G_i, \ldots, G_n) W_i - G_i), \quad (3.1)
\end{aligned}$$

where $W_i = V_i \alpha_i / c_i$. Since c_i / α_i is a constant, it has no impact on the strategic outcome, i.e., a game with payoffs described in (3.1) yields the same Nash equilibrium strategies as a game with payoffs expressed as the term in brackets in (3.1) (this is an example of the fact that a monotonic transformation of payoffs does not affect the maximum). In (3.1) all the heterogeneities are bundled in the valuations. It is important to note that the equilibrium efforts and payoffs in this game do not correspond to those in the original game. To calculate the true efforts, the number G_i must be divided by α_i, and the true equilibrium payoffs are the ones given by (3.1). On the other hand, the equilibrium probabilities correspond to those calculated using G_i.

Sometimes it is more convenient to combine the three sources of heterogeneity into the cost. By defining $G_i \equiv \alpha_i g_i$, payoffs can be expressed as

$$p_i(G_1, \ldots, G_i, \ldots, G_n) V_i - \frac{c_i}{\alpha_i} G_i = V_i \left(p_i(G_1, \ldots, G_i, \ldots, G_n) - \frac{c_i}{\alpha_i V_i} G_i \right). \quad (3.2)$$

Note that term V_i in the right-hand side of (3.2) is not relevant for finding the maximum. By defining $k_i = c_i / \alpha_i V_i$ as the new marginal cost, the three sources of heterogeneity are collapsed into heterogeneity in costs. The reader is invited to try a similar exercise in Exercise 3.1, where the three sources are combined into a single source in the CSF.

3.2 Two Contestants

We begin our analysis by considering two-person contests. This is because contests involving more than two contestants have a distinct qualitative nature that requires separate examination, which will be provided in later sections. In particular, in Sections 3.3 and 3.4, we will see that with three or more contestants, it is possible for a contestant to spend zero effort in equilibrium. However, under some reasonable assumptions, this is not possible in contests with only two contestants. For instance, suppose that the CSF is such that when $g_i = 0$ and $g_j \neq 0$ for some j, $p_i(g_i, g_j) = \mu_i \geq 0$.[1] This means that when one contestant is making no effort while the other is making a positive effort, the first contestant's probability of winning remains constant, regardless of the other contestant's efforts. This property is fulfilled by many of the CSFs considered in Chapter 2, such as All Pay Auction, Ratio, and Logit when $\phi(0) = 0$ (in these three cases $\mu_i = 0$) and the Ratio plus Luck CSF, in which μ_i may be positive.[2] Suppose that in equilibrium, contestant two makes no effort. Then her probability of winning remains constant, as does her adversary's probability of winning. But then, if contestant one reduces g_1, p_1 remains constant, reducing costs, and increasing contestant one's payoffs, which contradicts the assumption that we are in an equilibrium.

Another reason to focus on two-person contests is that they have important applications. Examples of such contests include US politics (Democrats and Republicans), litigation between two parties, wars between two countries, sports matches between two teams, etc.

We begin with a general setup, assuming that cost functions and the CSF are twice differentiable for strictly positive efforts and that the second-order conditions of payoff maximization are satisfied with strict inequality. Since the All Pay Auction lacks a pure strategy equilibrium, it is excluded from our next analysis and addressed later in the chapter. The existence of a Nash equilibrium in this general setting is complex, and the technical details are provided in the Appendix of this chapter. Here, we focus on the characteristics of Nash equilibria in two-person contests.

The best reply of contestant i, denoted by BR_i, is defined as

$$BR_i(g_j) = \{g_i \in [0, V_i] \mid \pi_i(g_i, g_j) \geq \pi_i(\bar{g}_i, g_j), \forall \bar{g}_i \in [0, V_i]\} \ i \in \{1, 2\}, i \neq j.$$

Let (g_1^*, g_2^*) be a Nash equilibrium, i.e., $g_1^* = BR_1(g_2^*)$ and $g_2^* = BR_2(g_1^*)$. The next proposition characterizes the slopes of the best replies at a Nash equilibrium where both efforts are strictly positive.

---

[1] This is a generalization of condition (III) in Section 2.7 of Chapter 2.
[2] On the other hand, CSFs that do not fulfill this property include the difference CSF, the CSF introduced by Amegashie, and the additive CSF.

PROPOSITION 3.1   *If the second-order conditions for payoff maximization hold with a strict inequality, the slopes of the best replies at the Nash equilibrium (g_1^*, g_2^*) either have different signs or are both equal to zero.*

Proof   Given that $p_1(\mathbf{g}) + p_2(\mathbf{g}) = 1$, at equilibrium

$$\frac{\partial p_1(g_1^*, g_2^*)}{\partial g_1} V_1 - c_1'(g_1^*) = 0 \text{ and } -\frac{\partial p_1(g_1^*, g_2^*)}{\partial g_2} V_2 - c_2'(g_2^*) = 0, \qquad (3.3)$$

where $c_i'(g_i)$ denotes the marginal cost of effort for player i. The slope of best replies can be obtained by differentiating the first-order conditions in (3.3). This process results in

$$\frac{d B R_1(g_2^*)}{dg_2} = -\frac{\frac{\partial^2 p_1(g_1^*, g_2^*)}{\partial g_1 \partial g_2} V_1}{\frac{\partial^2 p_1(g_1^*, g_2^*)}{\partial g_1^2} V_1 - c_1''(g_1^*)} \text{ and}$$

$$\frac{d B R_2(g_1^*)}{dg_1} = \frac{\frac{\partial^2 p_1(g_1^*, g_2^*)}{\partial g_2 \partial g_1} V_2}{-\frac{\partial^2 p_1(g_1^*, g_2^*)}{\partial g_2^2} V_2 - c_2''(g_2^*)}.$$

The second-order conditions of payoff maximization are

$$\frac{\partial^2 p_1(g_1^*, g_2^*)}{\partial g_1^2} V_1 - c_1''(g_1^*) < 0 \text{ and } -\frac{\partial^2 p_1(g_1^*, g_2^*)}{\partial g_2^2} V_2 - c_2''(g_2^*) < 0.$$

Thus,

$$sign \frac{d B R_1(g_2^*)}{dg_2} = sign \frac{\partial^2 p_1(g_1^*, g_2^*)}{\partial g_1 \partial g_2} = -sign \frac{d B R_2(g_1^*)}{dg_1}.$$

as desired.   □

Proposition 3.1 establishes the necessary conditions for an equilibrium in a two-person contest. It states that at equilibrium, if the strategies are locally strategic substitutes for one contestant, they must be locally strategic complements for the other contestant, or if the contestants are identical and the equilibrium is symmetric, the slopes of best replies must be zero, as it happens with the Tullock CSF. The scenario where both contestants have strictly increasing (or decreasing) best reply functions, which is common in the industrial organization literature, is not possible in two-person contests. This result was proven by Dixit (1987) for the case of $V_1 = V_2$ and identical linear costs.

Figure 3.1 illustrates the equilibrium with a Ratio Form CSF when the strong contestant has a value of $V_1 = 2$, the weak contestant has a value of $V_2 = 1$, and both contestants have a constant marginal cost of one.

Figure 3.1 shows that the equilibrium occurs in the decreasing part of the best reply of the weak contestant (contestant 2) and in the increasing part of the best reply of the strong contestant (contestant 1). This has important implications. An external shock that causes an upward shift in the best reply of the weak contestant (but still leaves her as the weak contestant) leads to both contestants exerting more effort than before in

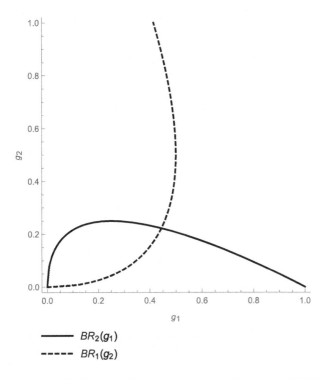

Figure 3.1 Equilibrium with two contestants, a Ratio Form CSF, $V_1 = 2, V_2 = 1$

the new equilibrium, thus exacerbating the conflict on both sides. On the other hand, if the shock benefits the strong contestant, only the strong contestant will increase their effort in the new equilibrium, while the weak contestant reduces theirs. Both implications are consequences of competitiveness.

A corollary of this result is that if best replies are identical, there can only be one symmetric equilibrium at most. At symmetric equilibrium $BR(g^*) - g^* = 0$. Since all best reply functions are identical, by Proposition 3.1, $dBR(g^*)/dg = 0$, meaning the slope of $BR(g) - g$ at any symmetric equilibrium is -1. Therefore, there cannot be two symmetric equilibria.

To gain further understanding, we return to a model where the equilibrium can be calculated. We simplify the heterogeneity in prize valuation into costs, which are assumed to be linear for simplicity and are written as $c_1 g_1$ and $c_2 g_2$. Recall that the actual cost has to be found by reverse engineering the cost found in equilibrium. The CSF is assumed to be a weighted Ratio Form, i.e.,

$$p_1(\mathbf{g}) = \frac{\alpha_1 g_1}{\alpha_1 g_1 + \alpha_2 g_2}, \quad p_2(\mathbf{g}) = 1 - p_1(\mathbf{g})$$

Collapsing all sources of heterogeneity into one simplifies the problem, but some important information may be lost in this process. In order to analyze the properties of the equilibrium, it is necessary to consider this information.

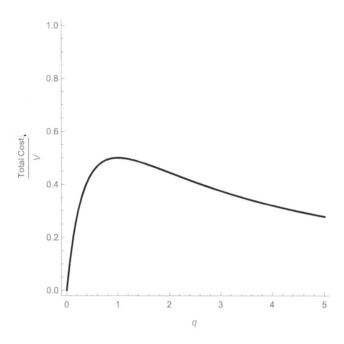

Figure 3.2 Total cost in equilibrium per unit value of the prize as a function of the advantage of player 1

To proceed, we will use a similar strategy as in Chapter 2. First, we eliminate $(0,0)$ as a possible equilibrium for the same reasons stated in Chapter 2. Then, we calculate a candidate equilibrium from the necessary condition of a Nash equilibrium. Finally, we demonstrate that this candidate is indeed an equilibrium.

Let $k = c_1/c_2$ and $a = \alpha_1/\alpha_2$. The parameter k represents the relative efficiency of contestant 1 in producing effort, with a high value of k indicating a higher marginal cost of effort for contestant 1 compared to contestant 2. The parameter a represents the bias of the CSF toward contestant 1, with a value greater than 1 indicating a biased jury in favor of contestant 1. This model will demonstrate the significance of relative magnitudes in absolute payoffs. The first-order condition of payoff maximization results in the following expression:

$$g_1^* = \frac{a}{c_2(a+k)^2}V \; ; \; g_2^* = k\frac{a}{c_2(a+k)^2}V.$$

The total costs in equilibrium, $c_1 g_1^* + c_2 g_2^*$, are given by

$$\frac{ak}{(a+k)^2}V + \frac{ak}{(a+k)^2}V = \frac{2ak}{(a+k)^2}V = \frac{2qV}{(q+1)^2}$$

where $q = a/k$ and represents a measure of contestant 1's advantage. Despite the asymmetries, when valuations are identical, costs are also identical. See Exercise 3.2 for a scenario where valuations and marginal costs differ. In Figure 3.2, the total cost per unit value of the prize is plotted as a function of q.

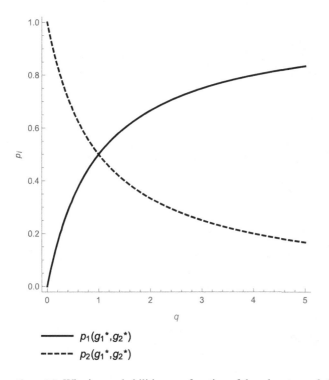

p_i

q

— $p_1(g_1^*, g_2^*)$

---- $p_2(g_1^*, g_2^*)$

Figure 3.3 Winning probabilities as a function of the advantage of player 1

We observe that the maximum rent dissipation occurs when $q = 1$ or $a = k$, meaning that the advantage of one player in costs is completely balanced by the advantage of the other player in the CSF. In this scenario, the contest is highly competitive, similar to a match between two top-tier tennis players. On the other hand, if there is inequality in the contest, the effort exerted will be minimal, similar to a match between a Champions League winner and a third-division team. The equilibrium probabilities are

$$p_1(\mathbf{g}^*) = \frac{\alpha_1 g_1^*}{\alpha_1 g_1^* + \alpha_2 g_2^*} = \frac{a g_1^*}{a g_1^* + g_2^*} = \frac{a}{a + \frac{g_2^*}{g_1^*}} = \frac{a}{a + k} = \frac{q}{q + 1};$$

$$p_2(\mathbf{g}^*) = 1 - p_1(\mathbf{g}^*) = \frac{k}{a + k} = \frac{1}{q + 1}.$$

Figure 3.3 illustrates these probabilities.

When the contest is skewed in favor of contestant 1, for instance, $c_1 < c_2$ and $\alpha_1 > \alpha_2$, the probability that this contestant wins the contest is larger than 0.5.

The payoffs in the unique Nash equilibrium are

$$\pi_1(\mathbf{g}^*) = \left(\frac{a}{a + k}\right)^2 V \text{ and } \pi_2(\mathbf{g}^*) = \left(\frac{k}{a + k}\right)^2 V$$

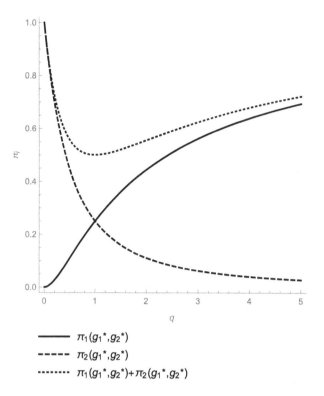

Figure 3.4 Equilibrium payoffs as a function of the advantage of player 1

that can be expressed as a function of q and V,

$$\pi_1(\mathbf{g}^*) = \left(\frac{q}{q+1}\right)^2 V \text{ and } \pi_2(\mathbf{g}^*) = \left(\frac{1}{q+1}\right)^2 V.$$

In Figure 3.4, the equilibrium payoffs for contestant 1, contestant 2, and the aggregate payoffs are plotted as a function of q with $V = 1$. The parameter q is interpreted as a measure of contestant 1's advantage, and when contestants have significant differences (e.g., q is close to 0 or a large number), costs are low, and individual payoffs reflect this advantage. It is also observed that when contestants are equal and costs are at their highest, payoffs reach a minimum.

The equilibrium in this model depends on two factors: the value of the prize and the contestants' relative efficiency. The latter is reminiscent of the Ricardian theory of international trade, in which equilibrium depends on comparative advantage (relative costs).

To conclude this section, we note that if the CSF is homogeneous of degree zero and marginal costs are constant and equal, in equilibrium the ratio of expenses equals the ratio of valuations. This can be seen from the first-order conditions, which states that

$$\frac{\partial p_1(g_1, g_2)}{\partial g_1} V_1 = 1 = -\frac{\partial p_1(g_1, g_2)}{\partial g_2} V_2.$$

The homogeneity of degree zero implies

$$\frac{\partial p_1(g_1, g_2)}{\partial g_1} g_1 + \frac{\partial p_1(g_1, g_2)}{\partial g_2} g_2 = 0.$$

Solving this system results in

$$\frac{g_1}{g_2} = \frac{V_1}{V_2}. \tag{3.4}$$

An interesting outcome of (3.4) is that if valuations are equal, then even if the CSF is skewed, both contestants will exert the same effort in equilibrium, provided their marginal costs are the same. This seems to contradict the results presented in the introduction to the chapter, which stated that all forms of asymmetry are equivalent. However, it should be remembered that these results do not mean that all asymmetries lead to the same equilibrium. In some cases, the substitutions imply that what is computed is not the equilibrium efforts, but a linear transformation of them. To find the true equilibrium, it is necessary to undo this transformation. This result illustrates this point very well by showing that, although all asymmetries result in strategically equivalent contests, they are not equivalent in terms of real payoffs and efforts.

3.3   Equilibrium with Heterogeneous Agents and Ratio Form CSF

In this section, we focus on the Ratio Form CSF.[3] Our focus will be on providing conditions for the existence of an equilibrium where all contestants invest positive effort. We will also explore how to extend these results to contests in which some contestants may be inactive in equilibrium.

To begin with, we consider a model in which valuations are the only source of heterogeneity. We need a new concept, namely the Harmonic Mean of V's denoted by H and defined as

$$H = \frac{n}{\sum_{j=1}^{n} \frac{1}{V_j}}. \tag{3.5}$$

If all contestants have identical valuations, $H = V$. The Harmonic mean is the reciprocal of the arithmetic mean of the reciprocals of valuations. It is different from other means like arithmetic or geometric. In particular, compared to the arithmetic mean, it tends to mitigate the impact of large valuations and increase the impact of small ones.

By multiplying both sides of (3.5) by V_i and rearranging terms,

$$V_i \sum_{j=1}^{n} \frac{1}{V_j} = \frac{n V_i}{H}.$$

---

[3] For an analysis including the Logit CSF, see Szidarovsky and Okuguchi (1997).

To ensure that all contestants are active in the equilibrium, we make the following assumption:

$$V_i > \frac{n-1}{n}H, \quad i \in \{1,2,\ldots,n\}. \tag{3.6}$$

Note that (3.6) always hold when contestants are identical or when $n = 2$. However, in general, it is a strong condition. With a larger number of contestants ($(n-1)/n$ close to one), the condition only holds when valuations are almost identical. Even with a small number of contestants, it is easy to find examples in which this assumption does not hold. For instance, if $V_1 = 3, V_2 = 2, V_3 = 1, H = 3/(1/3 + 0.5 + 1) \cong 1.66$ but $1 < (2/3)1.66 \simeq 1.1$, so contestant 3 does not meet (3.6). Exercise 3.5 requires the calculation of the equilibrium with these valuations.

PROPOSITION 3.2   *Assuming the Ratio Form CSF, there is a Nash equilibrium in which all contestants are active if and only if $V_i > (n-1)H/n$, $i \in \{1,2,\ldots,n\}$.*

Proof   We proceed as in Proposition 2.2 in Chapter 2. We first look for a suitable candidate for equilibrium and then we show that this candidate is indeed an equilibrium. To simplify notation, let $g \equiv \sum_{j=1}^{n} g_i$. Assuming interiority, the first-order conditions are

$$\frac{g - g_i}{g^2} = \frac{1}{V_i}$$

$$g - g_i = \frac{1}{V_i}g^2.$$

Adding over contestants

$$ng - g = g^2 \sum_{j=1}^{n} \frac{1}{V_j}.$$

Thus,

$$g^* = \frac{n-1}{\sum_{j=1}^{n} \frac{1}{V_j}} = \frac{(n-1)H}{n}.$$

And given that $g - g_i = \frac{1}{V_i}g^2$, then

$$g_i^* = \frac{(n-1)H}{n}\left(1 - \frac{(n-1)H}{nV_i}\right),$$

which is positive if and only if $nV_i/H \geq n-1$. Note also that winning probabilities and payoffs are given by

$$p_i^*(\boldsymbol{g}) = \frac{g_i^*}{g^*} = 1 - \frac{(n-1)H}{nV_i} \geq 0 \text{ if and only if } \frac{nV_i}{H} \geq n-1$$

$$\pi_i^*(\boldsymbol{g}) = \left(1 - \frac{(n-1)H}{nV_i}\right)\left(V_i - \frac{(n-1)H}{n}\right) \geq 0 \text{ if and only if } \frac{nV_i}{H} \geq n-1$$

where the last inequality comes from (3.5). Thus, g_i^* is a best reply for each contestant and given that the second-order conditions of payoff maximization hold, $(g_1^*, g_2^*, \ldots, g_n^*)$ is an equilibrium. $\qquad\square$

Now we consider the possibility that some contestants will be inactive in the equilibrium. For this purpose, we order the contestants such that $V_1 \geq V_2 \geq \cdots \geq V_n$. Intuition suggests that the most likely contestants to be inactive, i.e., to spend no effort, are those with lower valuations. First, we verify if the lowest valuation satisfies (3.6). If it does, all contestants are active in the equilibrium. If not, we remove the contestant with the lowest valuation and repeat the verification with the next lowest valuation. We repeat this process until all remaining contestants satisfy (3.6). Note that the condition for contestants to be active is always satisfied for $n = 2$. Thus, this algorithm will eventually stop. Let m denote the number of active contestants. The candidate equilibrium is the one found with n replaced by m. The effort of contestant i is given by

$$g_i^* = \frac{(m-1)H(m)}{m}\left\{1 - \frac{(m-1)H(m)}{mV_i}\right\},$$

where the harmonic mean H is written as a function of m since this number changes as we remove contestants from the contest. Finally, we must check if the first-order condition holds with inequality for contestants $m+1, \ldots, n$. See Nti (1997) for further details.

3.4   Effects of Rent-Seeking

Once we have secured the existence of equilibrium, it is time to consider the characteristics of such equilibrium. It is believed that rent-seeking can distort the allocation of resources. However, some argue that since all contestants engage in rent-seeking, the final outcome might not be affected.[4] To understand this, suppose that the probability of a contestant winning the prize in the absence of rent-seeking is q_i, while in the presence of rent-seeking, the probability depends on q_i and the rent-seeking efforts, mainly,

$$p_i(\mathbf{g}) = \frac{q_i g_i}{\sum_{j=1}^{n} q_j g_j} \text{ if } \sum_{j=1}^{n} q_j g_j > 0 \text{ and } p_i(\mathbf{g}) = \frac{1}{n} \text{ otherwise.} \qquad (3.7)$$

The motivation for this CSF is that rent-seeking efforts do not erase prior probabilities, it only enlarges or reduces them.

As discussed in Section 3.3, to ensure the existence of a Nash equilibrium with all contestants active, condition (3.6) is a necessary and sufficient requirement.

---

[4] Rent-Seeking is chosen here as a particular case of a contest. But the analysis of this section is equally applicable to any other form of contest.

Exercise 3.8 asks you to prove that, in order for the rent-seeking model under examination to have a Nash equilibrium with all contestants active, the following condition must be met:

$$q_i V_i > \frac{n-1}{\sum_{j=1}^{n} \frac{1}{q_j V_j}}. \tag{3.8}$$

To compute the Nash equilibrium under condition (3.8), let $S = \sum_{i=1}^{n} q_j g_j$, and consider the first-order condition for $i \in \{1, 2, \ldots, n\}$,

$$\frac{Sq_i - q_i^2 g_i}{S^2} V_i = 1, \quad q_i g_i = S - \frac{S^2}{q_i V_i}.$$

Adding up overall contestants,

$$nS - S = S^2 \sum_{j=1}^{n} \frac{1}{q_j V_j}$$

which implies that

$$S^* = \frac{n-1}{\sum_{j=1}^{n} \frac{1}{q_j V_j}}.$$

Thus, in a Nash equilibrium,

$$p_i(\mathbf{g}^*) = \frac{q_i g_i^*}{S^*} = 1 - \frac{n-1}{q_i V_i \sum_{j=1}^{n} \frac{1}{q_j V_j}}. \tag{3.9}$$

In general, we see that $p_i(\mathbf{g}^*) \neq q_i$. But if $n = 2$ and $V_1 = V_2 = V$,

$$p_i(\mathbf{g}^*) = \frac{q_i g_i^*}{S^*} = 1 - \frac{1}{1 + \frac{q_i}{q_j}} = q_i, i \in \{1, 2\}.$$

Therefore, in the case of two contestants, Rent-Seeking has no impact. See Corchón (2000) for a proof of this result for general Homogeneous of Degree Zero CSF. However, this conclusion does not hold for situations involving more than two contestants (see Exercise 3.9). All we can say is that:

PROPOSITION 3.3　*In a rent-seeking contest with n rent seekers and the CSF defined in (3.7), $p_i(\mathbf{g}^*) > p_j(\mathbf{g}^*)$ if and only if $q_i V_i > q_j V_j$.*

The proof of Proposition 3.3 comes directly from (3.9). In general, Rent-seeking makes a difference because a large prior pushes the luck of the contestant having it. Rent-seeking may also enhance efficiency because contestants with larger valuations have larger probabilities/shares of obtaining the prize. But this should be taken with some caution. Corrupt political parties may value office highly because they expect to extract a large return from it!

3.5   All Pay Auction with More Than Two Contestants

In Chapter 2, we have seen that the All Pay Auction models are extremely competitive contest in which the smallest difference in performance makes a big difference in results! In fact, the contestant with the smaller valuation earns zero in equilibrium. This suggests that there is not much gain in analyzing the case of n identical contestants because there is an equilibrium in which two of them are active – earning zero payoffs – and the rest are inactive, earning zero payoffs as well. We focus on the case in which at least one of the contestants with the largest valuations is different from the rest. We have the following result due to Hillman and Riley (1989).

PROPOSITION 3.4   *Suppose that $V_1 \geq V_2 > V_3 \geq \cdots \geq V_n$. Then there is a Nash equilibrium in which contestants 1 and 2 bid as in the two contestants case and the rest of the contestants bid zero. If $V_1 > V_2$, this equilibrium is unique.*

Proof   We will be content to give an intuition of how the proof works. Consider a candidate equilibrium where contestants 1 and 2 act as in the two contestants case. Suppose contestant 3 spends $\bar{g}_3$. Then, her expected payoffs are $\text{Prob}\{g_1 < \bar{g}_3\}\text{Prob}\{g_2 < \bar{g}_3\}V_3 - \bar{g}_3$. Since $\text{Prob}\{g_1 < \bar{g}_3\} < 1$, $V_3 < V_2$ and the expected payoffs of 2 are zero (or less because the expense by 3 might be positive), payoffs for 3 are necessarily negative if $\bar{g}_3 > 0$. Finally, if $V_1 > V_2$ strategies are those uniquely given by (2.1) and (2.2) in Chapter 2.   □

The very competitive All Pay Auction expels from the contests to all players that are not up to the standard of the second best! In other words, here, the third best is not even considered for the competition!

A full characterization of mixed strategy equilibrium is very technical and it is outside the scope of this book. The interested reader may consult it in Baye, Kovenock, and de Vries (1996).

3.6   Empirical Estimation of CSF

Having explored equilibrium and its characteristics, it is time to consider how these concepts fare in the real world.

Jia, Skaperdas, and Vaidya (2013) have surveyed the main challenges of applying contest theory to historical events. Along with the common technical difficulties in estimation faced by other branches of economics, we also face problems with data reliability and the lack of a straightforward method for converting it into efforts and winning probabilities, not to mention estimating valuations. Despite these limitations, choosing the correct CSF remains a challenge. As previously discussed, the form of the CSF significantly affects the characteristics of equilibria; therefore it is advisable to either test various CSFs or have a general functional form and let the data select the most suitable form.

Hwang (2012) considers the following CSF that he calls constant elasticity of augmentation (CEA):

$$p_i(\mathbf{g}) = \frac{\exp(\frac{k}{1-\rho}g_i^{1-\rho})}{\exp(\frac{k}{1-\rho}g_i^{1-\rho}) + \exp(\frac{k}{1-\rho}g_j^{1-\rho})} \quad \rho \in \mathbb{R}, k \in \mathbb{R}_+.$$

This CSF is a special case of a logit when $\phi(g_i) = \exp((k/(1-\rho))g_i^{1-\rho})$. When $\rho = 0$, we are back to the difference CSF. According to Hwang, "low ρ describes military technology in which the augmentation of the numerically superior side is very effective; the converse is true for a high ρ." Hwang interprets k as the "mass effect" that scales the differences between efforts. When k is close to zero, $\exp(k/(1-\rho))g_i^{1-\rho}$ is close to 1, and the probability of winning is close to $1/2$, meaning that the contest (war in this case) is decided randomly. When k is very large, the probability of winning tends to 1 when $g_i > g_j$ and to $1/2$ when $g_i = g_j$ so the CEA tends to the All Pay Auction. The parameter ρ is called the "elasticity of augmentation" and $1-\rho$ measures the elasticity of ϕ which, as we said before, measures the impact (or the merit) of g_i in the contest. Hwang estimates the elasticity of augmentation using actual battle data of the seventeenth-century European battles and World War II battles. He finds significant differences in ρ between these two scenarios. In the first case, ρ is close to one, while in the second case, it is close to half. This indicates that weapons play a more decisive role in modern wars compared to the seventeenth century, owing to factors such as improved organization and more accurate and specialized guns, etc.

Mildenberger and Pietri (2018) took a bold approach. To get around the data quality problem, they studied how contests play out in a virtual game where the data are perfect. Their paper empirically estimates four CSFs: ratio, logit, difference, and relative difference with $\alpha = 0.5$. In a database of 19,229 virtual battles, they show that the relative difference outperforms other existing forms of CSF.

Another approach to obtain reliable data is to simulate a contest in the lab. Experimental economics has a long pedigree starting with Chamberlin (1948) whose work was continued and refined by Vernon Smith who got the Nobel Prize in 2002. When experiments are run using the Ratio Form, CSF outcomes are not close to the theoretical predictions. Typically contestants spend more effort than the theoretical prediction. And even if payoff functions are identical, the variance of expenses is not negligible. Overspending is so notorious that some participants obtain negative expected payoffs! See Dechenaux, Kovenock, and Sheremeta (2015) for a detailed survey of all these issues. There are several explanations for this behavior.

1. **Utility of winning.** The motivation for this explanation comes from experiments in which auctioning a worthless prize incentives 40% of contestants to make a positive effort. In this case, the utility of the prize is not V, but $V + W_i$ where W_i is the utility of winning, yielding payoffs of $p_i(V + W_i) - g_i$. It is checked that subjects who exert higher efforts for the prize of zero also exert higher efforts for the positive monetary prize of 120. Another piece of evidence in favor of this explanation is that when p_i is announced as a share in the prize, predictions come much closer to observed data.

2. **Spiteful preferences and inequality aversion**. In this case, contestants obtain a negative utility from the success of another contestant. So if a contestant wins, she obtains $V - g_i$ but when losing she obtains $-S_i - g_i$. This yields payoffs of $p_i(V + S_i) - g_i - S_i$. Because S_i is given, this payoff function is strategically equivalent to the one in the case of the utility of winning. In both cases, having observed the expenses you can infer the value of W_i or S_i that makes the first-order condition of payoff maximization hold exactly. But, of course, this procedure does not elicit the true values of W_i or S_i but the values that make our model be correct.

3. **Behavioral explanations**. Overbidding also occurs in auctions and it has been shown that, in private-value auctions, it can be rationalized by level-k reasoning. Under this hypothesis, each contestant maximizes under the belief that all other contestants are one step less sophisticated than she is. Arve and Serena (2022) show that level-k reasoning can also explain overbidding in contests when there are more than two contestants or contestants are not identical.

Other explanations are mistakes and judgment errors and the origin of the endowment of effort. If the latter is obtained in a costly way, contestants tend to bid less than in the experiments quoted above.

3.7   Appendix: Existence of a Nash Equilibrium for Two-Person Games

Typically, proofs of the existence of an equilibrium assume that strategy spaces are compact and payoffs are continuous. However, as we have seen, if the CSF is homogeneous of degree zero, it is either undefined or discontinuous at the point where all expenses are zero. Therefore, the standard proof cannot be used in general for such cases. In this appendix, we address this issue specifically for the case when there are two contestants ($n = 2$).

Suppose that the payoffs are strictly concave with respect to the contestant's own strategy, twice continuously differentiable in $[0, V_1] \times [0, V_2] \setminus (0, 0)$, and can be written as

$$\pi_i(\mathbf{g}) = p_i(\mathbf{g})V_i - c_i(g_i).$$

We focus on the first-order condition of payoff maximization:

$$\frac{\partial p_i(\mathbf{g})}{\partial g_i}V_i - \frac{\partial c_i(\mathbf{g})}{\partial g_i} = 0. \tag{3.10}$$

If we can find a list of expenses such that (3.10) holds for both contestants, our concavity assumption implies that each action is maximizing the corresponding payoff and we have found a Nash equilibrium.

A possibility to find such a value of g_1 and g_2 is the following. Plug the best reply function of contestant 2 into the first-order conditions of payoff maximization of contestant 1, namely

$$\frac{\partial p_1(g_1, BR_2(g_1))}{\partial g_1} V_i - \frac{\partial c_1(g_1)}{\partial g_1} \tag{3.11}$$

and denote the expression in (3.11) as $T_1(g_1)$. Clearly T_1 is continuous for $g_1 > 0$. All we need is the existence of a couple of values of g_1, $\bar{g}_1$, and $\hat{g}_1$, such that

$$T_1(\bar{g}_1) > 0 \quad \text{and} \quad T_1(\hat{g}_1) < 0. \tag{3.12}$$

Then, the intermediate value theorem guarantees us the existence of a value of g_1, g_1^*, such that $T_1(g_1^*) = 0$. This leads us to the following result.

PROPOSITION 3.5   *Suppose that payoffs are strictly concave in its own strategy and twice continuously differentiable in $[0, V_1] \times [0, V_2] \setminus (0, 0)$. Under condition (3.12) a Nash equilibrium exists.*

Proof   The intermediate value theorem ensures the existence of g_1^* such that $T_1(g_1^*) = 0$. So, the first-order condition of payoff maximization is fulfilled and because strict concavity g_1^* maximizes payoffs of contestant 1. And g_2^* defined as $g_2^* = BR_2(g_1^*)$ maximizes payoffs of contestant 2. As a result, (g_1^*, g_2^*) constitutes a Nash equilibrium since each contestant's effort is the best response to the other's.   □

To look for the values of g_1 satisfying (3.12), it seems reasonable to look for a $\bar{g}_1$ close to zero since intuition suggests that when the effort is small, a contestant is willing to increase her own effort in an attempt to catch a larger share of the pie or increase the probability of winning the prize. A candidate for $\hat{g}_1$ may be found at very large values of g_1 (i.e., close to V_1) where it seems reasonable to assume that a decrease in expenses increases payoffs. In any case, any two values satisfying (3.12) work. Exercise 3.13 asks the reader to find $\bar{g}_1$ and $\hat{g}_1$ in the case of the Ratio Form CSF. Exercise 3.14 considers how a similar approach may work in contests with an arbitrary number of players.

3.8   Exercises

3.1   Consider a contest game with n contestants and payoffs

$$\pi_i(\mathbf{g}) = p_i(\alpha_1 g_1, \dots, \alpha_i g_i, \dots, \alpha_n g_n) V_i - c_i g_i.$$

Transform this game into one where all the asymmetries are collapsed in the CSF.

3.2   Compute the Nash equilibrium of a contest game with two contestants, linear cost, different valuations $V_1 \neq V_2$, and the Ratio Form CSF. Let the average and the variance of the valuations be defined as follows:

$$A = \frac{V_1 + V_2}{2}, \quad D = \frac{(V_1 - V_2)^2}{4}.$$

Prove that total expenses in equilibrium can be written as

$$g = g_1^* + g_2^* = \frac{A^2 - D}{2A}.$$

It should be noted that when the average valuations are kept constant, an increase in the variance of the valuations results in a decrease in the total expenses.

3.3 Consider an asymmetric contest with payoffs

$$\pi_i(\mathbf{g}) = \frac{\alpha_i g_i}{\sum_{j=1}^{n} \alpha_j g_j} - g_i.$$

(1) Show that a Nash equilibrium with all contestants active exists if and only if

$$\alpha_i > \frac{n-1}{\sum_{j=1}^{n} \frac{1}{\alpha_j}}.$$

(2) Prove that total effort in equilibrium can be written as

$$g^* = \sum_{i=1}^{n} g_i^* = \frac{n-1}{n} \left(1 - (n-1) \frac{\mathrm{Var}(\frac{1}{\alpha})}{\bar{X}^2} \right)$$

where

$$\bar{X} = \mathrm{mean}(1/\alpha) = (1/n) \sum_{j=1}^{n} (1/\alpha_j),$$

and

$$\mathrm{Var}(1/\alpha) = (1/n) \sum_{j=1}^{n} ((1/\alpha_j) - \bar{X})^2 = (1/n) \sum_{j=1}^{n} (1/\alpha_j)^2 - \bar{X}^2.$$

(3) Give an interpretation of this result.

3.4 Consider a game between two sellers, Seller 1 and Seller 2, each with a unit of a commodity. The profit from selling the commodity today is V_1 for Seller 1 and V_2 for Seller 2, where $V_1 > V_2$. If Seller 1 does not sell the commodity today, he can sell it tomorrow for a lower profit of V_1'. Seller 2 cannot sell tomorrow because that would result in negative profits, so he would prefer to keep the good that he values at 0 euros. Both sellers can influence the probability of selling today by making marketing expenses g_1 and g_2, respectively. The probability of selling today is

$$p_i(\mathbf{g}) = \begin{cases} \frac{g_i}{g_1 + g_2} & \text{if} \quad g_1 + g_2 > 0 \\ \frac{1}{2} & \text{if} \quad g_1 + g_2 = 0 \end{cases} \quad i = 1, 2.$$

Seller 1 does not need to spend marketing expenses to sell tomorrow. It is assumed that both sellers do not discount the future, so 1 euro today is equal to 1 euro tomorrow. Formulate this situation as a game in normal form.

(1) Find the Nash equilibrium of the game.
(2) Under what conditions will the marketing expenses of Seller 1 be higher than those of Seller 2 in the Nash equilibrium?

(3)   Can you answer question 2 simply by assuming that the CSF is homogeneous of degree zero?

3.5   Consider a contest between three contestants, with valuations for the prize as $V_1 = 3, V_2 = 2, V_3 = 1$. The probability of winning the prize depends on the effort, g_i, that each contestant makes in the contest. Assume that the marginal cost of effort is the same for all contestants, equal to one and that the CSF is the Ratio Form. Find the effort level that each contestant makes in the Nash equilibrium.

3.6   Consider a two-contestant contest with a prize value of $V = 1$ for both contestants. The marginal cost of effort for both contestants is 1. The CSF is the Relative Difference CSF with parameters $s = 1, \alpha = 1/2$, and $\beta = 1.5$. Prove that there is no pure strategy Nash equilibrium in this contest. Plot the best response functions of the two players on the same graph.

3.7   (This exercise extends the technique used in Exercise 2.7 to asymmetric games). Consider an aggregative game in which the payoffs of each player depend only on their own effort and the sum of all players' efforts, represented by g. Write the first-order condition as $T_i(g_i, g) = 0$. Assuming that the first-order condition can be written as $g_i = F_i(g)$ with F_i continuous. By defining $F(g) = \sum_{i=i}^{n} F_i(g)$, show that if F satisfies conditions (a) and (b) in Exercise 2.7 with $\mathbf{g}_{-i}$ substituted by g and B substituted by F, a Nash equilibrium exists.

3.8   Consider the rent-seeking model presented in Section 3.4. Show that a Nash equilibrium with all contestants active exists if and only if

$$q_i V_i > \frac{n-1}{\sum_{j=1}^{n} \frac{1}{q_j v_j}}.$$

3.9   Show by means of an example that when $n > 2$, rent-seeking matters (see Corchón, 2000).

3.10   Suppose that two countries – Country A and Country B – are in conflict over a disputed territory. The countries use efforts to increase their chances of winning control of the territory. The cost of effort is given by the function $C(g_i) = g_i$, $i \in \{A, B\}$. Assume that the countries have different valuations for the territory, with Country A valuing it at \$700 million and Country B valuing it at \$300 million. Country B has a maximum of \$50 million to expend in the conflict, but Country A does not face any financial constraint.

(1)   Using the Ratio Form CSF function, calculate the optimal effort levels for each country in the Nash equilibrium.
(2)   Plot the best replies for each country.
(3)   Suppose that the budget of Country B increases to \$100 million. How does this change the optimal effort levels and net benefits for each country? Explain your answer.

3.11   Marie and John are two students competing for a scholarship. Marie values the scholarship more than John, as she has a greater financial need. Marie values the scholarship at 8,000 euros, while John values it at 6,000 euros. The scholarship will be awarded to the student who submits the best essay. Both students must put in effort to write an essay, and the quality of the essay is directly proportional to the effort put in. Specifically, the quality of the essay is given by: $q = g/2$ where q is the quality of the essay, and g is the effort put in (measured in hours). The cost of effort is linear, with a cost of 20 euros per hour of effort.
(1)   Which mechanism would be most effective in encouraging both students to put in their best effort?
(2)   Compute the Nash equilibrium and interpret the result.

3.12   Develop a model for a political competition between two parties. Each party starts with a group of partisans who are loyal and will vote for their party regardless of the actions of the parties. The parties will need to expend resources to campaign and win over other voters.
(1)   Discuss all the ingredients of your model, strategies, prize, the CSF that you are going to use. (Take into account that the CSF should reflect the fixed votes that each party already has from its partisans.)
(2)   Solve the model and discuss the results.
(3)   Analyze how the results would change if the parties face financial constraints. How would these constraints affect their strategies and outcomes in the political competition?
(4)   Discuss the potential trade-offs and challenges each party might face in this scenario and how it might affect their overall performance.

3.13   Find the values $\bar{g}_1$ and $\hat{g}_1$ in (3.12) in the case of the Ratio Form CSF.

3.14   Consider an aggregative game characterized by payoffs $\pi_i(g_i, \sum_{j=1}^{n} g_j)$, wherein π_i is concave in g_i and differentiable for $\mathbf{g} \neq \mathbf{0}$. Assume that, from the first-order condition of payoff maximization, we can express g_i as a function of $\sum_{j=1}^{n} g_j$, denoted as $g_i = F_i(\sum_{j=1}^{n} g_j)$.
(1)   Find a condition similar to (3.12) such that the equation
$$\sum_{j=1}^{n} g_i = \sum_{j=1}^{n} F_i(\sum_{j=1}^{n} g_j) \text{ has a solution.}$$
(2)   Show how from the solution found in (1) above you can obtain a Nash equilibrium.

3.15   Consider a secession game where a group within a country may want to engage in secession to join a similar group in the annexing country. The annexing country decides whether or not to support the separatist ethnic group in the conflict. Assuming a Ratio CSF, find the equilibrium of such a game, see Hentschel (2022).

4 Foundations for Contest Success Functions

In this chapter, we provide foundations for the form of the various CSFs used so far. We will examine four approaches:

(1) **Noisy performance**. The outcome of a contest is driven by two factors: effort, and random elements such as weather, health, having a bad day, etc.
(2) **Axiomatics**. This approach derives the form of the CSF based on reasonable properties.
(3) **Planner.** A contest organizer decides the outcome. Randomness follows from the optimal policy of the planner or the incomplete information of contestants.
(4) **Bargaining and claims.** Contestants bargain about how to share the prize, taking into account the merits (efforts) or the claims that they have made in the contest.

We will delve into each of these four approaches in this chapter.[1]

4.1 Noisy Performance

The Noisy Performance approach was first introduced by Dixit (1987) and further developed by Hillman and Riley (1989). This approach posits that an individual's performance in a contest can be divided into two parts: effort and a random element, represented by the random variable ϵ_i. This random element accounts for external factors that can impact an individual's performance, such as physical or mental ability on a given day. Performance is therefore written as a function of both luck and effort, namely $h_i(\epsilon_i, g_i)$. Agent i wins the contest if and only if $h_i(\epsilon_i, g_i) > h_j(\epsilon_j, g_j)$ for any other contestant j.

For simplicity, let us consider two contestants. If noise enters additively in the function h_i, contestant i wins the contest if and only if

$$\epsilon_i + f_i(g_i) > \epsilon_j + f_j(g_j).$$

Let G be the cumulative distribution function of the difference between ϵ_j and ϵ_i. As you may recall from your statistics course, $G(f_i(g_i) - f_j(g_j))$ gives us the probability

---

[1] To this list, we can add persuasion. In this approach, the CSF appears as a result of contestants trying to persuade others; see Skaperdas and Vaidya (2012).

that $\epsilon_j - \epsilon_i$ is less than or equal to the value $f_i(g_i) - f_j(g_j)$. In other words, this is the probability that i wins the conflict. Hence, we obtain a generalized difference CSF,

$$p_i(\mathbf{g}) = G(f_i(g_i) - f_j(g_j)).$$

Refer to Exercise 4.1 to see how to find the relative difference CSF using this approach.

When the noise is perfectly correlated between contestants, $\epsilon_j = \epsilon_i$, contestant i wins the contest if and only if $f_i(g_i) > f_j(g_j)$. If $f_i = f_j = f$ and f is strictly increasing, this results in an All Pay Auction, where contestant i wins if and only if $g_i > g_j$.

Before we proceed, a caveat is necessary. Since the difference in noise is all that matters, there is a tendency to make assumptions about the distribution of the difference directly. However, we must be careful in doing so, as it is possible that such a distribution of the difference cannot be obtained from two independent and identically distributed (i.i.d.) random variables. For example, assuming that $\epsilon_j - \epsilon_i$ follows a uniform distribution is a bad assumption because there are no two specific i.i.d. noise terms such that their difference becomes uniformly distributed. Ewerhart and Serena (2023) list the distributions that have and do not have the property that the difference is distributed as the two original distributions. In the first group we have the Normal and the Logistic distributions. In the second group we have the Uniform (the difference of two uniform distributions yields the triangular distribution) and the Beta distributions.

A different possibility is that noise is multiplicative, so contestant i wins if and only if $\epsilon_i \phi(g_i) > \epsilon_j \phi(g_j)$, or equivalently, $\epsilon_j/\epsilon_i < \phi(g_i)/\phi(g_j)$. Hence,

$$p_i(\mathbf{g}) = G\left(\frac{\phi(g_i)}{\phi(g_j)}\right),$$

where G in this case is the accumulative distribution function of ϵ_j/ϵ_i.

This CSF resembles the Logit and the relative difference CSFs. Jia (2008) showed that, for $n > 2$, the CSF is Logit with $\phi(g_i) = g_i^\alpha$ if and only if each $\epsilon_i's$ is Inverse Exponential Distributed with $G(\theta) = \exp(-\gamma\theta^\alpha)$. The proof is very involved and is beyond the scope of this book.[2]

The consideration of noise affecting performance is very natural but it makes the CSF dependent on the distribution of the noise, about which, currently, we know very little. However, as technology advances, this may change. For example, if the noise comes from atmospheric factors like weather in sports or battles, it is likely that in the near future, we will have highly accurate weather forecasts for the next few days. Similarly, with advancements in tracking technology, it may soon be possible to monitor all internal variables that could impact an individual's performance.[3]

---

[2] Fu and Lu (2012a) extend this approach by allowing several prizes. All these contributions rely heavily on the techniques developed by McFadden (1974) in models of consumer choice.

[3] See MIT Technological Review, www.technologyreview.com/s/612055/dina-katabi-emerald-walls/. If this information is kept private, the game will be a Bayesian game (see Chapter 8).

4.2   Axiomatics

In the axiomatic approach, properties that a CSF must satisfy are postulated, and it explores the functional form that results from these properties. The seminal work in this area is Skaperdas (1996), where the following properties are postulated:

(P1) Imperfect discrimination: If $g_i > 0$, then $p_i(\mathbf{g}) > 0$.

This property indicates that all efforts, regardless of their magnitude – as long as it is strictly positive – result in a positive probability of reward. This excludes All Pay Auctions, where not all efforts are rewarded, and the linear difference CSF where a participant with significantly higher expenses compared to others is guaranteed to win. But the rest of CSFs considered so far exhibit this property.

(P2) Monotonicity: p_i increases in g_i and decreases in $g_j, j \neq i$.

It is reasonable to assume that a higher expenditure results in a greater likelihood (or share) of winning the prize, and that an increase in effort by competitors negatively affects one's chances of winning.

(P3) Anonymity: For any permutation $\pi: N \to N$, $p_i(g_1, \ldots, g_n) = p_{\pi(i)}(g_{\pi(1)}, \ldots, g_{\pi(n)})$ for all $i \in N$.

This property stipulates that only efforts are taken into account. As a result, if the ordering of contestants is altered, such as contestant 3 becoming contestant 10 and vice versa, their chances of winning remain unchanged in their new positions.

The next two properties explore a situation where some contestants from the original competition are restricted from participating. These properties examine the impact of this restriction on the winning probabilities of the remaining eligible contestants. Let $p_i^M(\mathbf{g})$ be the probability that i wins a contest in which only a subset M of the original contestants are allowed to compete.

(P4) Independence: $p_i^M(\mathbf{g})$, $i \in M$, is independent of g_j if $j \notin M$.

This property asserts that the efforts of disqualified contestants are not considered in determining the winner. For example, the budgets or physical efforts of teams that have been eliminated from the NBA Finals should not affect the outcome of the final, just as the budgets or physical efforts of teams not participating in the Champions League should not impact the outcome of that event.[4]

(P5) Consistency (IIA): Let M be a subset of N with at least two contestants,

$$p_i^M(\mathbf{g}) = \frac{p_i(\mathbf{g})}{\sum_{j \in M} p_j(\mathbf{g})} \text{ for all } \mathbf{g} \equiv (g_1, \ldots, g_i, \ldots, g_n).$$

This property is the most debated among all. It states that disqualifying a contestant should not alter the relative chances of victory among the remaining participants. This requires that the effect of the banned player on the others is symmetrical. See Exercise 4.2 for an example of a contest where Property 5 does not hold.

By utilizing these properties, Skaperdas (1996) established the following result:

---

[4] Budget of a nonparticipating team may influence the contest if it allows the acquisition of a player that otherwise would have been playing with a participating team.

PROPOSITION 4.1   *Properties (P1)–(P5) are satisfied if and only if the CSF is the Logit CSF. If, in addition, the CSF is homogeneous of degree zero, the Logit CSF is such that $\phi(g_i) = g_i^a$, $a > 0$.*

Clark and Riis (1998a) extended this result to the case where anonymity is not required and the CSF is homogeneous of degree zero. In such a case, the CSF obtained if the logit one with $\phi_i(g_i) = \alpha_i g_i^a$, $a > 0$ and $\alpha_i > 0$.

We encourage the reader to review the original papers for detailed proof of these results.

4.3   Contests Organized by a Planner

The outcomes of some contests occur naturally, such as those in research and development, sports, and war, while others – such as beauty contests, political competitions, and litigation – are the result of deliberate policy design by one or multiple contestants. In these contests, the CSF arises as a reduced form of a situation in which all contestants, including contestants and contest designers, act rationally. This section explores models in which this interaction leads to a random outcome.

A key question that arises is why a planner would have an interest in promoting randomness. Epstein and Nitzan (2006) provide an explanation: Suppose that the planner is concerned with contestants' payoffs and efforts. Interest in efforts may be rooted in the money generated by the event, as effort can be converted into financial gains. Furthermore, effort may serve as an indicator of the quality of the event or as a proxy for the welfare of external contestants observing the contest. Given two contestants with $V_1 \geq V_2$, it is postulated that the planner has the following payoff function

$$\alpha(\pi_1(\mathbf{g}) + \pi_2(\mathbf{g})) + (1 - \alpha)(g_1 + g_2), \quad \alpha \in [0, 1],$$

which is a linear convex combination of contestants' payoffs and efforts where α is the weight of payoffs. If α is close to one, the planner almost disregards efforts and if α is close to zero, efforts are very much appreciated by the planner. In case of no contest, the planner awards the prize to the contestant with the highest valuation. The planner prefers a random policy if and only if

$$\alpha(\pi_1(\mathbf{g}^*) + \pi_2(\mathbf{g}^*)) + (1 - \alpha)(g_1^* + g_2^*) > \alpha V_1$$

where asterisks refer to the equilibrium values in the contest. Taking into account the definition of contestants payoffs and assuming $p_1(\mathbf{g}^*) < 1$, the previous inequality can be written as

$$\frac{(1 - 2\alpha)(g_1^* + g_2^*)}{\alpha(1 - p_1(\mathbf{g}^*))} > V_1 - V_2. \tag{4.1}$$

To grasp the fundamentals, suppose that $V_1 \cong V_2$. If $\alpha < 1/2$, the left-hand side of (4.1) is always positive, so the planner prefers to run a contest, i.e., a policy of randomness. This is because the planner likes efforts so she chooses the contest instead of an effortless allocation of the prize. Conversely, when $\alpha > 1/2$, the planner is not very interested in efforts so she chooses no contest, which preserves payoffs. Exercise 4.3 asks you to compute the values of α for which randomness is the preferred policy for the contest with the Ratio Form CSF and the All Pay Auction with two contestants with different valuations.

The previous approach does not address the type of CSF that may arise in a contest. Let us consider this issue.

Consider two contestants and assume that the planner is only interested in efforts but has a bias. For example, if a theoretical economist competes against an applied economist for a chair, the bias represents the decider's preferences for theory versus applied work. Similarly, if contestants are from different parts of the world or different genders, the bias reflects the planner's preferences for nationality or gender. In litigation, the bias represents the opinion of the deciders (a judge or a jury) regarding similar cases. The bias, also known as type, is represented by a random variable θ which for simplicity is assumed to be uniformly distributed in the interval $[0, 1]$. Let $U_i(\theta, g_i)$ be the decider's payoff if the prize is awarded to contestant $i \in \{1, 2\}$. The function U_i is assumed to increase with g_i. Additionally, U_1 is assumed to decrease with θ while U_2 is assumed to increase with θ. Therefore, θ represents the planner's bias toward contestant 2.

In Figure 4.1, the utility functions of the planner are $U_1(\theta, g_1) = 0.5g_1 - 2\theta$ and $U_2(\theta, g_2) = \theta g_2$. When $g_1 = g_2 = 1$, the planner prefers contestant 1 for $\theta < 0.166$ and contestant 2 for the other values of θ. With $g_1 = g_2 = 2$, the intersection is at $\theta = 0.25$. Given that θ is uniformly distributed, the values of θ where the planner is indifferent between contestants are also the probability of contestant 1 winning.

The important fact is that contestants are uncertain about θ. This could be due to ignorance of the planner's identity, conflicting opinions from the planner, or uncertainty about the planner's true bias. Think, e.g., of the allocation of grants and professional prizes. In any case, the planner of type θ, after observing the efforts, awards the prize to contestant 1 if and only if $U_1(\theta, g_1) > U_2(\theta, g_2)$. However, since contestants are uncertain about θ, they view this inequality as occurring with some probability. Therefore, the probability of $U_1(\theta, g_1) > U_2(\theta, g_2)$ is equivalent to the probability of contestant 1 winning the contest.

As an illustration, let us consider $U_1(\theta, g_1) = V_1(\theta) + a_1g_1$ and $U_2(\theta, g_2) = V_2(\theta) + a_2g_2$, where $a_1, a_2 > 0$, V_1 strictly decreases with θ while V_2 strictly increases with θ. This means the planner has quasilinear preferences. To determine the planner's type who would be indifferent to the choice between both candidates, θ', given g_1 and g_2, we solve the equation

$$a_1g_1 - a_2g_2 = V_2(\theta) - V_1(\theta).$$

Let $z(\theta) = V_2(\theta) - V_1(\theta)$. Note that z is strictly increasing and therefore invertible. Hence, $\theta' = z^{-1}(a_1g_1 - a_2g_2)$. Given the expenses made by the candidates, for all types below θ' contestant 1 wins the contest. Since θ is uniformly distributed,

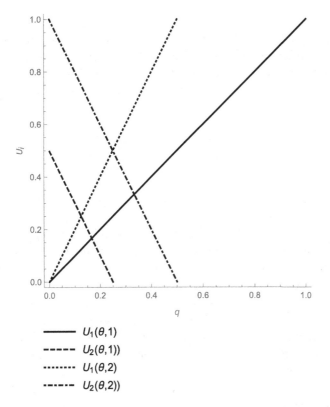

Figure 4.1 Utility functions of the planner as a function of the bias of the planner in favor of contestant 1 for $g_1 = g_2 = 1$ and $g_1 = g_2 = 2$

$p_1(g_1, g_2) = z^{-1}(a_1 g_1 - a_2 g_2)$, which is the difference form CSF considered in Chapter 2.[5]

Exercise 4.4 requests the reader to work out a special case of this construction to derive the Che and Gale CSF.

Suppose now that the utility function of a planner is multiplicatively separable in type and expenses, with $U_1(\theta, g_1) = (1 - \theta) f_1(g_1)$ and $U_2(\theta, g_2) = \theta f_2(g_2)$. If we find the type of planner for who is indifferent between contestants 1 and 2, the probability that contestant 1 wins the contest, $p_1(g_1, g_2)$, is calculated as $f_1(g_1)/(f_1(g_1) + f_2(g_2))$. This results in the Logit CSF. To find another CSF that can be derived in a similar manner, see Exercise 4.5.

The previous paragraphs suggest that by carefully selecting the form of the planner's utility function, any CSF can be derived. However, Corchón and Dahm (2010) demonstrate that this is mostly accurate only for two contestants. The situation becomes more complex when there are more contestants, as explained below.

---

[5] If $U_1(\theta, g_1)$ is always larger than $U_2(\theta, g_2)$, the probability of contestant 1 winning the contest is 1. If $U_1(\theta, g_1)$ is always smaller than $U_2(\theta, g_2)$, the probability of contestant 1 winning the contest is 0.

Assume three contestants with $U_i(1/2, g_i) \to \infty$ when $g_i \to \infty$, for $i \in \{1,3\}$. This assumption is fulfilled in the payoff functions used in the paragraph above whenever $f_i(g_i) \to \infty$ when $g_i \to \infty$. Additionally, U_1 is assumed to decrease with θ while U_3 is assumed to increase with θ and U_2 is continuous in θ and g_2. Let $\tilde{U}_2(g_2) = \max_\theta U_2(\theta, g_2)$, $\theta \in [0,1]$. By taking g_1 and g_3 large enough, say $\tilde{g}_1$ and $\tilde{g}_3$, we have that

$$U_1(\theta, \tilde{g}_1) > \tilde{U}_2(g_2), \forall \theta \in [0, 1/2)$$
$$U_3(\theta, \tilde{g}_3) > \tilde{U}_2(g_2), \forall \theta \in (1/2, 1].$$

Thus, contestant 2 never obtains the prize. Moreover, because $\tilde{U}_2(g_2)$ is continuous in g_2, small variations in g_2 do not affect either p_1 or p_3. Therefore, the Logit CSF cannot be obtained from payoff maximization. Note that in this example we keep the set of types one dimensional, but now we have three contestants. So now the type cannot be interpreted as a bias against a contestant in particular but as a bias against a particular class of contestants, i.e., based on sexism, race, etc.

In the previous approach, the CSF arises from the uncertainty about the planner's type. In particular, the way in which the planner judges the merits of expenses is unknown to the contestants. If this uncertainty disappears, the random element in the CSF also disappears, resulting in a, possibly asymmetric, All Pay Auction.

What if contestants know the type of the planner but the planner is unable to commit to a specific CSF? To address this scenario, assume again that the planner has preferences representable by a utility function. However, in this case, the planner cannot commit to a particular CSF and instead waits until the contestants have made their efforts before awarding the prize probabilistically, as in Epstein and Nitzan (2006). This creates a two-stage game, where the planner selects probabilities or shares in the second stage, while the contestants exert effort in the first stage. We will see that, once efforts have been made, the best reply of the planner is a mixed strategy mapping efforts into probabilities/shares. The best reply is the CSF. This approach avoids predictability of the planner's actions that would lead to an All Pay Auction.

Consider a generalized utilitarian planner whose payoff function is a constant elasticity of substitution function with the payoffs of contestants as arguments

$$W(\boldsymbol{p}, \boldsymbol{g}) = \begin{cases} \left(\sum_{i=1}^n (\pi_i(p_i, g_i))^{1-r} \right)^{1/(1-r)} & \text{if } r \neq 1 \\ \sum_{i=1}^n \ln(\pi_i(p_i, g_i)) & \text{if } r = 1 \end{cases} . \tag{4.2}$$

The positive parameter r represents the degree of inequality aversion of the planner. The utilitarian case corresponds to $r = 0$ in which the planner does not care about the distribution of payoffs, just about the sum. When $r = 1$, the planner cares about the product of payoffs as in the celebrated bargaining model of John Nash (1950b). When

r goes to infinity, the Rawlsian case arises and the concern is with the least well-off only.[6]

The planner maximizes $W(\boldsymbol{p}, \boldsymbol{g})$ as defined in (4.2) with $\pi_i(p_i, g_i) = p_i V_i - g_i$, taking $\boldsymbol{g}$ as given, subject to $\boldsymbol{p}$ nonnegative and adding up to one. It is instructive to start with the Bernoulli–Nash case in which $r = 1$. In this case the Lagrangian is

$$\sum_{i=1}^{n} \ln (p_i V_i - g_i) - \gamma \left(\sum_{i=1}^{n} p_i - 1 \right).$$

Looking at the first-order condition for an optimum, we obtain

$$(p_i V_i - g_i) V_n = (p_n V_n - g_n) V_i \text{ for } i \in \{1, \ldots, n-1\}.$$

Rearranging,

$$p_i = \frac{p_n V_n - g_n}{V_n} + \frac{g_i}{V_i} \text{ for } i \in \{1, \ldots, n-1\}.$$

Adding up overall contestants and taking into account $\sum_{i=1}^{n} p_i = 1$,

$$p_n(\boldsymbol{g}) = \frac{1 - \sum_{j=1}^{n} \left(g_j / V_j \right)}{n} + \frac{g_n}{V_n}$$

and replacing this in the previous equation, we obtain (4.3),

$$p_i(\boldsymbol{g}) = \frac{1 - \sum_{j=1}^{n} \left(g_j / V_j \right)}{n} + \frac{g_i}{V_i} \text{ for } i \in \{1, \ldots, n\} \tag{4.3}$$

which is linear in efforts. Thus, we arrive at a difference CSF. If $n = 2$, the CSF is

$$p_i(\boldsymbol{g}) = \frac{1}{2} + \frac{1}{2} \left(\frac{g_i}{V_i} - \frac{g_j}{V_j} \right) \text{ for } i \in \{1, 2\} \text{ and } j \neq i \tag{4.4}$$

in which the weights of efforts are the inverse of valuations.[7] Recall that the CSFs above are identical to the linear difference CSF in Che and Gale (2000) which when $p_i > 0$ for $i \in \{1, 2\}$ is defined as

$$p_i(\boldsymbol{g}) = \frac{1}{2} + s(g_i - g_j) \text{ for } i \in \{1, 2\} \text{ and } j \neq i, \tag{4.5}$$

where s is a positive scalar. In the case of two contestants (4.4) coincides with (4.5) if there is a common value V and $V = 1/2s$.

What is mildly surprising is that the case in which $r \neq 1$ and $r \in (0, \infty)$ yields a very similar CSF to the case $r = 1$ which is still linear in efforts. Specifically, from the first-order conditions, we obtain the following CSF

---

[6] These concepts are masterfully explained in Roemer (1996).

[7] In (4.4), for simplicity, we have not considered the issues arising from probabilities adding up to one and being nonnegative.

$$p_i(\mathbf{g}) = \frac{1 - \sum_{j=1}^{n}(g_j/V_j)}{\sum_{j=1}^{n}(V_j/V_i)^{\frac{1-r}{r}}} + g_i/V_i \text{ for } i \in \{1,\ldots,n\} \tag{4.6}$$

which is a generalization of (4.3). The proof is identical to the $r = 1$ case; see Exercise 4.7.[8] Note that in the Rawlsian case when $r \to \infty$, the CSF is

$$p_i(g_i, \mathbf{g}_{-i}) = \frac{1 - \sum_{j=1}^{n}(g_j/V_j)}{\sum_{j=1}^{n} V_i/V_j} + g_i/V_i \text{ for } i \in \{1,\ldots,n\}.$$

Other forms of the planner utility function yield similar results; see Exercise 4.8. This suggests that this approach will not be able to provide a foundation for the Logit CSF.[9] So let us try something different.

Suppose now that the planner is interested only in efforts. In particular she has a utility function which corresponds to a special case of the class postulated by Kahneman and Tversky (1979, p. 276) for regular prospects, namely

$$W(\mathbf{p}, \mathbf{g}) = \sum_{i=1}^{n} p_i^\alpha f_i(g_i)^{1-\alpha}, 1 > \alpha > 0. \tag{4.7}$$

The function $f_i(g_i)$ corresponds to how the planner evaluates the efforts of contestant i. This term is weighted by the probability that i wins the contest with exponents α and $1 - \alpha$, measuring the elasticity of the contest organizer's payoff with respect to effort and win probability. This reflects that contestants are perfect substitutes from the contest organizer's point of view and implies that the marginal product of a contestant's effort does not depend on the effort of others. Now we have the following result:

PROPOSITION 4.2   *The Logit CSF*

$$p_i(\mathbf{g}) = \frac{f_i(g_i)}{\sum_{j=1}^{n} f_j(g_j)} \text{ for } i \in \{1,\ldots,n\} \tag{4.8}$$

is the unique CSF that can be rationalized in mixed-strategies by a function fulfilling (4.7).

Proof Let us maximize $W(\mathbf{p}, \mathbf{g})$, $\mathbf{p} \in S = \{\mathbf{p} \in \Re_+^n / \sum_{j=1}^{n} p_j = 1\}$. Since $W(\mathbf{p}, \mathbf{g})$ is continuous on $\mathbf{p}$ and S is compact, a maximum exists. Since $W(\mathbf{p}, \mathbf{g})$ is strictly concave on $\mathbf{p}$ and S is convex, the maximum is unique. Consider the first-order conditions of the maximization with respect to $\mathbf{p}$

$$\alpha p_i^{\alpha-1} f_i(g_i)^{1-\alpha} - \lambda = 0, i \in \{1, 2, \ldots, n\}.$$

---

[8] A complete proof would be required to show that the second-order conditions of maximization hold. See Corchón and Dahm (2011).

[9] It can be shown that under pretty mild assumptions, no CSF can be rationalized in mixed strategies by a generalized utilitarian planner if it is either (i) homogeneous of degree zero or (ii) homogeneous of any degree and symmetric. See Corchón and Dahm (2011).

Clearly, the maximum is interior because if $p_i \rightarrow 0$, the left-hand side of the above equation goes to infinity. The above equations imply that

$$p_i^{\alpha-1} f_i(g_i)^{1-\alpha} = p_j^{\alpha-1} f_j(g_j)^{1-\alpha}, i, j \in \{1, 2, \ldots, n\}$$

which yield

$$p_i = \frac{f_i(g_i) p_n}{f_n(g_n)}, i \in \{1, 2, \ldots, n\}. \tag{4.9}$$

Substituting these equations in the simplex, we obtain that

$$p_n = \frac{f_n(g_n)}{\sum_{j=1}^{n} f_j(g_j)}.$$

Substituting this equation in (4.9), we obtain (4.8). □

4.4 Bargaining and Claims

In certain situations, contestants engage in negotiation regarding their individual shares. For example, consider several heirs discussing the division of a divisible inheritance, such as money or a plot of land, where their caregiving efforts for the deceased are publicly known. The question arises of how to fairly divide the inheritance. Another example is a coalition of countries that have won a war and must divide the spoils of victory.

The theory of bargaining seeks to answer the general question of how to divide a valuable "pie," such as an object or set of objects. Given contestants with utilities $u_1, u_2, \ldots, u_n$ belonging to a feasible utility set $\mathcal{U}$, the bargaining problem is to find a distribution of utilities within $\mathcal{U}$. John Nash (1950b) was one of the pioneers in answering this question. He was one of the fathers of the axiomatic method, which involves decomposing a solution into properties that it must fulfill. For a detailed analysis of Nash's contribution to bargaining, see the survey by Serrano (2021). Here, we will simply state his result. If certain properties of the solution hold, the distribution of utilities that maximizes the product of $u_i - d_i$ over the feasible utility set is obtained, where $\mathbf{d}$ represents the disagreement payoffs vector or the payoff vector if there is no agreement.

In Figure 4.2, a feasible utility set $\mathcal{U}$ is depicted, which is the set of points below the function $u_1 = 1 - 2u_2^2$. The disagreement payoffs are $\mathbf{d} = (d_1, d_2) = (0, 0)$. The figure also shows some of the indifference curves of the function $u_1 u_2$. In this case, the Nash solution gives utilities of 2/3 and 0.408 to contestants 1 and 2, respectively.

The asymmetric Nash bargaining solution maximizes $\Pi_{i=1}^{n} u_i^{\alpha_i}$ where $\alpha_i \geq 0$ reflect the bargaining power of contestant i. In Figure 4.2, one of the indifference curves of the function $u_1^{1/3} u_2$ is represented.

Let us examine how the Nash Bargaining Solution can be used to determine the distribution of a prize. We begin by assuming that if the contestants cannot reach an

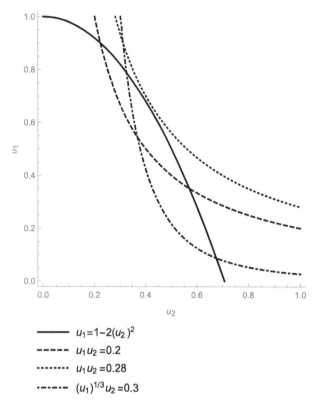

Legend:

$u_1 = 1 - 2(u_2)^2$

$u_1 u_2 = 0.2$

$u_1 u_2 = 0.28$

$(u_1)^{1/3} u_2 = 0.3$

Figure 4.2 Feasible utility set $\mathcal{U}$ and indifference curves for the functions $u_1 u_2$ and $u_1^{1/2} u_2$

agreement, the prize will not be shared, $\mathbf{d} = \mathbf{0}$. Given that efforts have already been made, they are sunk, and the contestants' utilities become the shares of the prize. The Nash Bargaining solution is found by solving the following maximization problem:

$$\max \prod_{i=1}^{n} p_i^{\alpha_i}, \quad p_i \geq 0, \ i \in \{1, 2, \ldots, n\}, \quad \sum_{i=1}^{n} p_i = 1.$$

The first-order conditions of this program are

$$p_j = \frac{\alpha_j}{\alpha_i} p_i \text{ for all } i, j \in \{1, 2, \ldots, n\}.$$

Suppose that the weights, α_i, are given by $\phi(g_i)$, where ϕ is strictly increasing and reflects the valuation of the efforts, i.e., the more effort, the more weight. Given that $\sum_{j=1}^{n} p_j = 1$,

$$p_i(\mathbf{g}) = \frac{\alpha_i}{\sum_{j=1}^{n} \alpha_j} = \frac{\phi(g_i)}{\sum_{j=1}^{n} \phi(g_j)}$$

which is the Logit CSF (see Dagan and Volij, 1993 and Corchón and Dahm, 2010). See Anbarci, Skaperdas, and Syropoulos (2002) for a comparison of the outcomes yielded by different bargaining solutions.

To conclude this section, we will provide a brief overview of how to obtain CSFs based on the theory of claims. This theory deals with dividing an object when there are claims on it. In the previously mentioned examples of war and inheritance, the claims are the efforts made by the countries in the war or the time spent by the contestants caring for the deceased person. Let $\phi(g_i)$ be the claim of contestant i, which is her aspiration, and assume $d = 0$. The proportional solution chooses shares $(p_1, \ldots, p_n)$ such that $p_i = t\phi(g_i)$ for some $t \geq 0$, meaning shares are proportional to claims. By summing up over contestants, $t = 1/\sum_{j=1}^{n} \phi(g_j)$. Hence, the share of contestant i is

$$p_i(\mathbf{g}) = t\phi(g_i) = \frac{\phi(g_i)}{\sum_{j=1}^{n} \phi(g_j)}.$$

The proportional solution to bargaining with claims leads to the Logit CSF (see Corchón and Dahm, 2010).

4.5 Exercises

4.1 Find the form in which noise and expenses yield the relative difference CSF. (Hint: Consider that performance of contestant i is given by $g_i + (g_1 + g_2)\epsilon_i$.)

4.2 Show an example in which the consistency property (P5), as described in Section 4.2, does not hold. (See Corchón, 2007, example 2.1.)

4.3 Compute equilibrium efforts in the All Pay Auction and in a contest with the Ratio Form CSF when V_1 and V_2 are different. Find the values of α for which the planner prefers the random contest.

4.4 Using the tools developed in Section 4.3, find $V_1(\theta)$, $V_2(\theta)$, a_1 and a_2 such that we obtain the difference-form CSF analyzed by Che and Gale (2000).

4.5 Let $U_1(\theta, g_1) = f_1(g_1)$ and $U_2(\theta, g_2) = 2\theta f_2(g_2)$ if $\theta \leq 1/2$ and $U_2(\theta, g_2) = f_2(g_2)/(2(1 - \theta))$ if $1/2 \leq \theta < 1$. Show that the CSF that arises from these utilities of the planner is $p_1(\mathbf{g}) = f_1(g_1)/(2f_2(g_2))$ if $f_1(g_1) \leq f_2(g_2)$ and $p_1(\mathbf{g}) = 1 - f_2(g_2)/(2f_1(g_1))$ otherwise. This expression is a generalization of the family of serial contests analyzed in Alcalde and Dahm (2007).

4.6 Suppose that three contestants are symmetrically distributed in the unit circle, which is now our set of types. Assume that contestants only compete with neighbors. If the prize is awarded to contestant i, the decider's payoffs are $U_1(\theta, g_1) - u - k|l_i - \theta| + g_1^\alpha$, where u, k, and α are positive numbers, l_i is the location of i in the circle and $\alpha < 1$. Derive the CSF that can be seen as an extension of Che and Gale's linear difference form. See Corchón and Dahm (2010), example 9.

4.7 Derive Equation (4.6) described in Section 4.3.

4.8 Suppose that the planner maximizes a constant absolute inequality aversion function (see Corchón and Dahm, 2011). Show that the CSF arising from this maximization is also linear in efforts.

4.9 Show that, for $n = 2$, the claim-egalitarian solution induces a generalization of the Che and Gale difference form contest success function (see Corchón and Dahm, 2010).

4.10 Describe the three bargaining solutions that are presented in Anbarci, Skaperdas, and Syropoulos (2002). Discuss the consequences of using each of these solutions as different division rules and the impact of this choice on the equilibrium investments in guns. Based on the article's findings, what recommendations would you make to parties involved in a negotiation in a conflict situation regarding the choice of bargaining solution and its impact on investments in guns?

4.11 Suppose that we use the noise performance approach to deduce the CSF in a two-person contest. Suppose the performance of contestant i is given by $h_i(\varepsilon_i, g_i) = \varepsilon_i + g_i^2$. Suppose that ε_1 and ε_2 are independent and uniformly distributed random variables. Find the CSF that yields this approach.

Part II

Extensions

5   Contests between Groups

In the preceding chapters, we analyzed contests that involved individual contestants. In these contests, contestans may consist of multiple units, such as an army composed of several battalions, as long as the aggregate effort is controlled by a single decision-making contestant. But this is not always the case. For instance, General Eisenhower served as the Supreme Commander of the Allied Expeditionary Force in the European theater during World War II, directing the Normandy landings and subsequent battles in France and Germany.[1] But on the other side of Europe, Stalin led the Soviet Union's battle against the Germans and took orders from no one. Not only in wars but also in politics, research and development, lobbying, and sports, contests are often played by groups of individuals.

This chapter explores the new issues that arise as a consequence of contests being played by groups. We present a model of two groups fighting for a prize in which effort is provided by the free will of contestants. The effort provided in this scenario is compared to the effort provided when dictated by the supreme commander of the group. We consider the validity of Mancur Olson's conjecture that small groups have the upper hand in lobbying. The conjecture is qualified by showing that it is true under certain conditions, but not in all circumstances. The CSF that would be chosen by the group is also discussed. The chapter concludes with the presentation of results from experiments on group contests, which validate some but not all of the predictions made by the theoretical models.

5.1   A Model of Contests between Groups

Assume two groups denoted by G_x and G_y with n_x and n_y members, respectively. Contests between more than two groups are possible (i.e., politics, R&D, sports), but we focus here on the simplest possible case. We take the members of the group as given. A possible extension of this model would be to consider that contestants can enter into the groups. For instance, a farmer can decide to join the American Farmer Association or not. In the simple model that we present here, we assume that groups were already formed and study their performance.

---

[1] The difficult relationship between Eisenhower and some of his subordinates (Montgomery, De Gaulle) was a well-known source of friction in the Allied command.

An Impact Function (IF, a name due to Wärneryd, 1998) converts the efforts of all members of a group (g_i for a typical contestant in G_x and g_j for a typical contestant in G_y) into the performance of this group, which is denoted, respectively, by X and Y. For simplicity, we assume that performance is just the sum of the efforts of the individuals inside the group. Thus, $X = \sum_{i \in \mathcal{G}_x} g_i$. Similarly, the performance of the second group is $Y = \sum_{j \in \mathcal{G}_y} g_j$. These IFs are called additive, and they represent the simplest way to aggregate efforts. Indeed, other forms of aggregation are possible. For instance, aggregate effort could be the best effort of a member of this group. This may be appropriate when positive or creative aspects are paramount to determining the success of the group. Thus, in a competition for the Most Valuable Player of a game, the best performance is what really counts. Chowdhury, Lee, and Sheremeta (2013) called this IF the best shot. In this case, $X = \max_{i \in G_x} \{g_i\}$ and similarly for Y. But it could be the other way around. In providing a dish for a contest, the worst side of the dish may be pivotal. Or when defending a front, the weakest defender is decisive. In these cases, $X = \min_{i \in \mathcal{G}_x} \{g_i\}$ and similarly for Y. This IF is called the weakest link (Lee, 2012). Also, efforts can be substitutes, as in the case of the additive IF, or complements. Kolmar and Rommeswinkel (2013) propose the CES form that encompasses both $X = (\sum_{i \in \mathcal{G}_x} g_i^\rho)^{1/\rho}$, see Exercise 5.1.

Knowing that all these variations are possible, let us stick with the simple case of an additive IF.

The probability that group $\mathcal{G}_x$ wins the contest, $p(X, Y)$, is assumed to increase with X and to decrease with Y. Similarly, $1 - p(X, Y)$ is the probability that group $\mathcal{G}_y$ wins the contest.

To start with, suppose that the prize is equally valued by all contestants in the contest and it is a public good. You may think of a law that affects all the lobbyists in a group equally. Or that the prize is awarded to a team like in the World Series or the Champions League. We will see that the nature of the prize, in particular – whether it is a public good (enjoyed by all members of the group) or a private good (which has to be divided among the members of the winning group) – is an important determinant of the characteristics of equilibrium. We postpone this discussion to Section 5.3.

So far, we have been content to assume that the cost of effort is linear in effort. We understood it as a simplification that allows us to focus on the CSF. But this assumption here is not appropriate anymore. This is because if the cost is linear and identical for all members in a group, given our assumption that IF is additive, individual efforts are perfect substitutes. Therefore, efforts of each member of the group are undetermined in equilibrium. Think of a group of three individuals that in equilibrium makes an aggregate effort of, say, 10 with individual efforts 2, 3, and 5. Any permutation of individual efforts is an equilibrium. Even worse, if individuals have different linear cost functions, the individual with the lowest cost may end up making the total aggregate effort. (See Baik, 1993 for the equivalent case of different valuations of the prize.) These two points will be formally proven in the next section. To avoid these oddities, we will work in this chapter with a strictly convex cost of effort, identical for all contestants and denoted by $C(g_k)$, $k \in \{i, j\}$. An example of this is $C(g_k) = g_k^a$ with $a > 1$. We remark that we do not consider organizational costs. All the costs borne by the members of a group are the private costs of efforts.

The previous discussion implies that we can define the payoffs for contestant i of group $\mathcal{G}_x$, and a contestant j of group $\mathcal{G}_y$, as $\pi_i(\mathbf{g}) = p(X,Y)V - C(g_i)$ and $\pi_j(\mathbf{g}) = (1 - p(X,Y))V - C(g_j)$.

Now we have to make an assumption about the coordination of the members of the group with regard to efforts. Our models in previous chapters can be interpreted as a contest among groups in which all members of a given group are making the effort they have been told to do, so we have perfect coordination. In the Marxian theory of social classes, each member of a class acts in accordance with the interests of this class. In this chapter, we will go to the other extreme and assume no coordination at all. In the parlance of contract theory, there are no binding contracts that can force individuals to make certain efforts. Each individual decides noncooperatively the effort that she puts into the coalition. This is, of course, an extreme assumption. Everybody who has been on a team knows that as long as efforts are, at least partially, visible, lazy players receive all sorts of incentives to increase effort. It is only in the limited case in which efforts are not visible that the assumption of individualistic behavior becomes more reasonable.[2] Our assumption can be regarded as a study of a polar case, valid as long as it sheds light on the problem, and allows us to focus on a new problem: the free-riding effect.

5.2   Free Riding

In this section, we compare the equilibrium efforts of a situation in which efforts are chosen noncooperatively with those that would be chosen by a perfectly informed supreme commander of this group.

Assuming an interior maximum, the first-order conditions for the payoff maximization of contestant i from group G_x and of contestant j from group G_y are as follows:

$$\frac{\partial p(X^*, Y^*)}{\partial X}V = C'(g_i^*), \, i \in \mathcal{G}_x, \quad -\frac{\partial p(X^*, Y^*)}{\partial Y}V = C'(g_j^*), \, j \in \mathcal{G}_y, \quad (5.1)$$

where stars represent a Nash equilibrium of this game.

Here we can see something we commented earlier: If $C(g_k)$ is linear, the previous equations only determine X and Y, leaving individual efforts totally undetermined. And if an unlucky contestant has a cost function that is below the cost functions of the rest, she/he must bear all the brunt of the effort because it is impossible that the first-order condition holds with equality for all contestants except the hapless one.

Consider now a supreme commander of group $\mathcal{G}_x$ who can dictate individual efforts. Following Vázquez-Sedano (2018), this contest is called Centralized. By

---

[2] However, equilibrium efforts can be anticipated. This is needed for Nash equilibrium to be a meaningful concept. In other words, efforts can be predicted, but they are not contractible.

simplicity, assume that the supreme commander is interested in maximizing the sum of all the payoffs of their subordinates. Using the superscript o to denote this solution, the first-order conditions are

$$n_x \frac{\partial p(X^o, Y^o)}{\partial X} V = C'(g_i^o), i \in \mathcal{G}_x, \quad -n_y \frac{\partial p(X^o, Y^o)}{\partial Y} V = C'(g_j^o), j \in \mathcal{G}_y. \quad (5.2)$$

Let us compare the centralized and decentralized cases. Considering both first-order conditions, (5.1) and (5.2), we have that for group $\mathcal{G}_x$,

$$\frac{C'(g_i^*)}{\frac{\partial p(X^*, Y^*)}{\partial X}} = V = \frac{1}{n_x} \frac{C'(g_j^o)}{\frac{\partial p(X^o, Y^o)}{\partial X}}$$

and a similar equation for group $\mathcal{G}_y$. Hence, the centralized and decentralized solutions cannot be the same. See Exercise 5.2 for more properties of the centralized solution. Exercise 5.3 asks you to prove that, under some conditions, the larger group underperforms in the decentralized contest with respect to the centralized contest. The free riding in the decentralized contest decreases the performance of this group. However, free riding in the small group is less severe. This group underperforms in the decentralized contest with respect to the centralized one if its size is sufficiently close to the larger group; otherwise, it outperforms.

This intuition takes us to the next section.

5.3   The Size of Groups and the Success of Conspiracies

Mancur Olson (1932–1988) was a prominent social scientist to whom we are indebted for his many brilliant contributions. Here is one of them. His book *The Logic of Collective Action: Public Goods and the Theory of Groups* (1965) was motivated by the difference between a stagnant UK and a buoyant Germany in the early 1960s. Also, recall that, at these times, Japan was growing at least twice as fast as the US.[3] So the question arises: Who won the war? Olson argues that politically stable societies tend to accumulate interest groups over the years. These groups infiltrate governments and drive their policies to suit their interests. And the working of such groups is detrimental to growth. Since Germany and Japan lost the war, the interest groups surrounding the Nazi Party and the Japanese Emperor were hit hard. On the contrary, the interest groups in the UK and the US thrived and even got some extra prestige for their contribution to victory. Crony capitalism flourished in Anglo-Saxon democracies. However, these interest groups were small. How can they be so decisive? We can find many commonsense answers like the superior organization of these groups or their privileged links with governments. But there must be something more. And here comes the crucial point in Olson's contribution. He conjectured that because of free

---

[3] In 1970, Germany's per capita GDP was 17% larger than the UK's.

riding in large decentralized groups, small decentralized groups exert *more* aggregate effort than large groups, which explains the success of the former.[4]

Is Olson's conjecture true? We will see that the theoretical answer is (a disappointing), it depends.[5] We start with a result due to Katz, Nitzan, and Rosenberg (1990) – see also Nti (1998) – that casts doubts on Olson's conjecture.

PROPOSITION 5.1 *Assume that the CSF is homogeneous of degree zero. Then $n_x > n_y$ implies $X^* > Y^*$ and $g_i^* < g_j^*$.*

Proof Looking at (5.1), we see that equilibrium is symmetric inside each group, so $g_i^* = X^*/n_x$ for all $i \in \mathcal{G}_x$ and $g_j^* = Y^*/n_y$ for all $j \in \mathcal{G}_y$. Hence,

$$\frac{\partial p(X^*, Y^*)}{\partial X} V = C'\left(\frac{X^*}{n_x}\right) \quad \text{and} \quad -\frac{\partial p(X^*, Y^*)}{\partial Y} V = C'\left(\frac{Y^*}{n_y}\right).$$

Suppose that $X^* \leq Y^*$ and $n_x > n_y$. Then, $X^*/n_x < Y^*/n_y$ and since $C'(g_k)$ is increasing $C'(X^*/n_x) < C'(Y^*/n_y)$. From the first-order conditions,

$$\frac{\partial p(X^*, Y^*)}{\partial X} < -\frac{\partial p(X^*, Y^*)}{\partial Y}.$$

Since the CSF is homogeneous of degree zero, given that p is increasing in X and $X^* \leq Y^*$, it follows that

$$\frac{\partial p(X^*, Y^*)}{\partial X} X^* = -\frac{\partial p(X^*, Y^*)}{\partial Y} Y^* \Rightarrow \frac{\partial p(X^*, Y^*)}{\partial X} \geq -\frac{\partial p(X^*, Y^*)}{\partial Y},$$

which contradicts the equation above. Thus, $X^* > Y^*$. By multiplying the first-order conditions by X^* and Y^*, respectively,

$$\frac{\partial p(X^*, Y^*)}{\partial X} X^* = \frac{C'(g_i^*)}{V} X^* \quad \text{and} \quad -\frac{\partial p(X^*, Y^*)}{\partial Y} Y^* = \frac{C'(g_j^*)}{V} Y^*.$$

By homogeneity of degree zero,

$$\frac{\partial p(X^*, Y^*)}{\partial X} X^* + \frac{\partial p(X^*, Y^*)}{\partial Y} Y^* = 0,$$

which implies that

$$C'(g_i^*) X^* = C'(g_j^*) Y^*.$$

Since $X^* > Y^*$, $C'(g_i^*) < C'(g_j^*)$ and since $C(g_k)$ is strictly convex $g_j^* > g_i^*$. □

The previous result says two things. First, a member of the larger group makes less effort than a member of the small group. Members of the large group, individually, do more free riding than the individual members of the small group. Second, numbers overwhelm free riding and the aggregate effort of the large group is finally larger than

---

[4] Olson admits that large groups (trade unions, farmer associations) can be successful. But he attributes this success either to coercion (legal or otherwise) or to the fact that these groups offer additional perks to their members.

[5] Olson claims (p. 106) that successful revolutions have been carried out by a small number of people. And that trade associations are actually controlled by a few individuals (p. 145).

the one made by the small group. Note that the CSF is not necessarily symmetric! Thus, asymmetries due to better links do not count here.

The previous result can be criticized on several fronts. For instance, we may assume that to make a real impact, individual efforts must be above a certain lower bound. Thus, the sum of many small efforts achieves nothing. Also, the assumption of identical costs and valuations may not reflect the reality of lobbying. And to form a group is costly. Larger groups are difficult to form and maintain, while the above result assumes an absence of any cost of group formation. Another factor that might explain the success of small groups is that they can exert social pressure more effectively than large groups.

Esteban-Marquillas and Ray (2001) noticed that the previous argument depended on the prize being entirely a public good (a law). The intuition is that if the prize is a private good, the members of the smaller group get more prize per capita than those in the larger group, possibly offsetting free-riding incentives.

To deal with the issue of private versus public goods, we write the prize of a contestant $i \in G_x$ as follows:

$$V_i = \frac{V}{n_x^{\alpha}} \quad 0 \le \alpha \le 1,$$

and similarly for a contestant $j \in G_y$,

$$V_j = \frac{V}{n_y^{\alpha}} \quad 0 \le \alpha \le 1.$$

When $\alpha = 1$, $V_i = V/n_x$ and $V_j = V/n_y$, the prize is a private good and is divided equally among the members of the group. When $\alpha = 0$, $V_i = V$ and $V_j = V$, the prize is a public good and we are back to the case we studied before.

Esteban-Marquillas and Ray (2001) proved the following result.

PROPOSITION 5.2 *Assume the CSF is homogeneous of degree zero and $C_i(g_i) = cg_i^{\beta}$, $\beta \ge 1$. The smaller group makes more effort than the larger group if and only if $\alpha + 1 > \beta$.*

Proof From the first-order conditions,

$$\frac{\partial p(X^*, Y^*)}{\partial X} V_x = c\beta \left(\frac{X^*}{n_x}\right)^{\beta-1} \quad \text{and} \quad -\frac{\partial p(X^*, Y^*)}{\partial Y} V_y = c\beta \left(\frac{Y^*}{n_y}\right)^{\beta-1}.$$

From the equations above and given that the CSF is homogeneous of degree zero, we get that

$$\frac{V_x Y^*}{V_y X^*} = \frac{\left(\frac{X^*}{n_x}\right)^{\beta-1}}{\left(\frac{Y^*}{n_y}\right)^{\beta-1}}.$$

Taking into account that $V_i = V/n_i^\alpha$ the equation above reads

$$\frac{n_y^\alpha Y^*}{n_x^\alpha X^*} = \frac{\left(\frac{X^*}{n_x}\right)^{\beta-1}}{\left(\frac{Y^*}{n_y}\right)^{\beta-1}}, \text{ which implies } \frac{Y^*}{X^*} = \left(\frac{n_x}{n_y}\right)^{\frac{\alpha-\beta+1}{\beta}}.$$

Suppose $n_x > n_y$, then $X^* < Y^*$ if and only if $\left(\frac{n_x}{n_y}\right)^{\frac{\alpha-\beta+1}{\beta}} > 1$, if and only if $\frac{\alpha-\beta+1}{\beta} \log\left(\frac{n_x}{n_y}\right) > 0$, if and only if $\alpha + 1 > \beta$. $\qquad\Box$

We see that this matter is considerably more complicated than envisioned by Olson. The validity of his conjecture depends on two things: the nature of the prize (α) and the cost of effort (β). Free riding in large groups really bites when the prize has an important private good aspect. But if an effort is very costly ($\beta > 2$), the members of the small group find the contest very hard to fight and their aggregate effort falls short of the aggregate effort of the large group. As it happens many times in economics, the devil is in the details.

Nitzan (1991a) showed that even if the prize is entirely a private good, what determines the size of free riding and, consequently, which group exerts a bigger effort, is the rule of prize distribution. To illustrate this effect, consider the reward to a member $i \in \mathcal{G}_x$ to be a linear combination of an egalitarian part, in which all members of the group are equally rewarded, and a relative contribution part. That is, the share of a perfectly divisible private good for a contestant $i \in \mathcal{G}_x$ is

$$\alpha \frac{g_i}{X} + (1-\alpha)\frac{1}{n_x}.$$

By assuming that the CSF is Ratio Form, payoffs are

$$\frac{X}{X+Y}\left(\alpha \frac{g_i}{X} + (1-\alpha)\frac{1}{n_x}\right)V - C(g_i).$$

Exercise 5.6 asks you to solve this model for linear costs. You will see that if $\alpha = 1$, the total effort in equilibrium, $X^* + Y^*$, is equal to the total effort obtained in a contest with $n_x + n_y$ contestants individually competing for a prize V. Therefore, the distribution of individuals among the groups does not influence the overall level of effort exerted in the contest. However, the total effort of a group is directly proportional to the number of contestants in the group. Thus, the reward rule creates positive incentives for individuals to participate in the group, counteracting the negative impact of free riding. As a result, the larger group is more likely to win the prize. If the prize is equally divided among all group members, i.e., $\alpha = 0$, the free-riding effect dominates. Consequently, if $n_x > n_y$, then $X^* < Y^*$, and therefore, the smaller group has a higher probability of winning the prize.

5.4   Endogenous Sharing Rules

A possible criticism of the way we modeled Olson's conjecture in the previous section is that we worked with a given distribution of the prize. But as long as groups possess a certain degree of autonomy, they would be able to choose the distribution that is more suitable to their interest. Think of a law firm that is competing to be the legal representative of a multinational in an antitrust case. Or an architecture firm that is fighting for a contract for the construction of a showcase skyscraper. In principle, these firms could make contracts with their employees on how to share the prize that might overcome the free-rider problem.

Ueda (2002) examines a two-stage contest game where each group simultaneously determines their sharing rule in the first stage to maximize the total payoff of the group. In the second stage, given the sharing rule, contestants decide on their effort levels. Payoffs for each contestant are given by

$$\pi_i(\mathbf{g}) = \frac{X}{X + Y}\left(\alpha_x \frac{g_i}{X} + (1 - \alpha_x)\frac{1}{n_x}\right)V - g_i, \ i \in \mathcal{G}_x;$$

$$\pi_j(\mathbf{g}) = \frac{Y}{X + Y}\left(\alpha_y \frac{g_i}{X} + (1 - \alpha_y)\frac{1}{n_y}\right)V - g_j, \ j \in \mathcal{G}_Y.$$

The equilibrium concept in this two-stage game is subgame perfect equilibrium. The following proposition due to Ueda (2002) characterizes this equilibrium.

PROPOSITION 5.3   *In the subgame perfect equilibrium of the two-stage contest game, both groups are active, and*

(1) If $n_x = n_y$, both groups choose the proportional sharing rule, $\alpha_x = \alpha_y = 1$.
(2) If $n_y > n_x$, $\alpha_x = 1$, and $1 - \alpha_y = (n_y - n_x)/(2n_x(n_y - 1))$. Furthermore, both groups have the same probability of winning.

Proof   The subgame perfect Nash equilibrium of the contest game is computed by backward induction. In the second stage of the game, given (α_x, α_y), contestants choose their effort. The Nash equilibrium in the second stage is given by the first-order conditions:

$$\alpha_x V \frac{(X + Y - g_i)}{(X + Y)^2} + (1 - \alpha_x)V \frac{Y}{n_x(X + Y)^2} \leq 1 \text{ for all } i \in \mathcal{G}_x; \qquad (5.3)$$

$$\alpha_y V \frac{(X + Y - g_j)}{(X + Y)^2} + (1 - \alpha_y)V \frac{X}{n_y(X + Y)^2} \leq 1 \text{ for all } j \in \mathcal{G}_Y. \qquad (5.4)$$

Exercise 5.8 asks you to compute the Nash equilibrium of the second stage. Here, we just focus on the key features of this Nash equilibrium which are relevant to the analysis of the first stage.

Let

$$\gamma_k = \alpha_k + \frac{(1 - \alpha_k)}{n_k}, \ k \in \{x, y\}.$$

(a) In equilibrium, all contestants in a group exert the same level of effort. Total equilibrium effort $X^* + Y^*$ is given by

$$\frac{X^* + Y^*}{V} = \max_{G \subseteq \{x,y\}} \frac{\sum_{k \in G} n_k \gamma_k - 1}{\sum_{k \in G} n_k}.$$

(b) Both groups exert positive effort in a Nash equilibrium if and only if

$$\gamma_k > \frac{n_x \gamma_x + n_y \gamma_y - 1}{n_x + n_y}.$$

(c) Only one group, say $\mathcal{G}_x$, exerts positive effort in equilibrium if and only if

$$\gamma_x - \frac{1}{n_x} \geq \gamma_y.$$

In the first stage, groups choose the sharing rule. Let us see first that in a subgame perfect equilibrium of the two-stage game, only one group active (monopolization) is not possible. Suppose this is the case. Assume that $\mathcal{G}_x$ is the active group. Then $\gamma_x - 1/n_x \geq \gamma_y$. But this should be consistent with the choice of the sharing rule in the first stage. The total payoff of group $\mathcal{G}_x$ is $\Pi_x = V - X$, since this is the unique group active, by (a) $X = V(n_x \gamma_x - 1)/n_x$. Hence, the first-order condition of payoff maximization is

$$\frac{\partial \Pi_x}{\gamma_x} = -1 \leq 0.$$

Therefore, $\gamma_x = 0$, which contradicts that $\gamma_x - 1/n_x \geq \gamma_y$. Therefore, in the subgame perfect equilibrium of the two-stage game, both groups are active. Hence, the first-order conditions (5.3) and (5.4) hold with equality. Summing up (5.3) for all $i \in \mathcal{G}_x$, and (5.4) for all $j \in \mathcal{G}_Y$,

$$\alpha_x V \frac{(n_x - 1)X + n_x Y}{(X + Y)^2} + (1 - \alpha_x)V \frac{Y}{(X + Y)^2} = n_x; \qquad (5.5)$$

$$\alpha_y V \frac{n_y X + (n_y - 1)Y}{(X + Y)^2} + (1 - \alpha_y)V \frac{X}{(X + Y)^2} = n_y. \qquad (5.6)$$

By rearranging the terms in (5.5) and (5.6), we obtain

$$n_x \left(\gamma_x - \frac{(X + Y)}{V} \right) = \frac{X}{(X + Y)}; \qquad (5.7)$$

$$n_y \left(\gamma_y - \frac{(X + Y)}{V} \right) = \frac{Y}{(X + Y)}. \qquad (5.8)$$

Thus, the total payoff of each group can be written as

$$\Pi_x = \frac{X}{(X + Y)}(V - (X + Y)) = V n_x \left(\gamma_x - \frac{(X + Y)}{V} \right)\left(1 - \frac{(X + Y)}{V} \right);$$

$$\Pi_y = \frac{Y}{(X + Y)}(V - (X + Y)) = V n_y \left(\gamma_y - \frac{(X + Y)}{V} \right)\left(1 - \frac{(X + Y)}{V} \right).$$

Since the total payoff is given by (a) and both groups are active, with performance of some algebra, $\partial \Pi_x / \gamma_x$ and $\partial \Pi_y / \gamma_y$ are given by

$$\frac{\partial \Pi_x}{\gamma_x} = n_x V \left[\left(1 - \frac{2n_x}{n_x + n_y} \right) \left(\gamma_x - \frac{n_x \gamma_x + n_y \gamma_y - 1}{n_x + n_y} \right) + \left(\frac{n_y}{n_x + n_y} \right) (1 - \gamma_x) \right];$$

$$\frac{\partial \Pi_y}{\gamma_y} = n_y V \left[\left(1 - \frac{2n_y}{n_x + n_y} \right) \left(\gamma_y - \frac{n_x \gamma_x + n_y \gamma_y - 1}{n_x + n_y} \right) + \left(\frac{n_x}{n_x + n_y} \right) (1 - \gamma_y) \right].$$

If $n_x = n_y$, the first-order conditions imply that $\gamma_x = \gamma_y = 1$, and consequently, $\alpha_x = \alpha_y = 1$. That is, both groups are meritocratic and both have the same probability of winning.

If $n_y > n_x$, $\partial \Pi_x / \gamma_x > 0$, and then, for group $\mathcal{G}_x$ is a dominant strategy to choose $\gamma_x = 1$, which implies $\alpha_x = 1$. The small group sharing rule is proportional to effort. For group $\mathcal{G}_Y$, $\partial \Pi_y / \gamma_y = 0$ gives

$$\frac{n_y - n_x}{2n_y n_x} = 1 - \gamma_y, \tag{5.9}$$

which if $\partial^2 \Pi_y / \gamma_y^2$ is negative (which you can verify), gives us the maximum, and consequently,

$$1 - \alpha_y = \frac{n_y - n_x}{2n_x (n_y - 1)}.$$

By using (5.7) and (5.8) and given that $\gamma_x = 1$ and γ_y is given by (5.9), we get that both groups have the same probability of winning. □

The preceding result indicates that if the prize is a private good, for a given (α_x, α_y), and the condition in part (c) above is satisfied, only one group is active in equilibrium. Ueda refers to this phenomenon as monopolization. Exercise 5.7 asks you to work on an example where this situation occurs. However, in the two-stage game where groups can choose the sharing rule, monopolization is never an equilibrium as proved by Proposition 5.3. In the subgame perfect equilibrium of the two-stage game, oligopolization is the outcome. This is because allowing the choice of the sharing rule prior to the choice of effort leads the small group to incentivize effort in a highly meritocratic manner, while the large group uses an intermediate sharing rule that partially rewards all members of the group equally. Both groups exert the same level of effort in equilibrium and obtain the same probability of winning. Once again, the Olson paradox does not arise, even if the good is a private good.

We now present other models of endogenous choice of sharing rules.

Nitzan and Ueda (2011) consider a divisible prize with mixed private-public good characteristics. Formally, if $\gamma \in [0, 1]$ represents the proportion of the prize with a private component and α_x represents the degree of meritocracy inside the group, the expected revenue for a contestant $i \in \mathcal{G}_x$ is given by:

$$\left[\left(\alpha_x \frac{g_i}{X} + (1 - \alpha_x) \frac{1}{n_x} \right) \gamma + (1 - \gamma) \right] V.$$

Another characteristic of their model is that groups might differ in marginal cost of effort. The groups determine endogenously the sharing rule by choosing the degree of meritocracy, (α_x, α_y). This choice is simultaneous to the choice of effort. They find that more efficient groups tend to be more equalitarian and larger group has a higher probability of winning.

Balard, Flamand, and Troumpounis (2015) examine a prize that comprises both a public and a private component (as in Nitzan and Ueda, 2011) and endogenize the sharing rule in a two-stage game similar to Ueda (2002), but with an unrestricted sharing rule, i.e., meritocracy is "unbounded," i.e., $a_x \in \mathbb{R}$, and the group can choose to allocate the private part of the prize in a way that could require worse-performing members of the group to transfer funds to better-performing members. They demonstrate that in a two-group contest, if the prize is sufficiently public, the large group uses its sharing rule to exclude the small group from the competition (monopolization arises). Conversely, when the degree of relative privateness is above a certain level, the small group not only participates but even outperforms the large group in terms of winning probabilities, leading to the emergence of the Olson paradox.

Vázquez-Sedano (2018) shows that in a decentralized contest where the prize is pure public good, each group can achieve the efforts corresponding to the centralized contests by means of transfers. Let us see how. The transfer received by contestant i in group $\mathcal{G}_x$ is $C(g_i) - \sum_{k \in \mathcal{G}_x} C(g_k)/n_x$. A similar transfer is received by each contestant of group $\mathcal{G}_y$. Note that these transfers add up to zero inside each group so they do not need external money to finance them. Now the payoff of contestant $i \in \mathcal{G}_x$ is

$$
p(X,Y)V - C(g_i) + C(g_i) - \sum_{k \in \mathcal{G}_x} \frac{C(g_k)}{n_x}
$$
$$
= p(X,Y)V - \sum_{k \in \mathcal{G}_x} \frac{C(g_k)}{n_x}
$$

but this payoff is strategically equivalent to $p(X,Y)Vn_x - \sum_{k \in \mathcal{G}_x} C(g_k)$. And the first-order conditions of payoff maximization in this decentralized contest with transfers are identical to the first-order conditions of an equilibrium in a centralized contest. If payoffs are strictly concave, then the effort chosen by the contestants is identical in both contests. The trick is to "nationalize" individual efforts and make each contestant in the group bear the full cost of effort. This brings together individual incentives and supreme commander wishes. A similar trick is used in mechanism design to encourage individuals to report their true preferences.[6] Exercise 5.4 asks you to generalize this transfer scheme to contestants with different cost functions and valuations.

A word of caution must be mentioned here. All the results presented in this chapter assume that all contestants have complete information, i.e., they know all the characteristics of everybody else in the game. Moreover, in the centralized contests, actions are perfectly controlled by supreme commanders. But it seems that these assumptions

---

[6] This is the basis of the celebrated Vickrey–Clarke–Groves mechanism. But there are differences. This mechanism is seldom balanced and incentives to report the true preferences (not efforts) in dominant strategies, not in a Nash equilibrium. See, e.g., Corchón (2009) for an exposition.

are a bit extreme for some applications, especially war. Extensions of the models presented in this chapter in scenarios involving private information are surveyed by Flamand and Troumpounis (2015).

To conclude this section, it is worth pointing out the existence of a substantial body of literature focused on experimental studies that simulate group contests. For a comprehensive survey, see Sheremeta (2018). As was found in individual contests (as presented in Section 3.6 of Chapter 3), the actual efforts in group contests are larger than those predicted by the Nash equilibrium. Additionally, significant variability in behavior is observed both within and between groups. The explanations for these behaviors are qualitatively similar to those presented in Section 3.6 of Chapter 3, including the utility of winning, spiteful preferences, and other behavioral factors.

Qualitative comparative statics predictions perform reasonably well, with individual efforts responding to the proportionality in rewards, and a more "competitive" CSF, as the All Pay Auction, incentivizes effort. When contestants are heterogeneous, stronger contestants tend to expend more effort, while weaker contestants are more likely to free ride. On the downside, empirical evidence suggests that, in general, larger groups tend to win more frequently, contradicting the Olson conjecture.

5.5   Exercises

5.1   Assume that the impact function of each group is CES, i.e., $X = (\sum_{k \in \mathcal{G}_x} g_i^\rho)^{1/\rho}$. Efforts inside each group might be complements or substitutes. The probability of success of group $\mathcal{G}_x$ denoted by p is

$$p = \frac{X}{X + Y}.$$

Costs are linear. Thus, payoffs of contestant i in group $\mathcal{G}_x$ are

$$\frac{X}{X + Y} - g_i.$$

(1)   Compute the Nash equilibrium in which each member of the group is free to contribute and all members of each group contribute with the same amount.

(2)   Take a close look at the properties of equilibrium when both groups have equal size.

5.2   Suppose the CSF is like in Exercise 5.1 and $C(g_k) = g_k^\beta$, $\beta > 1$ for all contestants.

(1)   Show that in the decentralized equilibrium, both groups choose the same individual effort, regardless of the number of members of each group.

(2)   Show the previous result for homogeneous of degree zero CSF and strictly convex cost functions.

(3)   Compare the centralized and the decentralized equilibria.

5.3   Following Section 5.2, suppose that $n_x > n_y$.

(1) Prove that, under some conditions, the total effort of the group $\mathcal{G}_x$ is smaller in the decentralized contest than in the centralized one.

(2) Prove that this is also the case for group $\mathcal{G}_y$ only if n_y is almost equal to n_x. Otherwise, the total effort of group $\mathcal{G}_y$ is bigger in the decentralized contest than in the centralized one (see Vázquez-Sedano, 2018).

5.4 Generalize the Vázquez-Sedano (2018) transfer scheme to a contest in which contestants have different cost functions and valuations.

5.5 Suppose that the prize is a private good. There are two kinds of efforts, internal (e_k) and external (g_k). The distribution within each group is proportional to the internal effort, which is interpreted as lobbying within the group. The probability of obtaining the prize is proportional to the sum of external efforts made by the members of the group. Suppose that $e_k + g_k = 1$, i.e., effort is spent either in the internal or the external conflict. Compute the Nash equilibrium of this game when both kinds of effort are chosen simultaneously and valuations are identical for all individuals (see Münster, 2007a).

5.6 Consider the model of Nitzan (1991a) with linear costs.

(1) Write the first-order conditions of payoff maximization. Assume that equilibrium is symmetric.

(2) Show that when the prize is allocated according to relative effort within the winning group, i.e., $a = 1$, the total effort in equilibrium, $X + Y$, is equal to the total effort obtained in a contest with $n_x + n_y$ contestants individually competing for a prize V. In this case, show that $n_x > n_y$ implies $X > Y$.

(3) Show that if the prize is equally divided among all group members, i.e., $\alpha = 0$, $X < Y$ if and only if $n_x > n_y$, and therefore, the smaller group has a higher probability of winning the prize.

(4) Find the Nash equilibrium in the case in which $\alpha \in (0, 1)$. Give an interpretation of the result.

5.7 Suppose that in the Nitzan (1991b) model, groups have different sharing rules. In particular, assume that group $\mathcal{G}_x$ is egalitarian, $\alpha = 0$, and that group $\mathcal{G}_y$ is meritocratic, $\alpha = 1$. Suppose also that $n_i \geq 2$, $i \in \{x, y\}$. Prove that, in a Nash equilibrium, only the meritocratic group is active (see Davis and Reilly, 1999). Recall that in a contest with two contestants, it is not possible to have an equilibrium with just one contestant exerting a positive effort. Discuss why this is not the case in this two-group contest model.

5.8 Suppose, like in Exercise 5.7, that groups have different sharing rules. Let $\alpha_x \in [0, 1]$ be the parameter that defines the sharing rule of group $\mathcal{G}_x$ and let $\alpha_y \in [0, 1]$ be the parameter that defines the sharing rule of group $\mathcal{G}_x$. Let

$$\gamma_k = \alpha_k + \frac{1 - \alpha_k}{n_k}, \quad k \in \{x, y\}.$$

(a) Show that $X^* + Y^*$ is the total effort in a Nash equilibrium if and only if

$$\frac{X^* + Y^*}{V} = \max_{G \subseteq \{x, y\}} \frac{\sum_{k \in G} n_k \gamma_k - 1}{\sum_{k \in G} n_k}.$$

(b) Show that both groups exert positive effort in a Nash equilibrium if and only if

$$\gamma_k > \frac{n_x \gamma_x + n_y \gamma_y - 1}{n_x + n_y}.$$

(c) Show that only one group, say $\mathcal{G}_x$, exerts positive effort in equilibrium if and only if

$$\gamma_x - \frac{1}{n_x} \geq \gamma_y.$$

Interpret the results. See Ueda (2002).

5.9 Using the model of Balard, Flamand, and Troumpounis (2015) with unbounded meritocracy, show the levels of γ for which monopolization occurs and the larger group excludes the smaller one from the competition. Explain the result.

5.10 This problem considers a simplified World War II scenario in Europe with three actors: Anglo-Saxons that act as a single contestant (subindex a, effort g_a), Soviets (subindex s, effort g_s), and Nazis (subindex n, effort g_n). The probability that allied Anglos and Soviets win the war (denoted by p) is given by a Ratio Form CSF where

$$p = \frac{g_a + g_s}{g_a + g_s + g_n}.$$

The prize is the territories conquered during the war that we assume is divided proportionally to efforts. Thus, if V is the territory conquered by the allied in case they win the war and W is the territory conquered by the Nazis,

$$V_a = V \frac{g_a}{g_a + g_s}, \quad V_s = V \frac{g_s}{g_a + g_s}, \quad V_n = W.$$

A repeated query of Stalin (leader of the Soviets) was that the allies did not make as much effort as they should. In other words, the Anglos free ride on the Soviets. Show that, in the case of this exercise, this objection was unfounded. Discuss in which case Stalin's objection could have been right.

5.11 Two teams are composed of n_A and n_B players. They compete for a prize of value V which can only be given to an individual. Think of two political parties in an election. There are two stages. In the first stage, teams announce (or do not) the individual who will be chosen to fight for the prize. If they select to announce the one who will be contended, only this person will make an effort. If they do not announce it, all persons in the team will think that, in case of winning, they will get the reward with probability $1/n_i$, $i = A, B$. Compute the subgame perfect Nash equilibrium.

5.12 Consider the model of Esteban-Marquillas and Ray (2001) presented in Section 5.3. Let the CSF be the Ratio Form and $C(g_i) = g_i^\beta$, $\beta \geq 1$.

(1) Calculate the Nash equilibrium efforts of this game and check that the results agree with Proposition 5.2.

(2) Calculate Nash equilibrium payoffs. Study how they depend on the number of contestants in each group and on the nature of the prize α.

5.13 Suppose a society with m agents that enjoy a good that is distributed among the agents in this society according to V/m^a. As in Esteban-Marquillas and Ray (2001), if $\alpha = 1$ the good is a perfectly divisible prize that is equally distributed among the members of the society, and if $\alpha = 0$, the good is public and enjoyed by all members of society. Assume that a subgroup of agents, referred to as the rebels, can challenge the ownership of this good. In this case, a conflict arises between the rebels and the rest of society, and the victor gets the entire good. If a conflict arises, the results of the contest are given by (1) and (2) obtained in Exercise 5.12.

(1) Determine the minimum number of agents who will rebel.

(2) Demonstrate that this number depends on the nature of the good, α.

(3) Show that the rebel group is more likely to be small when the good is private, $\alpha = 1$.

(4) Verify that the results correspond to the empirical findings of Mayoral and Ray (2022).

5.14 Intuition suggests that when contestants of a team perform sequentially, team performance may be plagued by free riding.

(1) Exhibit a model where such free riding arises in equilibrium.

(2) What kind of application of the result in (1) comes to the mind of the reader?
See Neugart and Richiardi (2013).

6   Sabotage

Cambridge Dictionary defines sabotage as "to damage or destroy equipment, weapons, or buildings in order to prevent the success of an enemy or competitor." In words more akin to our discipline, sabotage is a deliberate and costly act by an agent to damage the performance of another. Real-life examples of sabotage abound: The Luddites started destroying machinery in Nottingham (of Robin Hood's fame), England, but the movement spread rapidly and ended up in a rebellion that lasted from 1811 to 1816. Sabotage can also occur in the workplace (Lazear, 1989). Some authors attribute the decline of Microsoft since 2000 to the introduction of relative evaluations with top scorers receiving bonuses and bottom scorers being fired. This kind of evaluation destroys incentives to cooperate among employees and encourages sabotage. And we all are familiar with political campaigns in which, rather than advertising their own messages, parties blacken other parties' candidates proposed policies (Skaperdas and Grofman, 1995).

More generally, negative activities "exist not only in organizations but in virtually every competitive environment" (Chen, 2003). Chen points out that antitrust litigation can be used against large competitors by smaller rival companies. "Many competitors against Microsoft have developed products and filed antitrust suits simply to stop Microsoft." In a design competition for a new national stadium in Japan, architect Zaha Hadid accused her rivals of engaging in sabotage tactics by lobbying against her design, spreading false information about her work, and engaging in a smear campaign to undermine her chances of winning. Hadid claimed that the campaign was based on personal animosity rather than legitimate design concerns and that it violated the spirit of fair competition. In 2007, a group of hedge funds known as "Wolfpack" targeted the Chinese company Sino-Forest, which was listed on the Toronto Stock Exchange. The hedge funds accused Sino-Forest of fraudulently inflating its revenues and exaggerating its timber holdings, among other things. Wolfpack released a report detailing their accusations. Sino-Forest denied accusations, but the company's stock fell by more than 80%, and eventually declared bankruptcy. Wolfpack, on the other hand, made billions of dollars in profits from their short positions in Sino-Forest's stock. In 2018, Uber was accused of sabotaging Lyft, its primary competitor. The accusations were made by a former Uber employee, who alleged that Uber had used a program called "Hell" to track the location and availability of Lyft drivers. The program allowed Uber to identify drivers working for both companies and offered them incentives to work exclusively for Uber. The former employee claimed that the program had been used for several years and helped Uber gain a competitive advantage over Lyft.

Nalebuff and Stiglitz (1983) summarize the previous examples in a sentence: "In the competitive ... there are ... rewards from engaging in destructive activity if it can hurt one's rival more than oneself."

While it is sometimes believed that sabotage is an irrational act, driven by animosity rather than logical reasoning, in this chapter we explore the potential rational motivations for sabotage. We begin by presenting an example that illustrates the potential benefits of sabotage. We then introduce the basic sabotage model in contests and analyze the characteristics of equilibrium with and without sabotage. Finally, we discuss the consequences of sabotage and explore how it impacts the outcome of contests and which individuals are more likely to be targeted. Through this analysis, we hope to provide a better understanding of the role of sabotage in contests and shed light on its implications for strategic decision-making.

6.1   An Example

We start by assuming, like Chung (1996) and Amegashie (1999a), that the prize depends on effort. This is because we want to show that even if efforts increase the value of the prize, sabotage may occur in a world populated by rational agents. Moreover, in the examples of Luddites and Microsoft quoted above, the prize is the output that depends on the efforts of agents.

Suppose two agents, Andy and Beth, collect grapes according to the following production function of wine, $V(\mathbf{g}) = 10(g_1 + g_2)^{1/2}$. Now g_i is the productive effort of agent i that we call *performance*. Consumption, denoted by $C_i(g)$, is determined by the *Proportional Sharing Rule*.[1] Thus,

$$C_i(\mathbf{g}) = \frac{g_i}{g_1 + g_2} 10(g_1 + g_2)^{1/2}, \ i \in \{1,2\}.$$

In the framework used so far, it would correspond to the expected revenue of an agent. The output is distributed meritocratically according to relative performance. Let us compute the Nash equilibrium assuming that only productive effort is made. The payoff of agent i is

$$\pi_i(\mathbf{g}) = \frac{g_i}{g_1 + g_2} 10(g_1 + g_2)^{1/2} - g_i.$$

Then, the first-order condition of payoff maximization for agent 1 is

$$10 \frac{(g_1 + g_2)^{1/2} - 0.5(g_1 + g_2)^{-1/2} g_1}{g_1 + g_2} = 1$$

and since the second-order conditions hold, the Nash equilibrium is $g_1^* = g_2^* = 28.125$ and equilibrium payoffs are $5(2 \times 28.125)^{1/2} - 28.125 = 9.375$.

---

[1] The example is taken from Beviá and Corchón (2006).

Now suppose that by making a sabotage effort of 10 units, Andy can destroy the Beth's entire crop. If, by simplicity, a sabotage effort has the same cost as a productive effort, Andy's payoffs under sabotage are $10(28.125)^{1/2} - 38.125 = 14.908$. Thus, sabotage pays off despite the fact that it destroys part of the output that was shared and that sabotage is costly. This shows that the absence of sabotage is not an equilibrium.

To understand the previous result, let us go to the other extreme and assume that the sharing rule is *Egalitarian*, i.e.,

$$C_i(\mathbf{g}) = 10\frac{(g_1 + g_2)^{1/2}}{2}, \ i \in \{1,2\}.$$

This rule is blind to merit, in the sense that it allocates wine irrespective of relative inputs. The payoffs for agent i are now

$$\pi_i(\mathbf{g}) = 10\frac{(g_1 + g_2)^{1/2}}{2} - g_i.$$

Now the first-order conditions of the Nash equilibrium are

$$\frac{5}{2}(g_1 + g_2)^{-1/2} = 1.$$

In this case, $g_1^* = g_2^* = 25/8$. We see that agents make very little effort, since, in equilibrium, it is less rewarded than before. Again suppose that by making a sabotage of 10, Andy can destroy Beth's entire crop. But in this case, incentives to sabotage disappear entirely. Andy's payoffs are $5(g_1 + g_2)^{1/2} - g_1$, so they are increasing in g_2. The effect is so strong that even if sabotage had no cost, it is not a good strategy. How can it be?

Looking at how Beth's performance affects Andy's payoffs, we see that there are two separate effects:

- *Production effect.* An increase in Beth's performance produces an output that benefits Andy.
- *Distribution effect.* An increase in Beth's performance shifts the distribution of the output in Beth's favor.

In a contest with a fixed prize, the production effect does not exist. When the output is shared equally, the distribution effect does not exist either.

The previous example not only shows that rational sabotage is possible but that destructive activity is very likely when the contest is very meritocratic. Thus, meritocracy has a dark side too.

6.2   The Basic Model of Sabotage in Contest

This section presents a basic model of a contest with sabotage; we follow the model proposed by Konrad (2000) but extend it to accommodate asymmetries among contestants. The main change concerning our basic model spelled out in Chapters 1 to 3 is that now we have two kinds of efforts: the productive effort, g_i, which increases the probability that i wins the contest, and "sabotage effort," which reduces the performance of others. Let s_{ij} be the effort made by i to sabotage the performance of j. This effort decreases the probability that j wins the prize. In this model, contestant i chooses a vector of efforts $(g_i, s_{i1}, \ldots, s_{i(i-1)}, s_{i(i+1)}, \ldots, s_{in})$ instead of a single effort as in the basic model.

Assume that each contestant differs in productivity, and the impact of the productive effort is given by $\alpha_i g_i$ with $\alpha_i > 0$. The effective performance of i, denoted by R_i, is an increasing function of the own productive effort and a decreasing function in the vector of sabotage actions designed to lower i's performance. Write $R_i = R(\alpha_i g_i, s_{1i}, \ldots, s_{(i-1)i}, s_{(i+1)i}, \ldots, s_{ni})$. The value of the prize is equal for all contestants, V.

To make the model tractable, suppose that the sabotage efforts against i can be additively aggregated into a single number denoted by S_i. Thus, $S_i = \sum_{j=1, j \neq i}^{n} s_{ji}$. This reflects that sabotage is anonymous on the receiving end because what counts for effective performance is just the sum of sabotaging efforts. But the act of sabotage is not anonymous; it is aimed at particular contestants. The effective performance of contestant i can be written as $R_i = R(\alpha_i g_i, S_i)$ with $R(\alpha_i g_i, 0) = \alpha_i g_i$. Assume also that $R(\alpha_i g_i, S_i)$ is nondecreasing and concave in g_i (as it is in the no-sabotage case), nonincreasing and convex in S_i (so the marginal effect of sabotage is increasing), and continuously differentiable. An example of an effective performance satisfying the above conditions is

$$R(\alpha_i g_i, S_i) = \frac{\alpha_i g_i}{1 + \gamma S_i}, \quad \gamma \geq 0. \tag{6.1}$$

Note that if $\gamma = 0$, we return to the model without the possibility of sabotage.

The CSF is the Ratio Form but with efforts converted into effective performance. Thus,

$$p_i(R_1, \ldots, R_n) = \frac{R_i}{\sum_{j=1}^{n} R_j}.$$

Assuming that the marginal costs of positive efforts and sabotage are identical, payoffs are

$$\pi_i = \frac{R_i}{\sum_{j=1}^{n} R_j} V - g_i - \sum_{j=1, j \neq i}^{n} s_{ij}, \quad i \in \{1, \ldots, n\}. \tag{6.2}$$

A typical sabotage effort, s_{ik}, has two effects. First, it reduces the performance of contestant k, thereby increasing the probability of contestant i winning. Second, it increases the probability of winning for all other contestants except k, with only i bearing the cost. This effect is commonly known as the *dispersion effect* in sabotage, as named by Konrad (2000). Sabotage, in a sense, has a free-riding component. If an individual is competing against a highly talented player, she may want to sabotage the highly talented but may not want to do it herself as it would be a waste of her time.

6.3   Equilibrium with and without Sabotage

We first study the conditions under which sabotage, even though it is an option, is not an action chosen by contestants in equilibrium. This reveals the conditions under which the basic model developed in Part I is valid. This will also clarify the role of different ingredients in the production of sabotage.

Let us assume first that

$$\alpha_i > \frac{n-1}{\sum_{j=1}^{n} \frac{1}{\alpha_j}}. \tag{6.3}$$

This condition guarantees that in the absence of sabotage, all contestants will be active in equilibrium. The condition was already discussed in Exercise 3.3 in Chapter 3. When all contestants are equally productive, all α_i are identical, denoted by α, condition (6.3) collapses into $n > n - 1$ which always holds. Condition (6.3) can be expressed in a more compact way using the harmonic mean of productivities defined as

$$H = \frac{n}{\sum_{j=1}^{n} \frac{1}{\alpha_j}}.$$

If all contestants are identical, $H = \alpha$. By using the harmonic mean, condition (6.3) can be rewritten as

$$\alpha_i > \frac{n-1}{n} H.$$

See Equation (3.5) in Chapter 3 for a very similar condition when, instead of different productivities, contestants have different valuations.

PROPOSITION 6.1   *Suppose that condition (6.3) holds. If an equilibrium with all contestants active and all choosing zero sabotage exists, then*

$$-\frac{\partial R_i(g_i^o, 0)}{\partial S_i} \leq \frac{\frac{(n-1)H}{n}}{1 - \frac{(n-1)H}{\alpha_j n}} \text{ for all } j, i \in \{1, \ldots, n\}, j \neq i, \tag{6.4}$$

where g_i^0 is given by

$$g_i^o = \frac{(n-1)H}{\alpha_i n} \left(1 - \frac{(n-1)H}{\alpha_i n}\right) V. \tag{6.5}$$

Proof   When all contestants choose zero sabotage efforts, $R(\alpha_i g_i, 0) = \alpha_i g_i$; thus, an equilibrium with zero sabotage efforts, and under condition (6.3), implies that positive efforts should be

$$g_i^o = \frac{(n-1)H}{\alpha_i n} \left(1 - \frac{(n-1)H}{\alpha_i n}\right) V,$$

as in Section 3.3 of Chapter 3 when sabotage was not an option. A necessary condition for sabotage against i not to be profitable for contestant j requires $\partial \pi_j / \partial S_i \leq 0$ at $(g^o, 0)$. Using (6.2), we obtain that

$$-\frac{R_j(g_j^o,0)}{\left(\sum_{k=1}^n R_k(g_k^o,0)\right)^2}\frac{\partial R_i(g_i^o,0)}{\partial S_i}V - 1 \leq 0 \text{ for all } j,i \in \{1,\ldots,n\}, j \neq i. \quad (6.6)$$

Given that $R_k(g_k^o,0) = \alpha_k g_k^o$, using (6.5)

$$\sum_{k=1}^n R_k(g_k^o,0) = \frac{(n-1)H}{n}V.$$

Hence, using (6.5), condition (6.6) can be written as

$$-\frac{\partial R_i(g_i^o,0)}{\partial S_i} \leq \frac{\frac{(n-1)H}{n}}{1-\frac{(n-1)H}{\alpha_j n}} \text{ for all } j,i \in \{1,\ldots,n\}, j \neq i.$$

and the result follows. $\square$

In the symmetric case in which all contestants have the same productivity and $\alpha = 1$ for all $i \in \{1,\ldots,n\}$, condition (6.3) always holds and (6.4) simplifies to

$$-\frac{\partial R_i(g^0,0)}{\partial S_i} \leq n-1,$$

where $g^0 = (n-1)V/n^2$. For the symmetric case with the Logit CSF, see Konrad (2000).

The previous result leads to the following corollary.

COROLLARY 6.1 *If a Nash equilibrium exists and there exist i and j, with $j \neq i$ such that*

$$-\frac{\partial R_i(g_i^o,0)}{\partial S_i} > \frac{\frac{(n-1)H}{n}}{1-\frac{(n-1)H}{\alpha_j n}}$$

holds, then there is sabotage in equilibrium.

Proof The proof easily follows from contradiction, as if equilibrium does not involve sabotage, it would violate the necessary condition in Proposition 6.1. $\square$

To better understand the determinants of sabotage, we bring the effective performance of contestants presented in (6.1). With this parameterization in hand, the necessary condition for no sabotage in equilibrium (6.4) becomes

$$-\frac{\partial R_i(g_i^o,0)}{\partial S_i} = \alpha_i g_i^0 \gamma \leq \frac{\frac{(n-1)H}{n}}{1-\frac{(n-1)H}{\alpha_j n}},$$

and given that $\alpha_i g_i^o$ is given by (6.5), condition (6.4) can be written as

$$V < \frac{1}{\gamma\left(1-\frac{(n-1)H}{\alpha_j n}\right)\left(1-\frac{(n-1)H}{\alpha_i n}\right)} \text{ for all } i,j, i \neq j. \quad (6.7)$$

When all contestants are identical, $H = \alpha$ and (6.7) collapses into $V \leq n^2/\gamma$ which always holds for sufficiently large number of contestants. For $n = 2$, the necessary condition of no sabotage reduces to

$$V \le \frac{(\alpha_1 + \alpha_2)^2}{\gamma \alpha_1 \alpha_2}. \tag{6.8}$$

In Exercise 6.5, you are required to prove that this condition also becomes a sufficient condition for the existence of an equilibrium with no sabotage.

Condition (6.7) involves the variables that are relevant to understanding the role of sabotage in a contest. If the overall productivity of contestants increases (i.e., H increases), the right-hand side of (6.7) also increases, making an equilibrium with no sabotage more likely. The parameter γ represents the strength of the effect of sabotage on the effective performance of a contestant. The larger the value of γ, the more detrimental the effect of sabotage on a contestant's effective performance, and the more likely it is for sabotage to occur. An equilibrium with no sabotage is also more likely to occur when there are more contestants involved in a contest. The dispersion effect is accentuated as the number of contestants increases. A big prize might be a too-sweet candy and might motivate contestants to resort to sabotage to gain an advantage over their competitors. For instance, Corral, Prieto-Rodríguez, and Simmons (2010) tested this result empirically using the natural experiment of a rule change in Spanish football league. The rule change involved increasing the number of points awarded for a win from two to three, thereby increasing the prize at stake for winning a league match. The authors found that after the rule change, teams in a winning position were more likely to commit offenses that could result in the dismissal of a player. This suggests that the increase in the prize led to a higher likelihood of sabotage by teams in winning positions, as they may have felt a greater pressure to win.

Next, we examine the characteristics of equilibrium with sabotage. Initially, we limited our scrutiny to two contestants. It is pertinent to note that equilibrium outcomes may be substantially different when the number of contestants is increased, as demonstrated in Chapter 3. We will see that this is the case when there are more than two contestants.

PROPOSITION 6.2   *Suppose that $n = 2$, and the CSF is homogeneous of degree zero in (g_1, g_2). If an interior equilibrium with sabotage exists, then*

(a) *$g_1 = g_2$, and*
(b) *The marginal rate of substitution of the effective performance of each contestant between productive effort and sabotage is identical for both contestants.*

Proof   If an interior equilibrium with sabotage exists, it should be given by the first-order conditions of the payoff maximization. That is,

$$\frac{\partial \pi_1}{\partial g_1} = \frac{\partial p_1}{\partial R_1} \frac{\partial R_1}{\partial g_1} V - 1 = 0; \quad \frac{\partial \pi_2}{\partial g_2} = \frac{\partial p_2}{\partial R_2} \frac{\partial R_2}{\partial g_2} V - 1 = 0, \tag{6.9}$$

$$\frac{\partial \pi_1}{\partial S_2} = \frac{\partial p_1}{\partial R_2} \frac{\partial R_2}{\partial S_2} V - 1 = 0; \quad \frac{\partial \pi_2}{\partial S_1} = \frac{\partial p_2}{\partial R_1} \frac{\partial R_1}{\partial S_1} V - 1 = 0. \tag{6.10}$$

First, let us see that $g_1 = g_2$. From (6.9)

$$\frac{\partial p_1}{\partial R_1}\frac{\partial R_1}{\partial g_1} = \frac{\partial p_2}{\partial R_2}\frac{\partial R_2}{\partial g_2}. \tag{6.11}$$

Given that p_1 is homogeneous of degree zero in (g_1, g_2),

$$\frac{\partial p_1}{\partial R_1}\frac{\partial R_1}{\partial g_1}g_1 + \frac{\partial p_1}{\partial R_2}\frac{\partial R_2}{\partial g_2}g_2 = 0, \tag{6.12}$$

and given that $p_2(R_2, R_1) = 1 - p_1(R_1, R_2)$, $\partial p_2/\partial R_2 = -\partial p_1/\partial R_2$, by (6.11) and (6.12), we obtain

$$\frac{\partial p_1}{\partial R_1}\frac{\partial R_1}{\partial g_1} = \frac{\partial p_2}{\partial R_2}\frac{\partial R_2}{\partial g_2} = -\frac{\partial p_1}{\partial R_2}\frac{\partial R_2}{\partial g_2} = \frac{\partial p_1}{\partial R_1}\frac{\partial R_1}{\partial g_1}\frac{g_1}{g_2},$$

which implies that $g_1 = g_2$.

To prove the second part of the proposition, notice that from (6.9) and (6.10),

$$\frac{\partial p_1}{\partial R_1}\frac{\partial R_1}{\partial g_1} = \frac{\partial p_1}{\partial R_2}\frac{\partial R_2}{\partial S_2} = \frac{\partial p_2}{\partial R_1}\frac{\partial R_1}{\partial S_1} = \frac{\partial p_2}{\partial R_2}\frac{\partial R_2}{\partial g_2}. \tag{6.13}$$

Given that $p_2(R_2, R_1) = 1 - p_1(R_1, R_2)$, condition (6.13) becomes

$$\frac{\partial p_1}{\partial R_1}\frac{\partial R_1}{\partial g_1} = \frac{\partial p_1}{\partial R_2}\frac{\partial R_2}{\partial S_2} = -\frac{\partial p_1}{\partial R_1}\frac{\partial R_1}{\partial S_1} = -\frac{\partial p_1}{\partial R_2}\frac{\partial R_2}{\partial g_2},$$

which implies the following:

$$\frac{\partial R_1}{\partial g_1} = -\frac{\partial R_1}{\partial S_1}; \quad \frac{\partial R_2}{\partial g_2} = -\frac{\partial R_2}{\partial S_2}. \tag{6.14}$$

Hence, the marginal rate of substitution of the effective performance of each contestant between productive effort and sabotage is equal for both contestants, i.e.,

$$-\frac{\frac{\partial R_1}{\partial g_1}}{\frac{\partial R_1}{\partial S_1}} = -\frac{\frac{\partial R_2}{\partial g_2}}{\frac{\partial R_2}{\partial S_2}} = 1.$$

$\square$

In Equation (3.4) in Chapter 3, we see that when valuations are identical, expenses are identical too. This result and Proposition 6.2 part (a) do not require any symmetry of the CSF.

To show that an equilibrium with sabotage exists, in the subsequent analysis we will employ the effective performance function described in (6.1).

PROPOSITION 6.3 *Suppose that $n = 2$, $R_i(g_i, S_i) = \alpha_i g_i/(1 + \gamma S_i)$, and $p_i(R_i, R_j)$ is the Ratio Form CSF. Assume that $\alpha_1 \geq \alpha_2$ and*

$$\frac{(\alpha_1 + \alpha_2)^2}{\alpha_2\gamma\alpha_1} < V \leq \frac{(\alpha_1 + \alpha_2)^2}{\gamma\alpha_2(\alpha_1 - \alpha_2)}. \tag{6.15}$$

Then, an interior equilibrium with positive sabotage exists.
In equilibrium, $g_1 = g_2 = g^*$ and $S_1 = S_2 = S^*$ where

$$g^* = \frac{\alpha_1\alpha_2}{(\alpha_1 + \alpha_2)^2}V; \; S^* = \left(\frac{\alpha_2\gamma\alpha_1}{(\alpha_1 + \alpha_2)^2}V - 1\right)\frac{1}{\gamma}.$$

Proof   Since the concavity of payoffs cannot be guaranteed, we follow the strategy of the proof of the existence of equilibrium explained in the second approach in Section 2.7 of Chapter 2. We first identify a candidate equilibrium and then we show that this candidate is indeed an equilibrium.

Step 1. Finding a candidate equilibrium. Given that p_i is homogeneous of degree zero if an interior equilibrium with sabotage exists, then by Proposition 6.2, $g_1 = g_2$ and (6.14) holds. Hence,

$$\frac{\alpha_1}{(1 + \gamma S_1)} = \frac{\alpha_1 g_1 \gamma}{(1 + \gamma S_1)^2}; \; \frac{\alpha_2}{(1 + \gamma S_1)} = \frac{\alpha_2 g_2 \gamma}{(1 + \gamma S_2)^2}.$$

Which implies that

$$\frac{(1 + \gamma S_1)}{g_1} = \frac{(1 + \gamma S_2)}{g_2}.$$

Given that $g_1 = g_2 = g$, then $S_1 = S_2 = S$. From the first-order condition of payoff maximization of contestant 1 with respect to g_1,

$$\frac{\partial \pi_1}{\partial g_1} = \frac{\frac{\partial R_1}{\partial g_1}(R_2)}{(R_1 + R_2)^2}V - 1 = \frac{\alpha_1\alpha_2}{g(\alpha_1 + \alpha_2)^2}V - 1 = 0.$$

Thus,

$$g^* = \frac{\alpha_1\alpha_2}{(\alpha_1 + \alpha_2)^2}V.$$

And from the first-order condition of payoff maximization of contestant 1 with respect to S_2,

$$\frac{\partial \pi_1}{\partial S_2} = \frac{-\frac{\partial R_2}{\partial S_2}(R_1)}{(R_1 + R_2)^2}V - 1 = \frac{\alpha_2\gamma\alpha_1}{(1 + \gamma S)(\alpha_1 + \alpha_2)^2}V - 1 = 0.$$

Thus,

$$S^* = \left(\frac{\alpha_2\gamma\alpha_1}{(\alpha_1 + \alpha_2)^2}V - 1\right)\frac{1}{\gamma}.$$

Assumption (6.15) ensures that S^* is positive. Since payoffs are not necessarily concave, we go to step 2.

Step 2. Showing that the candidate equilibrium is indeed an equilibrium. When we plug the values of S_1 and g_2 found above in the payoffs of contestant 1, her payoffs are now a continuous function of S_2 and g_1. Thus, a maximum of 1's payoffs exist in the interval $[0, V]^2$. This maximum can only be located in the extremes or in the first-order conditions which yield a unique number. The last requirement corresponds to the observation made at the end of the proof of Proposition 2.4 that there is only one strategy that satisfies the first-order conditions. Clearly, the upper bound of the interval is never an optimal choice. Therefore, to ensure that (g^*, S^*) is an optimal choice for contestant 1, payoffs evaluated at the first-order conditions must be nonnegative. Repeating the same argument for contestant 2, we show that (g^*, S^*) is an equilibrium. The payoff for contestant i is given by

$$\pi_i(\mathbf{g}^*, \mathbf{S}^*) = \frac{\alpha_i}{\alpha_i + \alpha_j} V - \frac{\alpha_i \alpha_j}{(\alpha_i + \alpha_j)^2} V - \left(\frac{\alpha_i \gamma \alpha_j}{(\alpha_i + \alpha_j)^2} V - 1 \right) \frac{1}{\gamma}.$$

Simplifying,

$$\pi_i(\mathbf{g}^*, \mathbf{S}^*) = \frac{\alpha_i(\alpha_i - \alpha_j)}{(\alpha_i + \alpha_j)^2} V + \frac{1}{\gamma}.$$

For contestant 1, since $\alpha_1 \geq \alpha_2$, payoff is positive. For contestant 2, given that by (6.15), $V \leq (\alpha_1 + \alpha_2)^2 / (\gamma \alpha_2 (\alpha_1 - \alpha_2))$, $\pi_2(\mathbf{g}^*, \mathbf{S}^*) \geq 0$. Therefore, $(\mathbf{g}^*, \mathbf{S}^*)$ is a Nash equilibrium. □

Some remarks about the above proposition are in order: The left-hand side of the inequality (6.15) implies that the necessary condition for equilibrium without sabotage (condition (6.8)) is not satisfied. In simpler terms, if the value of the prize is too low, then neither contestant has any motivation to sabotage, and the equilibrium is like in Proposition 6.1. The right-hand side of the inequality (6.15) suggests that to obtain an interior equilibrium in pure strategies with sabotage, the differential in productivity between the contestants should not be excessively high. Hence, if the right-hand side of the inequality (6.15) does not hold, it could be that in a pure strategy equilibrium, one of the contestants chooses not to sabotage. Exercise 6.4 demands you prove that this is not possible either; therefore, under this situation, an equilibrium in pure strategies does not exist.

Finally, we will analyze the characteristics of an interior equilibrium with sabotage when there are more than two contestants participating in the contest.

PROPOSITION 6.4   *Suppose $n > 2$ and $R_i(g_i, S_i) = \alpha_i g_i / (1 + \gamma S_i)$. If there exists an interior equilibrium with sabotage, then $\alpha_i > \alpha_j$ implies that $S_i > S_j$. In other words, the most efficient contestant is the one who bears the greatest harm from sabotage.*

Proof   If an interior equilibrium with sabotage exists, it can be derived from the first-order conditions of payoff maximization given by

$$\frac{\partial \pi_i}{\partial S_j} = \frac{-\frac{\partial R_j}{\partial S_j} R_i}{(\sum_{k=1}^{n} R_k)^2} V - 1 = 0, \ i, j \in \{1, \ldots, n\}, \ i \neq j.$$

From the first-order conditions, we get

$$\frac{\partial R_j}{\partial S_j} = \frac{\partial R_k}{\partial S_k} \text{ for all } j, k \in \{1, \ldots, n\}, \ j \neq k.$$

Therefore,

$$\frac{\alpha_j g_k}{(1 + \gamma S_j)^2} = \frac{\alpha_k g_k}{(1 + \gamma S_k)^2} \text{ for all } j, k \in \{1, \ldots, n\}, \ j \neq k. \tag{6.16}$$

The first-order conditions with respect to g_i can be expressed as

$$\frac{\partial \pi_i}{\partial g_i} = \frac{\frac{\partial R_i}{\partial g_i}(\sum_{k=1}^{n} R_k - R_i)}{(\sum_{k=1}^{n} R_k)^2} V - 1 = 0, \; i, j, k \in N, \; i \neq j \neq k. \tag{6.17}$$

Let $X = \sum_{k=1}^{n} R_k$, then (6.17) can be written as

$$\frac{\partial R_i}{\partial g_i} X - \frac{\partial R_i}{\partial g_i} R_i = \frac{1}{V} X^2, i \in \{1, \ldots, n\}.$$

Given that $R_i = \alpha_i g_i/(1 + \gamma S_i)$, and $\partial R_i/\partial g_i = \alpha_i/(1 + \gamma S_i)$,

$$\frac{1}{(1 + \gamma S_i)} X - \frac{1}{\alpha_i V} X^2 = \frac{\alpha_i g_i}{(1 + \gamma S_i)^2}.$$

By using (6.16), we obtain

$$\frac{1}{(1 + \gamma S_i)} X - \frac{1}{\alpha_i V} X^2 = \frac{1}{(1 + \gamma S_j)} X - \frac{1}{\alpha_j V} X^2.$$

Hence,

$$\frac{1}{(1 + \gamma S_i)} - \frac{1}{(1 + \gamma S_j)} = \frac{X}{V}\left(\frac{1}{\alpha_i} - \frac{1}{\alpha_j}\right). \tag{6.18}$$

Thus, if $\alpha_i > \alpha_j$, condition (6.18) implies that $S_i > S_j$. □

This result warns us that the harm produced by the sabotage is not uniformly distributed among contestants. Sabotage, primarily, harms excellency.

6.4   Consequences of Sabotage

To close this chapter, we offer some remarks on the importance of sabotage on resource allocation. We see that sabotage is pervasive and makes us rethink about issues such as the efficiency of competition and meritocracy, group contests, affirmative action, and equilibrium in dynamic contest.

1. *Sabotage impairs the efficiency of competitive and meritocratic mechanisms.* Proposition 6.4 shows that with more than two contestants, the most skilled contestant is more vulnerable to sabotage. In a classic paper by Martin Shubik (1954), three players can fire bullets at each other, with bullets representing an extreme form of sabotage. Equilibrium properties depend on specific assumptions regarding the number of bullets fired by each player and the shooting order. However, in many cases, better shooters were less likely to survive.[2] Intuitively, skilled competitors pose a greater threat than unskilled competitors, thus making them a desirable target. This contradicts the concept that competitive systems favor the most competent individuals, suggesting that natural selection may favor those who engage in malicious behavior rather than those who are the most capable. A consequence of this is that talented contestants

---

[2] Shubik refers to this situation as Truel. For a thorough explanation and additional references, refer to Brams and Kilgour (1997).

may not want to participate in the contest if they anticipate being targeted for sabotage (Münster, 2007b). Thus, the possibility of sabotage may act as a barrier to attracting the most talented contestants to a particular contest. See Exercise 6.2. The same can be said about meritocratic payment schemes that yield incentives to sabotage those making a larger effort (Beviá and Corchón, 2006).

2. *Sabotage in group contests.* Gürtler (2008) shows that in team contests, teams direct their sabotage efforts exclusively toward the weakest member of the rival team. In his model, there are two crucial assumptions: an agent's contribution to the team's performance has decreasing returns, and contributions to the team's performance are complementary. Targeting the weakest agent yields the most significant reduction in the rival team's performance. First, because of decreasing returns, more able contestants, whose contributions are higher than those of their less able teammates, are less productive on the margin. Second, complementarity in production leads to a relatively stronger increase in the productivity of less able team members. Both effects imply that the weakest team member is on the most productive margin, making him the most attractive target for sabotage.

3. *Sabotage under affirmative action (AA).* Policies are aimed to level the playing field by providing assistance to less-advantaged contestants. In Chapter 12, Section 12.4.1, we examine the effects of these policies on productive efforts. However, it is unfortunate that AA policies may trigger sabotage. The reasoning behind this is that, by enhancing the performance of less competitive contestants, AA makes them better rivals, thereby making them a more appealing target for sabotage. This theoretical prediction is substantiated by empirical evidence from horse racing, where handicapping faster horses increases the likelihood of sabotage (Brown and Chowdhury, 2017). Similar findings have been reported in judo championships and laboratory experiments. Refer to the survey by Chowdhury and Gürtler (2015) for further details. Exercise 6.3 requires readers to theoretically prove this point.

4. *Sabotage in dynamic contests.* Although we will delve deeper into the topic of dynamic contests in Chapter 7, it is worth mentioning the effect that sabotage can have on dynamic situations. In dynamic contests, sabotage can have a significant impact on the continuation of the game and negatively affect the performance of the more skilled contestant. Being aware of the implications of the possibility of sabotage alerts us to how the contest should be organized to avoid adverse situations. Amegashie and Runkel (2007) consider a four-player two-stage elimination contest with sabotage using an All Pay Auction. They show that the least able player has a higher probability of winning if matched against the second most able player in the first stage. Gürtler and Münster (2010) consider a three-player, two-round tournament where players can choose whether or not to sabotage and invest productive effort in each round. They found that the leading player is sabotaged in the second round, discouraging investment in the first round. Gürtler, Münster, and Nieken (2013) propose a solution to the problem of sabotage in the tournament model presented by Gürtler and Münster (2010) by introducing an information policy where the manager does not communicate intermediate results; thus, contestants make sabotage choices without knowledge of the productive efforts invested by their competitors. Klunover (2023)

incorporates punishment into Gürtler and Münster (2010) two-round, three-player tournament model. He finds that the organizer should choose to punish in the second round, even if she could punish more than one player in the first round.

For more details on the subject, the interested reader can refer to the survey on sabotage in contests by Chowdhury and Gürtler (2015).

6.5   Exercises

6.1   As in the model of Beviá and Corchón (2006), show that if an agent is unwilling to sabotage another agent, she does not sabotage any agent of lower ability.

6.2   Show that in contests involving sabotage, the most able contestants may abstain from participation in the contest and the selected winner is the less able one with probability one (see Münster, 2007b).

6.3   Show that sabotage is higher in contests with Affirmative Action than in contests without Affirmative Action (see Brown and Chowdhury, 2017).

6.4   Suppose that $R_i(g_i, S_i) = \alpha_i g_i / (1 + \gamma S_i)$, and $p_i(R_i, R_j)$ is the Ratio Form CSF. Assume that

$$\frac{(\alpha_1 + \alpha_2)^2}{\alpha_2 \gamma \alpha_1} < \frac{(a_1 + a_2)^2}{\gamma \alpha_2 (\alpha_1 - \alpha_2)} < V.$$

Show that an equilibrium in pure strategies does not exist. Compute the equilibrium in mixed strategies.

6.5   Suppose that $R_i(g_i, S_i) = \alpha_i g_i / (1 + \gamma S_i)$, and $p_i(R_i, R_j)$ is the Ratio Form CSF. Assume that

$$V \leq \frac{(\alpha_1 + \alpha_2)^2}{\alpha_2 \gamma \alpha_1}.$$

Compute the Nash equilibrium and show that in equilibrium $S_1 = S_2 = 0$.

6.6   Suppose two contestants with valuations V_i, $i \in \{1,2\}$, and an effective performance function

$$R_i = \frac{\gamma_i g_i}{1 + \gamma_i s_{ji}}$$

where γ_i is the productivity of both the productive effort and sabotage. The CSF is the Ratio Form,

$$p_i(R_1, R_2) = \frac{R_i}{R_j + R_i}.$$

The marginal cost of productive effort is 1 for both contestants, and the marginal cost of sabotage is μ_i $i \in \{1,2\}$. The payoff of contestant i is

$$\pi_i = \frac{R_i}{R_j + R_j} V_i - g_i - \mu_i s_{ij}.$$

(1) Write payoffs as a function of $\gamma = \gamma_1/\gamma_2$.

(2) Give conditions that guarantee that an interior Nash equilibrium with sabotage exists. Compute the Nash equilibrium under those conditions.

(3) Show an example in which sabotage efforts are zero in equilibrium.

See Cohen and Nitzan (2021).

6.7 Suppose a contest where two contestants are competing for a prize worth V. Each contestant performs productive effort (g_i) and sabotage effort (s_i). Suppose that the contest is sequential. In the first stage, contestants exert sabotage and in the second stage, they exert productive effort. Sabotage increases the marginal cost of productive effort of the rival which is $1 + s_i$. The CSF is the Ratio Form with productive efforts as arguments.

(1) Write the payoffs of both contestants.

(2) Find the subgame perfect equilibrium of this game.

(3) Show that for a sufficiently high prize value, the ratio of sabotage effort to productive effort increases with an increase in the prize value.

See Amegashie (2012).

6.8 In the context of Amegashie's (2012) model described in Exercise 6.7, consider a scenario with three stages instead of two. In the first stage, a regulator decides on the level of monitoring effort, m_i, to be imposed on contestant i. Stages two and three follow as in Exercise 6.7. The monitor effort increases the marginal cost of sabotage for contestant i by $c_m m_i$. The total cost of sabotage by agent i is $(c + c_m m_i)s_i$. The regulator's payoff is represented by $R = g_1 + g_2 - m_1 - m_2$. Find the subgame perfect Nash equilibrium of this game and compare the results with Amegashie's findings. See Minchuk, Keren, and Hadad (2018).

6.9 Consider a contest between two contestants with identical abilities, where the prize is a monetary amount of $100. Suppose that each contestant can either put forth a "high" or "low" effort level. The cost of high effort is $50, while the cost of low effort is $0. If both contestants choose high effort, they split the prize equally. If only one contestant chooses high effort, he wins the entire prize. If both contestants choose low effort, the prize is split equally between them. Suppose that contestant 1 can sabotage contestant 2's effort at a cost of $10. If contestant 1 chooses to sabotage contestant 2's effort, then player 2's payoff is reduced by half.

(1) Write down the payoff functions for both contestants and find the Nash equilibrium of this game.

(2) Suppose instead that contestant 1 can sabotage contestant 2's effort at a cost of $20. How does the Nash equilibrium change?

(3) What is the minimum cost of sabotage that contestant 1 would need to make it optimal to sabotage contestant 2's effort, regardless of contestant 2's choice?

6.10 Suppose a contest between two teams. Each team has two members, an attacker (a) and a defender (d). The impact function of each team depends on the productive effort of each of its members and on sabotage from the members of the other team.

Suppose that an attacker can only sabotage a defender and a defender can only sabotage an attacker. Formally, the impact function of group $i \in \{1,2\}$ is given by

$$X_i = \frac{\alpha_i^a g_i^a}{1 + s_j^d} + \frac{\alpha_i^d g_i^d}{1 + s_j^a},$$

where α_i^k, $k \in \{a,d\}$, is the productivity of a member k of group i, g_i^k is the productive effort of a member k of group i, and s_j^d is the sabotage that a defender from group j exerts on an attacker of group i, and s_j^a is the sabotage that an attacker from group j exerts on a defender of group i. The marginal cost of productive effort is one for all contestants, and the marginal cost of sabotage for a contestant k from team i is μ_i^k. The payoffs for each contestant is

$$\pi_i^k = \frac{X_i}{X_i + X_j} V - g_i^k - \mu_i^k s_i^k, \ i \in \{1,2\}, k \in \{a,d\}.$$

Characterize the interior Nash equilibrium and provide conditions that guarantee its existence. Then prove that in the interior equilibrium, none of the team members free rides. To prove this, you may need to work out the equilibrium in a situation where sabotage is not a possibility. See Doğan, Keskin, and Sağlam (2019).

6.11 Develop a model that represents the case of Uber versus Lyft, as presented in the introduction of this chapter. Describe all the elements of the model and explain the assumptions that you choose.

7 Dynamic Contests

In the previous chapters, we assumed that contests occurred in one shot. This is adequate for modeling a decisive conflict in which the fate of the war is decided in a single battle, as in the Battle of Zama (202 BC) which ended Carthage's bid for supremacy in the Mediterranean; the Battle of Guadalete (711) that sealed the fate of Visigothic Spain; the Battle of Waterloo (1814), which put an end to the Napoleonic wars; or the Battle of Sedan (1870), which collapsed the French Second Empire. In terms of sports, the one-shot model would be adequate to analyze events such as the Super Bowl or the final Champions League. Also, one-shot contests may capture, in a reduced form, a dynamic situation, acting as a black box of a much more complex situation.

However, many contests are inherently dynamic and thus require a different modeling approach. Examples of such dynamic contests include electoral competition, in which candidates compete for votes in a series of elections over time; patent races, in which firms compete to be the first to develop and patent a new technology; sports leagues, in which teams compete against each other over a season to determine a champion; advertising campaigns, in which firms compete to capture market share over time; and wars not decided by a decisive battle, such as World Wars I and II, which were fought over several years and involved multiple battles and strategic moves.

Dynamic contest theory is a vast field, still emerging, and at present, we do not have anything close to a general picture. In this chapter, we will be content to analyze several examples of dynamic contests, namely:

(1) **Endogenous timing contests**. Contestants have the opportunity to choose between playing early or late.

(2) **Elimination contests**. Contestants compete in a series of pairwise matches, and the winner of each match advances to the next round while the loser is eliminated. The process continues until only one contestant remains who is declared the overall winner of the contest.

(3) **Races**. Contestants compete to achieve a certain number of victories. The first contestant to reach that number is declared the winner.

(4) **Contests with investments**. A contest where the contestants' efforts in the current period are an investment that can affect their chances of winning in future periods.

(5) **Repeated contests**. Contest where contestants play the same contest multiple times.[1]

Before delving into the formal discussion of each of these setups, it is important to note that the appropriate equilibrium concept for formalizing these dynamic contests requires some revamping. In dynamic games, the concept of Nash equilibrium is not sufficient as it fails to account for the sequential nature of the play. In particular, it could be that before the game is played, one of the contestants threatens with an action that, once we come to the date on which this action was supposed to occur, she does not have any intention to take it. To address this problem, these games are analyzed using the subgame perfect Nash equilibrium concept, which requires that the chosen actions constitute a Nash equilibrium in every subgame. This concept is explained in Fudenberg and Tirole (1991), pp 92–100.

7.1   Endogenous Timing Contests

In many contests, such as sporting events or auctions, the timing of moves is pre-determined and fixed. However, in other contests, such as political campaigns or strategic interactions between firms, the timing of moves may be endogenous. This means that contestants can choose when to move, and this decision can significantly affect the outcome of the contest. For instance, in a political campaign, the timing of a candidate's announcement of their candidacy or the release of a policy proposal can significantly affect their chances of winning. Similarly, in strategic interactions between firms, the timing of a firm's entry into a market or the release of a new product can have a substantial impact on its market share and profitability. Another example of endogenous timing in contests can be found in the context of patent races among firms. Firms can opt to enter the race early, invest more resources in research and development to secure the patent first, or wait and observe their competitors before deciding when to enter the race.

The 1934 celebrated model by Heinrich von Stackelberg (1901–1946) introduced the idea of leadership to our discipline.[2] One firm, the leader, announces and commits to a policy (price or quantity), and the remaining firm, called the follower, reacts optimally to this policy. Given the latter, the leader correctly anticipates the reaction of the follower and introduces it into its maximization program. In the original contribution, those who moved first or second were exogenous. It was implicitly assumed that the most important firm would be the natural leader. Hamilton and Slutsky (1990) studied how to endogenize the order of moves in the Cournot model. Baik and Shogren (1992) and Leininger (1993), building on Dixit (1987), studied this question in the framework

---

[1] Several important topics are not covered here like games with a variable reaction time see Leininger and Yang (1994); sequential Blotto games, see Snyder (1989); and Klumpp and Polborn (2006); entry prevention, see Gradstein (1995) and tug-of-war games, see Konrad and Kovenock (2005).

[2] Born in Moscow from a German Baltic nobility father and an Argentinian mother. Died in Madrid after designing the first degree in economics in Spain.

of contests. Subsequently, we will analyze a basic model to explore whether there are incentives for strong contestants to assume the role of the leader.

Suppose two contestants. Assume that the CSF is the weighted Ratio Form. For tractability reasons, we concentrate on this asymmetry in the CSF, but recall that this asymmetry can be understood as coming from different costs and valuations. Payoffs are given by

$$\pi_1(\boldsymbol{g}) = \frac{g_1}{g_1 + \theta g_2} V - g_1 \; ; \; \pi_2(\boldsymbol{g}) = \frac{\theta g_2}{g_1 + \theta g_2} V - g_2,$$

where $\theta \in (0, 1)$ reflects a handicap of contestant 2. Thus, contestant 1 is "strong" and contestant 2 is "weak." Contestants can act either in the first period (early) or in the second period (late). If a contestant chooses early and the other chooses late, we have the Stackelberg leader–follower situation. If both contestants choose to act in the same period, we have a simultaneous contest, as in the previous chapters.

Let us first compute efforts and payoffs once the period of action is chosen by each contestant.

If both move early or late, we have a simultaneous contest whose Nash equilibrium is

$$g_1^* = g_2^* = \frac{\theta V}{(1 + \theta)^2},$$

$$\pi_1(\boldsymbol{g}^*) = \frac{V}{(1 + \theta)^2}, \quad \pi_2(\boldsymbol{g}^*) = \frac{\theta^2 V}{(1 + \theta)^2}.$$

Now suppose that 1 moves early and 2 moves late, so 1 is the leader and 2 is the follower.

For a given g_1, the reaction of contestant 2 is given by the first-order conditions of payoff maximization. Thus, $\theta g_2 = g_1 - \sqrt{\theta g_1 V}$, whenever $g_1 - \sqrt{\theta g_1 V} > 0$, otherwise, $g_2 = 0$. The best reply for contestant 2 given g_1 is

$$BR_2(g_1) = \begin{cases} g_1 - \sqrt{\theta g_1 V} & \text{if} \quad g_1 < \theta V \\ 0 & \text{if} \quad g_1 \geq \theta V. \end{cases}$$

Contestant 1 incorporates this optimal reaction to its maximization program and chooses g_1 by maximizing π_1 defined as

$$\pi_1(g_1) = \begin{cases} \frac{g_1}{\sqrt{\theta g_1 V}} V - g_1 & \text{if} \quad g_1 < \theta V \\ V - g_1 & \text{if} \quad g_1 \geq \theta V. \end{cases}$$

Note that contestant 1 can prevent contestant 2 from entering the contest. As this will occur for any value of g_1 greater than or equal to θV, contestant 1's optimal choice is $g_1 = \theta V$, which minimizes the cost and keeps 2 out. In this case, contestant's 1's payoff would be $(1 - \theta)V$. For any other case, the optimal choice of contestant 1 is $g_1 = V/4\theta$. Note that $V/4\theta < \theta V$ if and only if $\theta \in (0.5, 1)$. Thus, we need to distinguish between $\theta \in (0.5, 1)$, and $\theta \in (0, 0.5)$.

Table 7.1 Payoff matrix for two players making early or late moves with θ in the range (0.5, 1)

$\theta \in (0.5, 1)$	2 moves early	2 moves late
1 moves early	$\left(\frac{V}{(1+\theta)^2}, \frac{\theta^2 V}{(1+\theta)^2}\right)$	$\left(\frac{V}{4\theta}, \frac{(2\theta-1)^2 V}{4\theta^2}\right)$
1 moves late	$\left(\frac{V(2-\theta)^2}{4}, \frac{\theta V}{4}\right)$	$\left(\frac{V}{(1+\theta)^2}, \frac{\theta^2 V}{(1+\theta)^2}\right)$

Case 1. $\theta \in (0.5, 1)$.

In this case, the equilibrium of this leader–follower game is

$$g_1^{LF} = \frac{V}{4\theta}, \quad g_2^{LF} = \frac{V(2\theta-1)}{4\theta^2}, \quad p_1(g^{LF}) = \frac{1}{2\theta}$$

$$\pi_1(g^{LF}) = \frac{V}{4\theta}, \quad \pi_2(g^{LF}) = \frac{(2\theta-1)^2 V}{4\theta^2},$$

where the superscript LF refers to contestant 1 being the leader and 2 the follower. Note that $g_2^{LF} > 0$. There is no preemptive equilibrium that keeps 2 out of the competition. This occurs because $\pi_1(\theta V) = (1 - \theta)V$, which is smaller than $\pi_1(g^{LF}) = V/4\theta$.

Case 2. $\theta \in (0, 0.5)$.

In this case, we cannot have an interior equilibrium. In equilibrium $g_2 = 0$, $g_1 = \theta V$, $\pi_1 = (1 - \theta)V$, and $\pi_2 = 0$.

Now suppose that 2 moves early and 1 moves late, so 2 is the leader and 1 is the follower.

The equilibrium of this follower–leader game is similarly calculated and is found to be

$$g_1^{FL} = \frac{\theta V(2-\theta)}{4}, \quad g_2^{FL} = \frac{V\theta}{4}, \quad p_1(g^{LF}) = \frac{2-\theta}{2},$$

$$\pi_1(g^{LF}) = \frac{V(2-\theta)^2}{4}, \quad \pi_2(g^{LF}) = \frac{\theta V}{4},$$

where the superscript FL refers to contestant 1 being the follower and 2 the leader. Exercise 7.3 asks you to demonstrate that if contestant 2 is the leader, there is no preemptive equilibrium that would prevent the contestant 1 from entering the contest.

We have all the necessary components to analyze the incentives for moving early or late. Let us begin by examining the case where $\theta \in (0.5, 1)$. In Table 7.1, we plug the payoffs calculated above into each of the four possibilities.

In each cell, payoffs at the first place refer to contestant 1, and those in the second place refer to contestant 2. Note that for the weak contestant, to move early is a dominant strategy because

$$\frac{\theta^2}{(1+\theta)^2} > \frac{(2\theta-1)^2}{4\theta^2} \quad \text{and} \quad \frac{\theta}{4} > \frac{\theta^2}{(1+\theta)^2}.$$

Table 7.2 Payoff matrix for two players making early or late moves with θ in the range $(0, 0.5)$

$\theta \in (0, 0.5)$	2 moves early	2 moves late
1 moves early	$\left(\frac{V}{(1+\theta)^2}, \frac{\theta^2 V}{(1+\theta)^2}\right)$	$((1-\theta)V, 0)$
1 moves late	$\left(\frac{V(2-\theta)^2}{4}, \frac{\theta V}{4}\right)$	$\left(\frac{V}{(1+\theta)^2}, \frac{\theta^2 V}{(1+\theta)^2}\right)$

To end the analysis of the game, contestant 1 just has to compare $V/(1+\theta)^2$ and $V(2-\theta)^2/4$. Simple calculations show that to move second is optimal for her.

Let us consider now the case where $\theta \in (0, 0.5)$. In Table 7.2, we plug the payoffs calculated above into each of the four possibilities.

As before, note that for the weak contestant, to move early is a dominant strategy because $\theta^2 V/(1+\theta)^2 > 0$, and $\theta V/4 > \theta^2 V/(1+\theta)^2$. And, given this, it is optimal for contestant 1 to move second.

The interpretation of those results is that the weak contestant tries to compensate for her handicap by throwing the first punch, irrespective of what the strong contestant may do. In other words, the situation is sufficiently bad for the handicapped contestant to accept the role of a follower.

Summing up we have the following result.

PROPOSITION 7.1 *In the leader–follower game with the weighted Ratio Form CSF, the handicapped contestant moves first and the strong contestant moves second.*

In this game, contestants do not have incentives to play simultaneously unless $\theta = 1$, i.e., unless they are identical. (In this case contestants are totally indifferent between moving early or late.) Comparing this equilibrium with the simultaneous Nash equilibrium, we see that:

(1) Payoffs in this equilibrium for both contestants are larger than those in the simultaneous contest (see Exercise 7.1).
(2) Aggregate effort spent in this equilibrium is smaller than the one spent in the simultaneous contest (see Exercise 7.2, part (1)).
(3) Aggregate effort is larger when the strong contestant moves first than when the weak contestant moves first (see Exercise 7.2, part (2)).

The first point suggests that endogenous moves facilitate a form of tacit collusion among competitors, resulting in larger payoffs than those achievable under simultaneous moves. This phenomenon can be explained by the second point, which posits that contestants exert less effort in equilibrium under endogenous moves compared to simultaneous moves. This observation can be traced back to Proposition 3.1 and Figure 3.1 in Chapter 3, which reveal that under simultaneous moves, strategies are strategic substitutes for the weaker contestant and strategic complements for the stronger contestant. Consequently, when starting from a Nash equilibrium, reduced effort by the weaker contestant leads to less effort by the stronger contestant, thereby increasing payoffs. Conversely, reduced effort by the stronger contestant prompts more effort by the weaker contestant, which is disadvantageous for payoffs.[3]

The model we have examined can be extended to include more general CSFs, asymmetric information, prizes with endogenous values, and more contestants and periods.

(1) **More general CSFs.** Gao, Lu, and Wang (2023) analyzed the leader–follower game with a generalized Tullock CSF with competitiveness parameter $\epsilon \in (0, +\infty)$. They demonstrated that if $\epsilon < 1$, an interior equilibrium exists regardless of who takes the lead, and there is no preemptive equilibrium. However, if $\epsilon \geq 1$ and the strong contestant leads, a preemptive equilibrium can occur. In the model we presented here, this is the case when $\theta \in (0, 0.5)$. Exercise 7.3 asks you to prove this fact. Moreover, they showed that a preemptive equilibrium is also possible for a middle range of $\epsilon > 1$ when the weak contestant leads, provided that the weak contestant is not extremely weak. The intuition behind this is that in a highly competitive contest (a high ϵ), competition becomes a risky undertaking, and the leader prefers to preempt. However, this strategy is expensive because it necessitates a significant effort on the leader's part. Although Gao, Lu, and Wang (2023) conducted an exhaustive analysis to characterize all equilibria in the leader–follower contest, they did not examine the endogenous choice related to whether or not to take on the leadership role, which remains an open question in their general framework.

(2) **Asymmetric information.** Fu (2006) analyzed rent-seeking contests with one-sided information asymmetry and allowed contestants to choose the timing of their actions. In equilibrium, the informed contestant never moves first, and there is a sequential equilibrium where the uninformed contestant moves first. This is because the uninformed contestant can lower her bid and reduce the potential for overbidding due to uncertainty softening competition. Thus, asymmetric information performs the same role as the difference in abilities in the previous analysis. In Chapter 8, we will revisit this situation after introducing the main components of asymmetric information (see Exercise 8.15).

(3) **Endogenous prize.** Hoffmann and Rota-Graziosi (2012) provided a theory of endogenous timing and worked out a number of special cases under the assumption that the value of the prize might decrease with effort. For instance, war efforts may destroy part of the prize (cities, crops). In this case, strategies can be strategic complements or substitutes for both contestants which is impossible when the prize is fixed (see Proposition 3.1 in Chapter 3). Under some circumstances, contestants may have incentives to play simultaneously or the strong contestant may have incentives to move first. These findings serve to take the results presented in this section with some caution (see also the survey by Hoffmann and Rota-Graziosi, 2018).

---

[3] Note that the equilibrium of the game in Tables 7.1 and 7.2 is not only a Nash equilibrium, but is a Dominant Strategy of a game in which we have successively eliminated all dominated strategies. This solution concept is called Dominant Solvability (see Osborne and Rubinstein, 1994, p. 63).

(4) **More contestants and periods**. The sequential contests discussed so far have exclusively considered two contestants and two periods. There is limited knowledge concerning sequential contests involving additional periods where n contestants take actions sequentially. The challenge resides in the resolution of these contests, wherein backward induction requires the computation of optimal response functions for each period and their subsequent recursive substitution. This renders the analysis of such multiperiod sequential contests at times intractable. Glazer and Hassin (2000) analyzed the equilibrium in a sequential three-contestant Tullock contest with an exogenous order of moves. They showed that early movers may not always secure higher profits compared to later movers and that the total profits are lower than in a contest where contestants move simultaneously. Kahana and Klunover (2018), using aggregative games techniques, showed the existence and uniqueness of subgame perfect equilibrium in a sequential contest with n identical contestants. Hinnosaar (2023) examines a model of sequential contests where effort choices are made by n contestants sequentially, but the efforts are not observable by subsequent contestants. The model incorporates a fixed and common knowledge disclosure information rule, as well as a fixed order of contestant arrivals. The disclosure rule determines the time at which the choices made in previous periods are revealed. The author characterizes equilibria for these sequential contests and investigates how the availability of information about other contestants' efforts influences the equilibrium behavior. By employing a specific solution method (see Exercise 7.4), the author establishes the existence and uniqueness of equilibria and demonstrates that the information about other contestants' efforts strictly increase the total effort. The optimal contest design depends on the desirability of efforts, leading to contests with either full transparency or hidden efforts. Furthermore, the analysis reveals a strict earlier-mover advantage, wherein contestants who move earlier in sequential contests choose greater efforts and achieve higher payoffs compared to later contestants.

7.2   Elimination Contests

Elimination contests are commonly seen in various domains, including sports, beauty contests, and procurement processes. These contests typically involve multiple rounds where a certain number of participants are eliminated in each round until a winner is determined. The concept of elimination contests and their outcomes has been explored extensively. Sherwin Rosen (1938–2001), in his influential paper published in 1986, explains an intriguing pattern observed in multistage contests: the concentration of prizes in the later stages, particularly the final.

To illustrate this phenomenon, let us consider examples from the sports world. In the 2019 Wimbledon tennis tournament, the champion earned a staggering $2,983,748, while the runner-up received $1,491,874. The losing semifinalists were awarded $746,572, and those exiting in the quarterfinals $373,286. Similarly, in the illustrious Champions League football competition, the financial rewards escalate significantly as teams progress through the stages. The winning team can potentially earn up to 82 million euros, while those only participating in the group stage receive 15 million euros.[4] Drawing upon Rosen's observations, it becomes apparent that in many career-oriented competitions, such as managerial roles, individuals often climb the ladder by starting from lower-level positions.

To capture the essence of an elimination contest, we will consider a straightforward model involving four identical contestants. This model allows for a maximum of two elimination rounds, with each round consisting of pairwise matches between the contestants. We assume the Ratio Form CSF. The structure of prizes is as follows: V_{FW} is the final prize for the winner of the competition; V_{FL} is the final prize for the winner runner up in the final; V_S is the prize for playing the semifinal. The organization has M dollars to spend. The budget constraint of the organization is

$$V_{FW} + V_{FL} + 4V_S \leq M.$$

Let g^F be the vector of efforts in the final match. In the final, the payoff of a finalist is

$$\pi_i(g^F) = p_i(g^F)V_{FW} + (1 - p_i(g^F))V_{FL} - g_i^F$$
$$= p_i(g^F)(V_{FW} - V_{FL}) + V_{FL} - g_i^F.$$

This is akin to a game with prize $V_{FW} - V_{FL}$ since V_{FL} is a constant that does not influence efforts. The difference $V_{FW} - V_{FL}$ represents the marginal prize or incremental reward for advancing toward the final. Given that p_i is the Ratio CSF, in equilibrium, in the final round both contestants make an effort of $(V_{FW} - V_{FL})/4$ and they have an expected payoff of $\pi_i(g^F) = (V_{FW} - V_{FL})/4 + V_{FL}$. Let g^S be the vector of efforts in the semifinal. In the first round, the payoff of a semifinalist is

$$\pi_i(g^S) = p_i(g^S)\pi_i(g^F) + V_S - g_i^S.$$

In equilibrium, contestant i effort is $\pi_i^F(g^F)/4$. Total effort is

$$\frac{V_{Fw} - V_{FL}}{4} + V_{FL} + \frac{V_{Fw} - V_{FL}}{2}$$
$$= \frac{V_{Fw} - V_{FL} + 4V_{FL} + 2V_{Fw} - 2V_{FL}}{4}$$
$$\frac{3V_{Fw} + V_{FL}}{4}.$$

Clearly, since in the budget constraint the marginal cost of any effort is identical but the marginal revenue of the prize of the winner is larger than the marginal revenue of any other effort, total effort is maximized over the budget constraint when $V_S = V_{FL} = 0$ and $V_{Fw} = M$, i.e., the winner takes all. Formally,

[4] It is worth noting that the Champions League follows a specific structure, wherein soccer teams from European countries are divided into groups of four. These teams play against each other twice, resulting in six games for each team. The winner of each game is awarded three points, while the loser gets none. A draw grants each team a single point. The two teams with the highest scores in each group advance to the next round, known as the round of 16, where pairings are determined through a lottery. The progression continues until the final stage, where the ultimate champion is crowned.

PROPOSITION 7.2   *In the elimination game explained above, a unique prize for the winner of the competition maximizes aggregate effort.*

When participants are competing at an early stage, the grand prize serves as a significant motivating factor. This prize remains in their minds throughout the entire game, driving their efforts at every stage. If there were prizes awarded merely for participation or playing, it would actually disincentive effort. This effect was observed during the 2019 Wimbledon tournament when an increase in the prize for participating in the first round led to several contestants withdrawing from their matches. But a word of caution is advisable here. The above analysis assumes risk-neutral contestants. It is possible that if contestants are risk-averse, the reward scheme that maximizes aggregate effort would include a less extreme prize distribution, as it happens in the standard principal–agent problem with moral hazard.

There are several noteworthy extensions of the preceding result.

(1) **Heterogeneous contestants**. The analysis presented so far assumes that all contestants in the elimination tournament are identical. However, it is also possible to extend the analysis to the case where contestants have different abilities or skills. In such scenarios, the prize differentials between rounds also play a crucial role. Rosen (1986) demonstrated that an increase in the prize differential between rounds has the effect of increasing the probability of the stronger contestant winning the tournament. Exercise 7.7 asks you to prove this fact in a simple case.

(2) **Multiple stages**. Fu and Lu (2012b) analyzed elimination contests where a group of identical contestants competes in multiple stages, with participants being successively eliminated from the race at each stage. The survivors from each stage compete against all remaining contestants to advance further in the competition. At each stage, the competition can be modeled as a nested contest with multiple winners (see Clark and Riis, 1996, 1998b). Fu and Lu (2012b) proved that the optimal contest strategy involves eliminating one contestant at each stage, ultimately culminating in a finale where a single winner emerges to claim the entire prize. Exercise 7.8 requires you to prove this assertion for the specific scenario involving four contestants and the Tullock CSF.

Finally, a study conducted by Gilsdorf and Sukhatme (2008) analyzed a comprehensive data set comprising 2,632 individual matches across 68 tournaments during the 2001 men's professional tennis circuit. The study found a positive and statistically significant effect of increases in prize money differentials on the stronger contestant's probability of winning the match.

7.3   Races

A race is a series of matches in which the winner of a given number of matches wins the race. Examples are a tennis match, in which winning two (sometimes three) sets ensures victory, or NBA finals in which the winner of four matches is the champion.

In some chess tournaments, contestants compete in a series of matches. The contestant who wins the most matches or accumulates the most points over the tournament becomes the winner. US primaries and presidential elections are a variation of races in which the value of each match depends on the size of the corresponding state. With the increasing involvement of private companies, there is a growing race in the field of space exploration. Companies like SpaceX, Blue Origin, and Virgin Galactic are competing to achieve milestones such as manned missions to Mars, space tourism, or establishing a lunar base. In industries and markets, companies strive to outpace each other in developing and launching innovative products or services. For example, the competition between tech giants like Apple and Samsung to release the latest and most advanced smartphones can be seen as a technology race.[5]

We start with a couple of conjectures on the main characteristics of equilibrium in this class of contests.

- The **Discouragement effect** which says that if the distance among competitors in the final rounds is too large, laggards throw the towel.
- The **New Hampshire effect**, originally coined in political science, which says that, in political races, campaigning is very intensive in first districts (like New Hampshire). The early winner has a larger probability of winning in further districts.

The New Hampshire effect and the Discouragement effect can be regarded as two sides of the same coin because once one of the contestants has secured a beefy lead, the incentive of other contestants to expend effort is low.

There is considerable evidence of the New Hampshire effect. In US primaries, winning in New Hampshire increases a candidate's share of the final count by 27 percentage points (see Mayer, 2004). In sports, Krumer and Lechner (2017) gather data on all FIFA World Cups and UEFA European Championships 1996–2014. They find that the team playing the first match of each round, namely in the first and the third matches, has, on average, 17% more probability to qualify for the next stage than the other teams.[6]

We now present a theoretical model in which the New Hampshire effect arises very naturally. It is based on a contribution by Klumpp and Polborn (2006). For simplicity, suppose that to win the contest you need to win in at least two districts out of three. We assume that the CSF satisfies the following properties:

- Homogeneity of Degree Zero;
- Symmetry;
- Differentiable when g is strictly positive;
- Allows for the existence of a one-shot symmetric equilibrium in pure strategies.

---

[5] The topic of R&D races has produced an important body of literature that cannot be surveyed here, see Reinganum (1989).

[6] Apesteguia and Palacios-Huerta (2010) find that in soccer, "when a match is drawn but a winner is needed" … "teams that take the first kick in the sequence win the penalty shoot-out 60.5 percent of the time." But they attribute this to psychological pressure.

The traditional Ratio Form CSF satisfies all these properties. To simplify notation, take $V = 1$.

Coming back to our game, we start with the third round. To reach the third round, the only possibility is that each contestant has won one previous round. Since this round is final because there is no future, we can use Nash equilibrium as a solution concept because it is a one-shot contest. As we already know, in equilibrium $g_1^3 = g_2^3 = g^3$, and

$$\pi_1(g_1^3, g_2^3) = \pi_2(g_2^3, g_1^3) = \frac{1}{2} - g^3,$$

where the superscript indicates the round in which the action is chosen.

Now we go to the second round. Without loss of generality, suppose contestant 1 has won in round 1. Thus,

$$\pi_1(g_1^2, g_2^2) = p_1(g_1^2, g_2^2) + (1 - p_1(g_1^2, g_2^2))\pi_1(g_1^3, g_2^3) - g_1^2$$

$$= p_1(g_1^2, g_2^2)\left(\frac{1}{2} + g^3\right) + \pi_1(g_1^3, g_2^3) - g_1^2;$$

$$\pi_2(g_2^2, g_1^2) = p_2(g_2^2, g_1^2)\pi_2(g_2^3, g_1^3) - g_2^2$$

$$= p_2(g_2^2, g_1^2)\left(\frac{1}{2} - g^3\right) - g_2^2.$$

So we see that this is identical to a simultaneous game in which prizes are no longer identical: It is $1/2 + g^3$ for the winner of the first round and $1/2 - g^3$ for the loser of the first round. (The term π_1^3 in the payoffs of the winner is a constant and can be disregarded in the maximization.)

By homogeneity of degree zero, in the equilibrium in the second round, the ratio of expenses equals the ratio of valuations (see (3.4) in Chapter 3) and so $g_1^2/g_2^2 = (1/2 + g^3)/(1/2 - g^3) > 1$. Because of symmetry of CSF, $p_1(g_1^2, g_2^2) > p_2(g_2^2, g_1^2)$. Summarizing:

PROPOSITION 7.3   *In the race considered above, there are both Discouragement* $(g_1^2 > g_2^2)$ *and New Hampshire* $(p_1(g_1^2, g_2^2) > p_2(g_2^2, g_1^2))$ *effects.*

As Fu, Lu, and Pan (2015) explain, early winners "value the battle more and therefore are more likely to win. A laggard has to continue to sink costly effort into the third battle if he wins the current one, which dissipates his future rent, thereby attenuating his incentive to remain in the contest." Exercise 7.9 asks you to compute equilibrium when the CSF is Ratio Form.

The previous observation motivated Fu, Lu, and Pan (2015) to consider a variation of the previous game in which the contest is played by a team. Each member of the team participates in just one battle. They call this situation a "Team Race." As examples of this situation, we have "House of Representatives and Senate elections in US and India's electoral politics which are dominated by two alliances led by two parties which require the success of allied regional parties."[7] To explain the basics, we now present a simplified version of this paper, keeping the assumptions made above.

There are two teams with three contestants each. There are three battles. A team wins if it wins two battles. The prize is a public good for the team. To simplify notation, we set $V = 1$. Note that the difference with the previous contest is that a contestant fighting in battle t does not take into account the effort that a teammate will make in battle $t + 1$.

As before, let us start by analyzing the final round. Again this round only occurs when both teams are tied. And since this is the end of the contests, we have that in a Nash equilibrium

$$g_1^3 = g_2^3 = g^3; \ \pi_1(g_1^3, g_2^3) = \pi_2(g_2^3, g_1^3) = \frac{1}{2} - g^3,$$

as before. Now consider the second round and, without loss of generality, assume that candidate 1 has won in round 1. Payoffs for the contestants in this battle are

$$\pi_1(g_1^2, g_2^2) = p_1(g_1^2, g_2^2) + (1 - p_1(g_1^2, g_2^2))\frac{1}{2} - g_1^2$$

$$= p_1(g_1^2, g_2^2)\frac{1}{2} + \frac{1}{2} - g_1^2$$

$$\pi_2(g_2^2, g_1^2) = p_2(g_2^2, g_1^2)\frac{1}{2} - g_2^2.$$

We see that the prize is identical for both contestants and so by homogeneity of degree zero of the CSF, in the equilibrium in the second round, $g_1^2/g_2^2 = 1$ and because symmetry of the CSF, $p_1(g_1^2, g_2^2) = p_2(g_2^2, g_1^2)$. Thus, in this game there are neither discouragement nor New Hampshire effects. The reason is that contestants do not interiorize the effort that other members of the team have to make in the continuation game.

Summarizing:

PROPOSITION 7.4 *In a race involving two teams, where each team member participates in just one battle, neither the discouragement effect nor the New Hampshire effect is observed.*

Several extensions of the previous results are worth mentioning.

(1) **More general temporal structures**. Another result in Lu, Fu, and Pan (2015) is that all temporal structures of team contests (i.e., simultaneous, sequential, etc.) yield the same expected aggregate effort. (Exercise 7.10 asks you to prove this fact.) However, expected winners' efforts – a natural objective in R&D races, elections, and sports – are not the same in all structures. Barbieri and Serena

---

[7] Additional examples include: the Tennis Davis Cup in which two teams composed of five players play five matches, four individuals, and a double comes close to our framework. But in the Davis Cup a player can play up to three matches. In golf, the Ryder Cup is a prestigious team competition where golfers from Europe and the United States compete against each other. Each player participates in a series of individual matches against opponents from the opposing team, and the team that accumulates the most points from these matches claims victory.

(2019) show that "among all possible temporal structures, expected winners' efforts are maximized by a fully simultaneous contest and minimized by a fully sequential contest." Hinnosaar (2023) shows that more information about other contestants' efforts increases total effort. Total effort is maximized with full transparency and minimized with no transparency. (Exercise 7.11 asks you to prove this fact.)

(2) **Different payoff functions**. Sela (2011) considers a race of a three-stage All Pay Auction with two contestants in which contestants do not want to lose quickly. In other words, contestants prefer to lose the race by putting up a good fight in the second stage rather than throwing in the towel. Sela shows how this preference improves efforts to the point in which the discouragement effect is reversed.

7.4 Effort as an Investment for the Future

So far, each stage of the games considered is governed by identical rules to the ones played before or after. In the NBA finals, or the Soccer World Champions, despite history matters, all games are played by the same rules. It is time to consider a situation in which the efforts of today have an impact on the rules of the game of tomorrow. In the parlance of historians, history shapes the rules of the current conflict. In war, success today means more territory and more resources tomorrow. During the Cold War, the term Domino Theory was coined, according to which if one country fell into communist hands, surrounding countries would follow suit. Large firms have access to better financial facilities that allow them to build a better brand tomorrow. In sports, success today implies more supporters and more revenue, which allows a better performance tomorrow.

The literature on these kinds of conflicts started with the contributions of Münster (2007c), Möller (2012), Clark and Nilssen (2013), and Beviá and Corchón (2013). The first paper considers a stage in which only investment decisions are taken. The contest is played in the second stage. The second and third papers analyze the optimal distribution of a given prize in a contest played twice. The planner faces a trade-off since a large prize in the first period makes contestants fitter in the second but leaves a small prize to fight for.[8] See Exercise 7.15 for the Möller model. The last paper focuses on the characteristics of the path of equilibrium actions in a contest played in two periods, where the strength of the contestants in the second period depends on the realization of the contest in the first period. This is the model explained below.

Consider a conflict between two contestants that lasts for two periods denoted by the superscript t. Contestants fight for a divisible prize with a value V each period whose value is independent of the conflict. Think of two countries fighting for territory. Or two teams – Oxford and Cambridge – fighting in a boat race each year. Or

---

[8] These papers assume two contestants. See Clark, Nilssen, and Sand (2020) for an extension to n contestants.

two political parties fighting for some seats in a hung parliament that will give them more power to impulse or to veto laws.

Effort of contestant i in period t is denoted by g_i^t. Contestant 1 ends each period with a fraction $p^t(\boldsymbol{g^t})$ of the prize. So $1 - p^t(\boldsymbol{g^t})$ is the fraction controlled by contestant 2 at the end of period t. Payoffs for i in t are

$$\pi_i^t(\boldsymbol{g^t}) = p_i^t(\boldsymbol{g^t})V - g_i^t, \ i \in \{1,2\}, \text{ with } p_1^t = p^t \text{ and } p_2^t = 1 - p^t.$$

Payoffs for the whole game are $\sum_{t=1}^{2} \delta^{t-1}\pi_i^t(\boldsymbol{g^t})$ denoted by Π_i where $\delta \in [0,1]$ is the common discount rate. Contrarily to what happens in Races and Elimination contests, payoffs are delivered in each period.

The CSF is a weighted Ratio Form,

$$p^t(\boldsymbol{g^t}) = \frac{\alpha^t g_1^t}{\alpha^t g_1^t + (1 - \alpha^t)g_2^t} \text{ if } \sum_{i=1}^{2} g_i^t > 0; \ p^t = \alpha^t \text{ otherwise,}$$

where $\alpha^t \in (0,1)$ is the relative strength of contestant 1 at t. The reader can think of the relative influence of contestant 1 as $\alpha^t g_i^t$, which is a Cobb–Douglas production function of the influence of i by means of strength and effort. The main difference with the conflicts considered so far is that here α^t varies with time.

The strength evolves according to a transition function, which says how the relative strength (strength in the sequel) of a contestant in the second period depends (positively) on her share of the prize in the first period. For simplicity, we choose the affine form, namely

$$\alpha^2 = ap^1 + b, \ a = 1 - 2b, \ a \in (0,1), \ b \in (0, 0.5).$$

The parameter a measures the importance of the share in the previous period. If $a = 0$ – so $b = 0.5$ – we are back to the symmetric case considered in previous sections in which weights in the CSF are constant. The parameter b is the strength of country 1, which does not depend on the share. We can think of technology, social values, etc. The condition $a = 1 - 2b$ makes sure that the strength in period two is between zero and one. And implies that when the first contest ends evenly ($p^1(\boldsymbol{g^1}) = 0.5$) tomorrow' strength is even too ($\alpha^2 = 0.5$). Figure 7.1 shows the transition function $\alpha^2 = 0.5p^1 + 0.25$.

The *Investment Effect* is the effect of today's performance on tomorrow's strength. Incentives to expend more effort today are enhanced by the existence of additional periods. In the example in Figure 7.1, an increase in today's performance that raises the fraction of the prize from 0.3 to 0.5 increases the strength of this contestant in the second period by 0.1 points.

This contest has a unique subgame perfect Nash equilibrium. The proof is tedious and will be skipped here. The important thing is that this simple model allows us to discuss the interplay between Discouragement and Investment Effects. We have already seen that in the former, weak contestants make little effort. Both effects drive efforts in different directions so the question is, which effect is stronger? Clearly, in

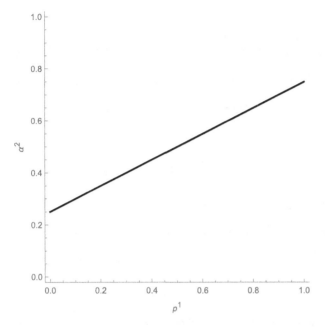

Figure 7.1 Transition function $\alpha^2 = 0.5p^1 + 0.25$

period 2 there is no future, so the investment effect does not exist. Thus, let us focus on period 1.

Consider the following example in which $a = 1$, $b = 0$, $V = 10$, and $\delta = 1$ which is represented in Figure 7.2.

The dotted line is the equilibrium effort of contestant 1 if the future did not exist, i.e., in a one-shot game. We see that when the contest is very asymmetric (α^1 close to zero or one), the effort of contestant 1 is small. This is because when she is weak, her chances of winning are slim. (think of yourself playing a tennis match against Nadal) and when she is strong, a little effort secures a good performance (think of Nadal playing a tennis match against you). As we already know, incentives to spend effort are maximized in many contests, including this one, when contestants are identical.

Now look at the solid line which represents the effort of contestant 1 in the first period in a subgame perfect Nash equilibrium. This line intersects twice with the dotted line representing effort in a one-shot situation. We see that for $\alpha^1 \in (0, 0.3) \cup (0.7, 1)$ the discouragement effect wins. In other words, when the contest is very biased, even if contestants understand that today's efforts influence tomorrow's outcomes, the Discouragement Effect wins because of the strong imbalance. But when contestants are sufficiently similar ($\alpha^1 \in (0.3, 0.7)$), this effect is small and the Investment effect prevails. The dashed line represents the effort of contestant 2 in the first period. Observe that this line is the mirror image of the line representing the efforts of contestant 1. What we said about contestant 1 can be applied, mutatis mutandis to contestant 2. These results generalize to the model considered here. Given $a, \delta > 0$, there exist $\alpha^* \in (0, 1/2)$ such that for all $\alpha \in (0, \alpha^*)$ the equilibrium effort of

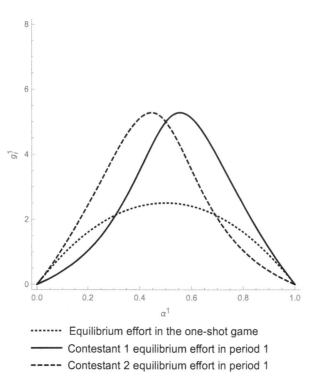

Figure 7.2 Efforts as functions of strength

contestant 1 in period 1 is smaller than the equilibrium effort in the one-shot game. Similarly for contestant 2.

An effect that may occur in this kind of model is the *Matthew Effect*. The name comes from a quotation from Matthew the evangelist "For to everyone who has will more be given, and he will have abundance; but from him who has not, even what he has will be taken away." In sociology, the *Matthew Effect* (or accumulated advantage) is the occurrence that "the rich get richer and the poor get poorer." It was coined by Robert K. Merton (1968). In education, early success in acquiring reading skills usually leads to later successes in reading as the learner grows, while failing to learn to read before the third or fourth year of schooling may be indicative of lifelong problems in learning new skills. In science, already famous authors get more recognition in joint papers than relatively unknown coauthors. Similar occurrences happen in citations, arts, celebrities, etc. The difference with the New Hampshire effect explained in Section 7.3 is that there the constituent game is the same period after period. Here early winners shift the prize allocation rule (i.e., the CSF) in their favor. Empirical evidence of the Matthew effect is presented in Perc (2014).

An example is the *Domino Effect* which happens when a contestant is having initially more than half of the prize, she will have an even larger share in the second period. This term was used during the Cold War to back up American military interventions in countries in which communism was a threat. We say that there is a Domino

Effect when contestant 1 is having initially more than half of the prize ($p^1 > 1/2$); she will have even a larger share in the second period ($p^2 > p^1$). We have the following:

PROPOSITION 7.5 *In the model explained above, there is no Domino Effect.*

Proof In the second stage, it is readily calculated that $p^2 = \alpha^2$. But then, notice that

$$p^2 = ap^1 + b = (1 - 2b)p^1 + b. \tag{7.1}$$

Rearranging (7.1), we obtain

$$p^2 - p^1 = b(1 - 2p^1).$$

We have two cases. In the extreme case in which only the outcome in the first period is relevant to determine the strength of the next period (i.e., $b = 0$), $p^1 = p^2$ so shares are invariant in time. In any other case, $b > 0$ and $p^1 > 1/2$ implies $p^2 < p^1$. $\square$

This result suggests that protracted conflicts tend to end up in an impasse in which contestants have to spend resources period after period in order to maintain their position. Examples like the Roman Empire versus Germanic tribes or the one versus the Persian Empire, the World War I (until the entry of the US into the conflict), or the Cold War come to our minds. However, a full proof of this conjecture would take a model with several periods which is not attempted here. See Neary (1997) and Luo and Xin (2018) for an extension of this model to endogenous prizes and Exercise 7.16 for a generalization to more general transition functions.

The class of models in this section suggests that when the prize is indivisible and the contest is repeated many times, sooner or later, losers in most contests will become bankrupt. Think of architectural firms competing regularly for supply plans for new buildings, aircraft engineering corporations competing to supply new airliners, or empires fighting for a border territory. In fact Kennedy (1987) pointed out financial overburden as the main cause of the decline of empires with Spain, France, and the UK as leading examples. In some cases, advancing the problems to come, a contestant in dire straits may behave very aggressively, trying to obtain quickly a decisive victory since in a long fight she will end up bankrupt. Beviá and Corchón (2016) call this situation the *Despair Effect*. A further consequence of potential bankruptcies is that contestants with big pockets may prey on contestants in financial distress by making expenses that others cannot follow. Some say that Reagan' Star Wars program accomplished this during the last years of the Cold War. Gelder and Kovenock (2017) examined experimentally strategic patterns of competition in a best-of-seven-wins dynamic contest. They found that a sizable number of contestants that after losing preliminary battles make a last stand or escalate.

7.5   Repeated Contests

So far we have assumed that the contestants act in a noncooperative way. However, there is evidence suggesting that in repeated procurement (either private or public) contestants collude in several ways. One of the most common is *bid rigging*. This happens when some firms do not submit a competitive bid – or no bid at all – to allow other firms to win the contract. For instance, bidders may take turns to share the spoils. And sometimes they create phony companies to cover their tracks.[9] The occurrence of such behavior has prompted the US Department of Justice's Antitrust Division to establish on November 5, 2019, the Procurement Collusion Strike Force (PCFS), a new task force designed to detect criminal anticompetitive behavior in government procurements. Maci (2012) estimated that the cost of bid rigging in the EU is between 13 and 37 billion euros. In Korea, estimates of bid rigging amount to a whopping 15.5% of total expenses in the construction industry (Lee and Hahn, 2002).

In this section, we present a stylized model of bid rigging in contests. Suppose two firms that live an indefinite number of periods and are the only suppliers of an item. Each period the supplier of this item is allocated by a contest. If a firm makes no expenses in a period, it loses the contract for this period. We will not specify the CSF of this contest but it suffices to denote by V^O the payoffs obtained in case they play noncooperatively. For instance, with the Ratio Form CSF and identical firms, $V^O = V/4$. By simplicity, we assume that these payoffs are the same for both firms. Firms discount the future at a rate δ.

Firms take turns to bid. One firm makes a ridiculously low bid and the other firm makes no bid at all. Of course, this is an idealization. In real life, such behavior would trigger a judicial response. But here, we are analyzing a limited case that once understood will allow us to confront more realistic scenarios. To further streamline the presentation, we assume that the bid of the winning firm can be approximated by zero.

Firms use grim trigger strategies as in the pioneering contribution of the late James Friedman (1936–2016) (see Fudenberg and Tirole, 1991, pp. 154–155). Collusion works as follows. Firm 1 bids (almost) zero and wins the contests in even periods and firm 2 bids (almost) zero and wins the contests in odd periods. In any other period, firms bid zero. If someone breaks this agreement, both contestants play noncooperatively from then on to the end of time. In other words, when the agreement is broken once, contestants never expect a further agreement.

If contestant 2 follows this strategy, it collects $\delta V + \delta^3 V + \delta^5 V + \cdots = \delta V(1 + \delta^2 + \delta^4 + \cdots)$. And assuming that $\delta < 1$ the previous sum amounts to

$$\frac{\delta V}{1 - \delta^2}.$$

For this strategy to be a subgame perfect Nash equilibrium it must be that no contestant has incentives to betray the agreement by switching to an action not prescribed by this strategy. Betrayal, which takes the form of bidding a ridiculously low bid (but larger than one made by contestant 1) in a period in which she was supposed not to bid at all, yields the contestant 2 (almost) V today and $\delta V^O + \delta^2 V^O + \delta^3 V^O + \cdots$ in the future. All together this move amounts to

$$V + \frac{\delta V^O}{1 - \delta}.$$

Thus, for the collusive action to be profitable for the contestant 2 in a subgame perfect Nash equilibrium,

$$\frac{\delta V}{1 - \delta^2} \geq V + \frac{\delta V^O}{1 - \delta} \quad \text{or}$$

$$\delta(1 + \delta) \geq \frac{V}{V - V^O}. \tag{7.2}$$

Note that the left-hand side of (7.2) is always smaller than 2. Thus if $2V^O > V$ collusion cannot be supported by this scheme. If the contest is played with a Ratio Form CSF, $V^O = V/4$ so for any δ below 0.75831 collusion is not a subgame perfect Nash equilibrium of this game. It is left as an exercise to show that if the incentive equation holds for firm 2, it also holds for firm 1 (see Exercise 7.17).

One of the pioneering papers exploring infinitely repeated contests is Leininger and Yang (1994). The authors specifically concentrate on a scenario involving homogenous contestants. Their primary objective centers around comparing expenditures in repeated contests to those in static contests. Through their analysis, they demonstrate that collusion in a rent-seeking contest is advantageous as it diminishes wasteful expenditures when contrasted with a static rent-seeking contest. Leininger and Yang's work sheds light on the benefits of sustained cooperation and its potential impact on reducing inefficiencies in rent-seeking contests.

Shaffer and Shogren (2008) focused on heterogeneous contestants, and they compared expenditures within the same infinitely repeated contest for different degrees of heterogeneity between the contestants. Collusion becomes more viable and sustainable when the contestants exhibit a higher level of equality compared to situations with lower equality. Consequently, the total expenditures on rent-seeking activities may decrease when the contestants possess a more balanced level of capabilities. This finding starkly contrasts with the conventional outcome observed in the existing literature on static rent-seeking contests, where increasing disparities between contestants typically lead to higher aggregate expenditures.

7.6   Exercises

7.1 Show that aggregate payoffs under endogenous moves are larger than those in simultaneous Nash equilibrium.

7.2 Show that: (1) Aggregate effort spent under endogenous moves is smaller than that spent in simultaneous Nash equilibrium. (2) Aggregate effort is larger when the strong contestant moves first than when the weak contestant moves first.

7.3 Show that if the weaker contestant is the leader, there is no preemptive equilibrium that can prevent the stronger contestant from participating in the contest, however, if the strong contestant leads, a preemptive equilibrium can occur when $\theta \in (0, 0.5)$.

7.4 In sequential contests with a finite number of contestants, the computation of equilibria typically involves the use of backward induction, a process that involves determining optimal response functions for each period and recursively substituting them. However, as the number of contestants increases, this conventional method may occasionally prove infeasible. Hinnosaar (2023) proposed an innovative approach to addressing this issue by characterizing optimal response functions through the employment of inverse functions, an approach he refers to as the Inverted Best-Response Method. Apply this methodology to a sequential contest involving four identical contestants who arrive in a sequential manner, with their exertion of effort being instantaneously observed.

7.5 In a two-contestant Tullock contest with endogenous moves, the planner of the contest requires the contestants to pay a cost per unit of effort. The cost for first movers is $c \in (0, 1)$, and for second movers is $c = 1$. The planner cannot distinguish the strong contestant from the weak one. The contest organizer's objective is to set the level of c that yields the maximum possible payoff for her, taking into account that she prefers effort to be exercised earlier than later. Show that there exists no c that generates the first-best outcome. However, there is a range of c that can induce both contestants to move early. See Protopappas (2023).

7.6 Consider the elimination contest with four identical contestants and the Ratio Form CSF. Suppose that we have a budget M to be distributed between the prize of the semifinal, V_{SF} and the prize of the final, V_F. (1) Which is the optimal allocation of prizes if the objective is to maximize total effort? (2) Compare this with the structure of the prizes that give the same effort in the final as in the semifinal. (3) What structure gives you the lowest discouragement? Discuss your result.

7.7 Consider two elimination rounds, where each round involves pairwise matches between four contestants with different skills ($\alpha_1 < \alpha_2 < \alpha_3 < \alpha_4$). Suppose there is a budget M to be allocated between the prize of the semifinal, V_{SF} and the prize of the final, V_F. Suppose also that the CSF in each match is the weighted Ratio Form CSF. Show how the pairwise matches in the first round should be arranged and how the budget M should be distributed to maximize the probability of the strongest contestant winning the final.

7.8 Following the model of Fu and Lu (2012b) but with four contestants and the Ratio Form CSF, prove that the optimal contest strategy involves eliminating one contestant at each stage, with the prize being concentrated in the winner of the final. Interpret the result.

7.9 Compute the subgame perfect Nash equilibrium for the Race model in Section 7.3 with the Ratio Form CSF.

7.10 Consider a race model involving two teams, with three contestants in each team. In this scenario, each contestant participates in just one battle. The objective of this exercise is to demonstrate that regardless of the temporal structure chosen for the team contest (e.g., simultaneous or sequential), all structures yield the same expected aggregate effort (see Fu, Lu, and Pan, 2015).

7.11 Using the same setting as in Exercise 7.10, prove that if the objective is to maximize the expected winner effort, the optimal temporal structure is a fully simultaneous contest. Additionally, prove that the sequential structure minimizes the expected winner effort. Provide an interpretation of the results (see Barbieri and Serena, 2019).

7.12 In the race model, discuss how the introduction of a prize in every stage makes the discouragement effect less powerful.

7.13 Two countries fight for the ownership of a resource valued V by both. In the first stage, country 1 chooses between war (W) or to settle the conflict in an international court (S). Country 2 always wants to settle peacefully. In each possible contest, W or S, the CSF is $p_1(\mathbf{g}) = \alpha^K g_1/(\alpha_1^K g_1 + g_2)$ for $K \in \{W, S\}$, i.e., the importance of the countries in the CSF depends on the kind of contest they fight. Costs are $c_i^K g_i$ for contestants $i \in \{1, 2\}$ and contests $K \in \{W, S\}$ reflecting the different marginal costs of W and P. Calculate the subgame perfect Nash equilibrium of this game and find conditions under which country 1 prefers war even if $c_1^W > c_1^S$.

7.14 Two contestants, incumbent and entrant, fight for the ownership of an object which in each period has a value of 1. The defeated contestant disappears and is substituted by the victorious entrant who becomes the incumbent tomorrow. All contestants discount the future by δ. Assuming a Ratio Form CSF, find the Markov perfect equilibrium[10] efforts in this game with an infinite horizon. Comment on the role of δ (see Konrad, 2009, pp. 178–180).

7.15 Suppose a two-period contest with a Ratio Form CSF with constant strengths and in which the marginal cost of effort in period 2 is $1 + \alpha V$ where V is the prize received by this contestant in period 1. Contestants do not derive direct utility from the prizes awarded in the contest 1. Assuming that the planner has one unit of resources to spend on prizes in both periods, find the policy that maximizes total efforts (see Möller, 2012).

7.16 Following the model described in Section 7.4, keep the assumption that CSF is a weighted Ratio Form, but now assume that the transition function is just a concave and continuous function $f(p^1)$ such that $f(0.5) = 0.5$. Show that, provided a subgame perfect Nash equilibrium exists, there is no Matthew effect.

7.17 Show that if (7.2) holds, the first firm has incentives to keep the collusive agreement. Explain why.

---

[10] For the concept of a Markov perfect equilibrium, see Fudenberg and Tirole (1991), chapter 13.

7.18   Show that in an infinitely repeated contest with two symmetric contestants and a Ratio Form CSF, using grim trigger strategies, the collusive outcome where both contestants exert zero effort can be sustained as a subgame perfect equilibrium if the discount factor (δ) exceeds 2/3.

7.19   Using the model of Shaffer and Shogren (2008), prove that, for any discount rate, the underdog is more inclined to defect from the collusive outcome because he has relatively less at stake compared to the favorite. Give the intuition of the result and explain the role of all the parameters in the model.

7.20   Two contestants play twice the same contest. Suppose that the CSF is the Ratio Form. Contestant 1 starts the first contest with resources $V/4$ and contestant 2 starts with resources $kV/4$ with $k \geq 3$. Contestants cannot spend more resources than they have. The resources obtained in the first period are carried to the second period. Suppose that both contestants spend $V/4$ in the first period. Thus, with probability $1/2$, 1 wins V, so both can participate in the second contest. With a probability of $1/2$, contestant 1 loses, and she cannot participate in the second contest. Her expected payoff in both periods is

$$\frac{1}{2}\left(V + \frac{V}{4}\right) + \frac{1}{2}0 = \frac{5}{8}V.$$

Show that when p_i is the proportion of the prize received and both contestants spend $V/4$ in the first period, both can participate in the second contest and if each contestant spends $V/4$ in this second contest, expected payoffs in both periods for contestant 1 are $3V/4$.

7.21   Consider a three-stage game. In the first stage, contestants choose to dope or not. If a contestant is doped, her performance is enhanced. In the second stage, each contestant is inspected with a given probability. Those found doped are expelled from the contest. In the third stage, the remaining contestants enter into a contest with a Ratio Form CSF.
(1)   Write the first-order condition of the Nash equilibrium in the last stage of the game.
(2)   Outline the conditions on the probability of detection that prevent doping. See Ryvkin (2013).

8 Asymmetric Information

So far, we have explored contests using the tools offered by Nash equilibrium and its extensions. One interpretation of the Nash equilibrium presumes that all players know all game characteristics, i.e., strategies and payoffs of all involved. This constitutes a game of complete information. Another interpretation suggests that Nash equilibrium is a steady state in a learning process, where players, through repeated engagement in the same game, familiarize themselves with the strategies employed by their competitors. Regardless of the interpretation chosen, a fundamental characteristic of Nash equilibrium is its consistency as a prediction – if all players foresee a particular set of strategies, no player is incentivized to deviate from this prediction (Fudenberg and Tirole, 1991, p. 13).

Military strategists advocate that generals should prepare their forces for any potential adversary action, as opposed to what the adversary will likely do. Put simply, it is unwise to precisely predict others' actions because this prediction may fail. A quick modelling of this recommendation would be the following. Imagine two contestants, where contestant 1 believes contestant 2 will execute efforts $g_2^1, g_2^2, \ldots, g_2^k$ with probabilities $p_2^1, p_2^2, \ldots, p_2^k$. She can then compute the action that optimizes her expected utility (or a variant thereof), and vice versa for contestant 2. But, where do these probabilities and efforts originate?

In three path-breaking papers published in 1967–1968, John Harsanyi (1920–2000) provided an answer.[1] Each player has an information set. Each element of this set contains a description of all the information the player holds. This description constitutes a player's type. Now a player's action depends on her type. For example, consider individuals in the stock market. Depending on the information they have, they might become sellers or buyers of a specific share or remain inactive. Thus, a strategy is not merely an action; it is a function from the information set to the set of actions. An equilibrium, referred to as a Bayesian equilibrium, generalizes the idea behind a Nash equilibrium. Namely, it is a list of strategies where for each player's type, the action suggested by this strategy is the one that optimizes the player's expected utility. Once again, an equilibrium represents a consistent prediction now applicable to games of *incomplete information*, also referred to as games of *asymmetric information*. When all players have only one type, a Bayesian equilibrium becomes a Nash equilibrium.

---

[1] A special case of this model was put forward by William Vickrey (1914–1996) in 1961.

Equipped with this primer on modeling a game where players are uncertain about others' characteristics, we return to the domain of contests. In this framework, contestants might have incomplete information regarding three aspects: the CSF, prize valuations, and other contestants' costs. The subsequent list presents examples of asymmetric information in contests.

(1) **Political campaigns**: In a political competition, the incumbent party may know the value of office better than the challenger party.

(2) **Public examination**: In a public examination, one of the candidates may know better the value of the contested position because she has relatives or friends in this job.

(3) **Oil exploration**: Two companies are fighting for drilling rights in areas suspected to have oil. If one company has conducted preliminary seismic surveys or has other data suggesting the presence of oil, it will have a better idea of the tract's value. A less informed competitor may only have a vague idea about the amount of oil in the tract.

(4) **Product launch**: A company launching a new product may have insights into a competitor's value for launching a similar product based on the competitor's market strategies, past launch data, etc., while the competitor might not know how much value the company places on the new product launch.

(5) **Research and development (R&D) competition**: Two companies may compete to develop a new product or technology. Each company knows its own valuation of the potential market but does not know the competitor's valuation.

(6) **Startup funding competition**: Multiple startups might be competing for the same funding from a venture capitalist. They each won't know the marginal cost of effort (time spent preparing the pitch, resources spent on prototypes and market research, etc.) that the others are incurring.

In Examples 1 through 4, one contestant possesses more precise information than the other. In the limit, when one of the contestant knows all relevant characteristics but the other contestant does not, we have a one-sided asymmetric information game. In Examples 1, 2, and 3, the value of the prize is common; that is, the office, the job, or oil holds the same value for both contestants. In contrast, in Example 4, the contestants assign different valuations to the prize.

In Examples 5 and 6, neither contestant has precise information about their opponent, a scenario referred to in the literature as two-sided asymmetric information.

In the next two sections of this chapter, we analyze a simplified model of one-sided asymmetric information and its equilibrium properties. We expand this exploration to include a two-sided asymmetric information model. Throughout these analyses, we contrast the effects of asymmetric information with scenarios that have complete information.

8.1   One-Sided Asymmetric Information

In this section, we present a simplified model of a common value contest with one-sided asymmetric information based on Wärneryd (2003).

There are two contestants: I, who is informed, and U, who is uninformed. The prize can take either a high value, denoted by V_H, or a low value, denoted by V_L. The informed contestant can be of two types, H or L. Contestant U does not know the precise value of the prize and attaches a probability of q to the prize having a high value V_H and a probability of $1 - q$ to the prize having a low value V_L.

As the information is asymmetric, the contestants' strategies depend on their information. Contestant U, being uninformed, has only one type; therefore, his effort is represented by a single effort, g_U. However, the effort made by contestant I depends on her information, written as $g_I(V)$ where $V \in \{V_H, V_L\}$. The CSF is the Ratio Form.

The payoff for the informed contestant, contingent on the realization of V, depends on $(g_I(V), g_U)$, and is given by[2]

$$\pi_I = \frac{g_I(V)}{g_U + g_I(V)} V - g_I(V), \ V \in \{V_H, V_L\}.$$

The expected payoff for the uninformed contestant depends on $(g_U, g_I(V_H), g_I(V_L))$ and is given by

$$E\pi_U = q \left(\frac{g_U}{g_U + g_I(V_H)} V_H - g_U \right) + (1 - q) \left(\frac{g_U}{g_U + g_I(V_L)} V_L - g_U \right).$$

From the first-order condition for contestant I,

$$\frac{g_U}{(g_U + g_I(V))^2} V = 1, \ V \in \{V_H, V_L\},$$

we can derive contestant I's best response

$$g_I(V) = \sqrt{g_U V} - g_U \ \text{ if } g_U \leq V$$
$$g_I(V) = 0 \ \text{ otherwise}$$
$$V \in \{V_H, V_L\}.$$

Contestant U's action is also determined from the first-order condition:

$$q \frac{g_I(V_H)}{(g_U + g_I(V_H))^2} V_H + (1 - q) \frac{g_I(V_L)}{(g_U + g_I(V_L))^2} V_L = 1.$$

In this scenario, we have three unknowns: U's effort, and I's efforts under both high and low prize values. We also have three equations derived from the first-order conditions of I's payoff maximization and from the first-order condition- of U's expected payoff maximization. The solution to this system of equations provides a Bayesian equilibrium for this asymmetric information contest.

The following proposition shows the existence of a Bayesian equilibrium.

PROPOSITION 8.1   *There exists $\hat{q} \in [0, 1]$ such that*
(Case 1) if $q < \hat{q}$, both informed types are active in equilibrium and
(Case 2) if $q \geq \hat{q}$ only the informed high type is active.

Proof   First, let us see that $g_I(V_H) = g_I(V_L) = 0$ cannot be an equilibrium. This is because U can get the prize for sure with a positive effort. But, decreasing effort

---

[2] To simplify notation, we skip the arguments of payoffs.

increases payoffs, so there is no best reply to both informed types inactive. Thus, in equilibrium, either both informed types are active or only the high type is active.

(**Case 1**) Both informed types are active.

By applying the first-order conditions for the maximization of expected payoff for the uninformed contestant, and taking into account the best response from the informed contestant, we arrive at the following equation:

$$q\frac{\sqrt{V_H}}{\sqrt{g_U}} + (1-q)\frac{\sqrt{V_L}}{\sqrt{g_U}} = 2.$$

Solving this equation, we find that

$$g_U^* = \frac{\left(q\sqrt{V_H} + (1-q)\sqrt{V_L}\right)^2}{4}.$$ (8.1)

For this to be an equilibrium, we require that $g_U^* < V_L$, namely,

$$q < \frac{\sqrt{V_L/V_H}}{1 - \sqrt{V_L/V_H}}$$ (8.2)

where $\hat{q}$ is the right-hand side of (8.2). It turns out that if $V_H < 4V_L$ this inequality holds for all q because the right-hand side is larger than 1. Given that $g_I(V) = \sqrt{g_U^* V} - g_U^*$ and $g_U^* < V_L$, $g_I(V)$ is always positive for $V \in \{V_H, V_L\}$ and consequently, π_I is also positive. Finally, it is not difficult to see that $E\pi_U$ is also positive.

(**Case 2**) Only the informed high type is active.

In this case, the first-order conditions for the maximization of expected payoff for the uninformed contestant are

$$q\frac{g_I(V_H)}{(g_U + g_I(V_H))^2}V_H = 1.$$

Taking into account the best response from the informed contestant, we arrive at

$$g_U^* = \frac{q^2 V_H}{(1+q)^2}.$$ (8.3)

For this to be consistent with the lower type expending nothing, it must be that $q \geq \hat{q}$. Finally, we derive

$$g_I(V_H) = \sqrt{g_U^* V_H} - g_U^* = \frac{q V_H}{(1+q)^2}.$$ (8.4)

$\square$

Wärneryd (2003) extended the above results to logit contests in which contestant have a common value drawn from a continuous distribution (see Exercise 8.6). Hurley and Shogren (1998) consider a Tullock contest with one-sided asymmetric information but with private values (see Exercise 8.8).

8.2   Characteristics of Equilibrium in One-Sided Asymmetric Information

We first focus on the difference of efforts between the two contestants.

PROPOSITION 8.2   *In equilibrium, both contestants do the same effort in expectation.*

Proof   When in equilibrium both informed types are active, $q \in (0, 1)$, $V_H > V_L$, g_U^* is given by (8.1), and the expected effort for the informed contestant, $q g_I(V_H) + (1 - q) g_I(V_L)$, is equal to

$$q \left(\sqrt{g_U^* V_H} - g_U^* \right) + (1 - q) \left(\sqrt{g_U^* V_L} - g_U^* \right)$$
$$= \frac{\left(q \sqrt{V_H} + (1 - q) \sqrt{V_L} \right)^2}{4} = g_U^*.$$

For the case where only the informed high-type contestant is active, g_U^* is given by (8.3), and the expected effort for the informed contestant is $q g_I(V_H)$, where $g_I(V_H)$ is given by (8.4). Thus, $q g_I(V_H) = g_U^*$.   □

This is the incomplete information counterpart of a result obtained in Chapter 3 showing that if valuations are identical, no matter how skewed the CSF may be, equilibrium is symmetric. You can check that when q is equal to 0 or 1, i.e., information asymmetry disappears, the result above is just the result in Chapter 3.

Next, we compare efforts under Nash (symmetric information) and Bayesian (asymmetric information) equilibria.

PROPOSITION 8.3   *Total expected effort is lower in the one-sided asymmetric information scenario than under the symmetric information scenario.*

Proof   Expected effort for a contestant in the symmetric information case when both contestants are informed is $\tilde{V}/4$ (as we show in Chapter 2) where $\tilde{V} = q V_H + (1 - q) V_L$. Expected effort for a contestant in the asymmetric information scenario when both types are active (case 1) is identical and given by (8.1). We have that

$$g_U^* = \frac{\left(q \sqrt{V_H} + (1 - q) \sqrt{V_L} \right)^2}{4} \le \frac{\tilde{V}}{4}.$$

This follows because, by Jensen's inequality, $q \sqrt{V_H} + (1 - q) \sqrt{V_L} \le \sqrt{q V_H + (1 - q) V_L}$. Furthermore, for $q \in (0, 1)$ and $V_H > V_L$, the inequality is strict. In case 2, $g_U = (q^2 V_H)/(1 + q)^2$ which is also smaller than $\tilde{V}/4$.   □

A consequence of this result is that an informed planner running a contest with an informed and an uninformed contestant will opt to disclose information to maximize total effort. But the matter is subtle when both contestants are incompletely informed, as we will see in the next section.

With respect to expected payoffs, we have the following result.

PROPOSITION 8.4   *(a) The uninformed contestant is worse off in expectation that in symmetric information scenario. (b) The informed contestant is strictly better off in expectation than in the symmetric information scenario.*

Proof (a) In the symmetric information scenario, the expected payoff for each contestant is $\tilde{V}/4$. In the asymmetric information scenario, the expected payoff of the uninformed player is

$$E\pi_U = \frac{qg_U}{\sqrt{g_U V_H}}V_H + \frac{(1-q)g_U}{\sqrt{g_U V_H}}V_L - g_U$$
$$= q\sqrt{g_U V_H} + (1-q)\sqrt{g_U V_H} - g_U$$
$$< \sqrt{g_U}\sqrt{\tilde{V}} - g_U < \sqrt{\frac{\tilde{V}}{4}}\sqrt{\tilde{V}} - \frac{\tilde{V}}{4} = \frac{\tilde{V}}{4}.$$

We have taken into account that $\sqrt{g_U}\sqrt{\tilde{V}} - g_U$ is increasing for $g_U < \tilde{V}/4$. Thus, the uninformed contestant is worse off under asymmetric information.

(b) Let us see that the informed contestant is strictly better off in expectation than in the symmetric scenario. To see this, recall that $Eg_I(V) = g_U$, and

$$E\pi_I + E\pi_U = \tilde{V} - 2g_U.$$

Since $g_U < \tilde{V}/4$,

$$E\pi_I + E\pi_U > \tilde{V} - \frac{\tilde{V}}{2} = \frac{\tilde{V}}{2}.$$

Given that $E\pi_U < \tilde{V}/4$, then $E\pi_I > \tilde{V}/4$. □

Additional results are discussed in Exercises 8.3 and 8.4. In these exercises, we ask the readers to demonstrate that in a common value Tullock contest, contestants with informational advantages are rewarded. In other words, a contestant's equilibrium payoff is higher than that of less informed competitors.

In any contest, the loser always has negative ex-post payoffs, while the winner gets nonnegative ex-post payoffs. With one-sided asymmetric information, if contestant I wins, her ex-post payoffs are always nonnegative. This, however, might not be the case for the uninformed contestant, U. The following proposition examines the behavior of ex-post payoffs.

PROPOSITION 8.5   *Even in the event of a win, the uninformed contestant could potentially face negative ex-post payoffs.*

Proof Consider a scenario where U wins and V_L occurs. In case 1, U's ex-post payoff is negative if and only if

$$V_L < \frac{\left(q\sqrt{V_H} + (1-q)\sqrt{V_L}\right)^2}{4} \Leftrightarrow \sqrt{\frac{V_L}{V_H}} < \frac{q}{1+q}.$$

This is ruled out by (8.2), so if both types are active, U's ex-post payoff, regardless of the V value realization, is always positive if he wins. In case 2, U's ex-post payoff is negative if and only if

$$V_L < \frac{q^2 V_H}{(1+q)^2} \Leftrightarrow \sqrt{\frac{V_L}{V_H}} < \frac{q}{1+q}.$$

The above inequality is always satisfied in case 2. Therefore, in case 2, U's ex-post payoff is negative. Thus, the uninformed contestant must have sufficient funds to cover potential losses in a worst-case scenario to avoid bankruptcy. □

Having explored the behavior of one-sided asymmetric information in contests and established the existence and properties of equilibrium, we now shift our focus to the domain of two-sided asymmetric information.

8.3   Two-Sided Asymmetric Information

In a contest involving two-sided asymmetric information, neither of the contestants possesses complete information about their opponent. In this section, we introduce a simplified model of such a contest, built upon the framework proposed in Malueg and Yates (2004).

Consider two contestants, A and B. As in the previous section, the CSF is the Ratio Form. The value of the prize for each contestant, V_A and V_B, can either be high, V_H, or low, V_L, with equal probability. While each contestant is aware of their own valuation, they are uncertain about the other's. However, contestants do have knowledge of the joint probability distribution of valuations, as in Table 8.1.

Note that V_A and V_B may be correlated. Parameter $q = 0$ corresponds to perfect negative correlation, while $q = 1$ correspond to perfect positive correlation. If $q = 1/2$, V_A and V_B are independent.

Each contestant uses his personal information and the prior distribution to update his beliefs regarding the other contestant's value.

A strategy for each contestant is determined by their respective types. Hence, for contestant A, a strategy is represented as $(g_A(V_H), g_A(V_L))$. Likewise, for contestant B, a strategy is expressed as $(g_B(V_H), g_B(V_L))$.

Expected payoffs for each contestant are

$$E\pi_A = P(V_B = V_H \mid V_A)\frac{g_A(V_A)}{g_A(V_A) + g_B(V_H)}V_A$$
$$+ P(V_B = V_L \mid V_A)\frac{g_A(V_A)}{g_A(V_A) + g_B(V_L)}V_A - g_A(V_A);$$

Table 8.1   Joint probability distribution of valuations

V_B	V_A		
		V_L	V_H
	V_L	$\frac{1}{2}q$	$\frac{1}{2}(1-q)$
	V_H	$\frac{1}{2}(1-q)$	$\frac{1}{2}q$

$$E\pi_B = P(V_A = V_H \mid V_B)\frac{g_B(V_B)}{g_A(V_H) + g_B(V_B)}V_B$$

$$+ P(V_A = V_L \mid V_B)\frac{g_B(V_B)}{g_A(V_L) + g_B(V_B)}V_B - g_B(V_B).$$

Here $P(V_i = V_k \mid V_j)$ represents the conditional probability that a contestant i, $i \in \{A, B\}$, has a valuation V_k, $V_k \in \{V_H, V_L\}$, given that contestant j, $j \in \{A, B\}$, $j \neq i$, has a valuation V_j. Thus,

$$P(V_i = V_H \mid V_j = V_H) = P(V_i = V_L \mid V_j = V_L) = q, \ i, j \in \{A, B\}, i \neq j,$$

and

$$P(V_i = V_H \mid V_j = V_L) = P(V_i = V_L \mid V_j = V_H) = 1 - q, \ i, j \in \{A, B\}, i \neq j.$$

To simplify the analysis, consider the case where all types are active in equilibrium. The subsequent proposition illustrates that in a symmetric Bayesian equilibrium, both types of contestants expend effort proportional to the prize's value, with the proportion being identical for both types.

PROPOSITION 8.6   *In a symmetric Bayesian equilibrium*

$$\frac{g_A(V_H)}{V_H} = \frac{g_A(V_L)}{V_L} = q\frac{1}{4} + (1 - q)\frac{\frac{V_L}{V_H}}{\left(1 + \frac{V_L}{V_H}\right)^2}.$$

Proof   Considering the first-order conditions for contestant A:

$$P(V_B = V_H \mid V_A)\frac{g_B(V_H)}{(g_A(V_A) + g_B(V_H))^2} + P(V_B = V_L \mid V_A)\frac{g_B(V_L)}{(g_A(V_A) + g_B(V_L))^2} = \frac{1}{V_A}. \tag{8.5}$$

(1) If $V_A = V_L$, from (8.5), in a symmetric equilibrium,

$$\frac{g_A(V_L)}{V_L} = q\frac{1}{4} + (1 - q)\frac{g_A(V_H)g_A(V_L)}{(g_A(V_L) + g_A(V_H))^2}. \tag{8.6}$$

(2) If $V_A = V_H$, from (8.5), in a symmetric equilibrium,

$$\frac{g_A(V_H)}{V_H} = q\frac{1}{4} + (1 - q)\frac{g_A(V_H)g_A(V_L)}{(g_A(V_H) + g_B(V_L))^2}. \tag{8.7}$$

Since the right-hand side of (8.6) and the right-hand side of (8.7) are identical,

$$\frac{g_A(V_L)}{V_L} = \frac{g_A(V_H)}{V_H}.$$

From (8.6) and (8.7),

$$\frac{g_A(V_H)}{V_H} = \frac{g_A(V_L)}{V_L} = q\frac{1}{4} + (1 - q)\frac{\frac{V_L}{V_H}}{\left(1 + \frac{V_L}{V_H}\right)^2}. \tag{8.8}$$

Let us denote the proportionality factor, the right-hand side of (8.8), by k. In order to verify that (8.8) truly represents a Bayesian equilibrium, it is crucial to ensure that both types of contestants anticipate positive profits. If not, one type might find it more advantageous to refrain from participating in the contest. Let us represent the expected payoff of a high-type A with the notation $E\pi_A^H$. Similarly, for a low-type A, the expected payoff is denoted as $E\pi_A^L$. Thus,

$$E\pi_A^H = \left(q\frac{1}{2} + (1-q)\frac{V_H}{V_H + V_L} - k\right)V_H,$$

$$E\pi_A^L = \left((1-q)\frac{V_L}{V_L + V_H} + q\frac{1}{2} - k\right)V_L.$$

Observe that if $E\pi_A^L > 0$, then $E\pi_A^H > 0$. Thus, let us examine the circumstances under which $E\pi_A^L > 0$, That is,

$$(1-q)\frac{V_L}{V_L + V_H} + q\frac{1}{2} > k. \tag{8.9}$$

It is not difficult to see that (8.9) holds for all value of the parameters (see Exercise 8.9). In conclusion, (8.8) characterizes the symmetric Bayesian equilibrium. □

In equilibrium, both types of contestants expend effort in proportion to their respective value prizes. Notably, the factor of proportionality remains the same for both contestants.

Considering that the analysis is confined to the symmetric Bayesian equilibrium, efforts are solely dependent on types. For the purpose of simplifying notation in subsequent discussions, efforts in the Bayesian equilibrium will henceforth be represented as $g(V_H)$ and $g(V_L)$.

For a more comprehensive examination of the existence and uniqueness of a Bayesian equilibrium in broader contests with incomplete information, the interested reader can refer to the works of Einy et al. (2015) and Ewerhart and Quartieri (2020).

8.4 Characteristics of Equilibrium in Two-Sided Asymmetric Information

In this section, we investigate the properties of equilibrium to elucidate the role of two-sided asymmetric information. The following proposition reveals that the effort exerted by both types of contestants rises with an increase in the probability that the prize value realization coincides for both contestants. Similarly, effort intensifies with an increase in the prize value ratio, V_L/V_H. This is because more similar valuations means a more competitive contest, so contestants have to fight harder.

PROPOSITION 8.7   (a) *Effort of each type increases with q. (b) Effort of each type also increases with V_L/V_H.*

Proof   The proof of the proposition is derived directly from (8.8) by showing that the proportionality factor k is increasing in both q and V_L/V_H. □

To compare the total effort in a scenario with symmetric information versus a scenario with two-sided asymmetric information, let us refer back to Chapters 2 and

3. In those chapters, we discussed the efforts in a Nash equilibrium under symmetric information, which for the Ratio Form CSF are as follows:

1. If both contestants are high types

$$g^{HH} = \frac{1}{4}V_H.$$

2. If both contestants are low types

$$g^{LL} = \frac{1}{4}V_H.$$

3. If one contestant is a high type and the other is a low type

$$\frac{g^{HL}}{V_H} = \frac{g^{LH}}{V_L} = \frac{\frac{V_L}{V_H}}{\left(1 + \frac{V_L}{V_H}\right)^2}.$$

PROPOSITION 8.8   (a) *Assume that* $q \in (0, 1)$, *and* $V_H > V_L$. *Then, the total effort – under two-sided asymmetric information and under symmetric information – can be ordered as follows:*

$$2g(V_L) < 2g^{LL} < g^{HL} + g^{LH} < g(V_L) + g(V_H) < 2g(V_H) < 2g^{HH}.$$

(b) Conditional on contestants' value, the expected effort under symmetric information is equal to the expected effort under two-sided asymmetric information, that is

$$g(V_L) = qg^{LL} + (1-q)g^{LH}; \; g(V_H) = qg^{HH} + (1-q)g^{HL}.$$

(c) The ex ante expected payoff – under two-sided asymmetric information and under symmetric information – are identical.

Proof   The proof of (a) and (b) can be derived directly through straightforward comparisons between points 1, 2, and 3 above Proposition 8.8 and (8.8). The proof of (c) can be derived from (b) and the fact that the ex ante expected probability of winning the prize for a high type is given by:

$$\frac{1}{2}q + (1-q)\frac{g(V_H)}{g(V_H) + g(V_L)},$$

by (8.8),

$$\frac{1}{2}q + (1-q)\frac{V_H}{V_H + V_L}.$$

Note that this result is identical to the ex ante expected probability of winning under symmetric information. A similar analysis applies to a low type.   □

To end this section let us consider the optimal disclosure of information by a contest organizer who knows the types of all contestants and aims to maximize total effort. Examples of this situation are:

(1) **Sports tournaments**: Here, the coach or organizer may possess comprehensive information about the abilities of all teams or athletes. In contrast, each team or athlete only knows about their own capabilities, remaining unaware of the abilities of others.

(2) **Startup funding competition**: In this setting, the organizer or a panel of investors might understand the business models, market sizes, and potential growth of all competing startups. Each startup, however, only has detailed knowledge about its own business and lacks information about the other competitors.

In these contexts, the organizer has the option to disclose pertinent information to all participants. According to the ordering of total efforts presented in Proposition 8.8, the organizer would like to disclose information when competition is balanced (where $g(V_L) < g^{LL}$, and $g(V_H) < g^{HH}$), and choose not to disclose information when competition is imbalanced (where $g^{HL} + g^{LH} < g(V_L) + g(V_H)$). Knowing a competitor shares the same "type" stimulates effort. This is because participants feel more motivated to compete when they perceive the playing field to be more even. However, this disclosure policy may not be optimal as it would lead contestants to have complete information even when their types differ.

Serena (2022) tackled this issue of information disclosure where the draws of types are independent (equivalent to $q = 1/2$ in the context of this section) and the probabilities of each type can differ (in the context of this section, both types share equal probability). Serena (2022) demonstrated that the policy which maximizes total effort involves full disclosure only when both contestants are of a high type. In such instances, the organizer essentially is saying to both contestants "look, don't fantasize with the idea that your opponent is weak and a little effort will make you the winner. Your contestant is as strong as you are, so you better wake up and pull out all stops!" If a contestant is weak and the other strong or both are weak, the organizer retains the secret to maintain the impression that a substantial effort is required to win the contest.

A different story arises when the organizer is committed to disclosing information before learning the contestants' types. In this case, prior probabilities matter. When the probability of a high type is substantial, unveiling the contest becomes advantageous because there is a high likelihood that both contestants will be high types and will compete vigorously. Serena (2022) established that as long as the probability of a contestant being of high type exceeds 0.5, information disclosure enhances overall effort (see Exercise 8.11).

To conclude, a crucial matter arises: whether the complete information contests model serves as a valid approximation for contests with a little bit of incomplete information. If it does, then the model presented in Part I of this book could be cautiously applied to scenarios where contestants possess limited knowledge about each other's characteristics. Einy, Moreno, and Sela (2020) offer a qualified response to this question. Assuming a Ratio Form CSF, they show that if a sequence of contests with incomplete information converges to a contest with complete information, then any limit point of the sequence of Bayesian equilibria represents an equilibrium with complete information. Moreover, if the Bayesian equilibrium is unique, the function linking information to equilibrium allocations is continuous everywhere. This result lends support to the notion that complete information contests can be considered an idealization of contests with a small degree of asymmetric information.

Summing up, this chapter has presented simplified models of asymmetric informa-tion, providing you with a foundational understanding you can apply to other models explored in this part of the book, including group contests, sabotage, and dynamic contests. Exercises 8.13 through 8.17 will help you to understand the consequences of incorporating asymmetric information into these models.

8.5   Exercises

8.1   Prove that in the case where only the informed high type is active, the unin-formed contestant probability of winning is greater than $1/2$. A fully anticipated "winners course" may occur! This is confirmed by proposition 7 in Aiche et al. (2019) showing very generally that "in the interior equilibrium of a two-contestants contest and a Ratio Form CSF, a contestant with an information advantage wins the prize less frequently than his opponent." This is so because the informed contestant shirks effort when the prize has a low value whereas the uninformed contestant puts out all the stops to win a prize that for her has larger expected value. But these authors show by means of an example that this result does not carry to contests with more than two contestants (see Exercise 8.2).

8.2   Show by means of an example (with eight contestants!) that informed contestants may, in equilibrium, win the prize more frequently than uninformed contestants (see Aiche et al., 2019, example 2).

8.3   Show that in the interior equilibrium of two-contestant contests with the Ratio Form CSF, the expected payoff of a contestant with an information advantage is greater than or equal to that of his opponent.

8.4   Show that in a common value Tullock contest with more than two contestants, information advantages are rewarded, that is, a contestant's equilibrium payoff is greater than that of worse-informed contestants (see Aiche et al., 2018).

8.5   Show that when valuations can take k values denoted by $V_1, V_2, \ldots, V_k$ with probabilities $q_1, q_2, \ldots, q_k$ both contestants make the same expected effort. Assume two contestants and a homogeneous of degree zero CSF. Follow the same steps as in the main text.

8.6   Prove the result mentioned in Exercise 8.4 (that information advantages are rewarded) holds when V is distributed according to a continuous cumulative distri-bution F with support $[\underline{V}, \infty)$ (see Wärneryd, 2003).

8.7   Prove the result mentioned in Exercise 8.4 (that information advantages are rewarded) holds if the CSF is

$$p_i(g_i, g_j) = \frac{\varphi(g_i)}{\varphi(g_i) + \varphi(g_j)}, i \in \{I, U\},$$

whenever φ is an increasing and concave function and $\Phi(g) = \varphi(g)/\varphi'(g)$ is convex (Wärneryd, 2003).

8.8 Consider a one-sided asymmetric information Tullock contest with two contestants, I and U, with different valuations of the prize. Contestant I knows his valuation and the valuation of the opponent (V_I and V_U), but contestant U only knows his valuation V_U and he thinks that the valuation of contestant I can be high (V_I^H) with probability q or low (V_I^L) with probability $1 - q$. Prove that, if both types are active in equilibrium, the effort of the uninformed contestant is:

$$g_U^* = \frac{\left(q \frac{V_U}{V_I^H} \sqrt{V_H} + (1 - q) \frac{V_U}{V_I^L} \sqrt{V_L}\right)^2}{\left(1 + q \frac{V_U}{V_I^H} + (1 - q) \frac{V_U}{V_I^L}\right)^2}.$$

8.9 In the two-sided asymmetric information contest described in the text, show that $E\pi_A^L$ is positive when $g_A(V_A)$ and $g_A(V_L)$ are given by (8.8).

8.10 In the context of the two-sided asymmetric information contest model introduced in this chapter, suppose that the CSF adopts a generalized Ratio Form with a parameter ϵ. Prove that, if a pure strategy Nash equilibrium exists under public information conditions, a symmetric pure strategy Bayesian equilibrium also exists under two-sided asymmetric information (see Malueg and Yates, 2004).

8.11 Consider Serena's (2022) model but with the Ratio Form CSF. Prove that if the contest organizer must commit to a disclosure policy before the types are realized, complete information disclosure will occur only when the probability of being a high type exceeds 0.5.

8.12 Baliga and Sjöström (2012) present a version of the Hawk and Dove game (see Fudenberg and Tirole, 1991, p. 18) with asymmetric information. Payoffs are:

	$Hawk$	$Dove$
$Hawk$	$-c_1, -c_2$	$V - c_1, -d$
$Dove$	$-d, V - c_2$	$0, 0$

If both contestants are Doves, peace prevails. To be a Hawk entails a cost of c_i, $i = 1, 2$ and if the opponent is a Dove wins the prize. But if both are Hawks, a serious conflict arises and both get a negative payoff of d.

(1) Solve the game when both contestants know c_1 and c_2. Find conditions under which (Hawk, Hawk) is always an equilibrium. Find conditions under which there is another equilibrium in which both contestants take the Dove action.

(2) Now suppose that each contestant knows her own cost but has only a probabilistic assessment of the cost of her rival. Costs are independently drawn from the same distribution. Let F denote the continuously differentiable cumulative distribution function, with support $[\underline{c}, \bar{c}]$ and strictly increasing. Players use cutoff strategies such that they choose Hawk if and only if the cost is sufficiently low. (Actually they remark that there is no loss of generality in

using this strategy). Thus, a strategy is identified with its cutoff point. Find the Bayesian equilibrium of this game.

8.13   Consider the group contest model discussed in Chapter 5. Incorporate an element of asymmetric information into this basic model by selecting a parameter that would logically be subject to incomplete information. Provide examples that demonstrate the rationale for this chosen element of incomplete information. Determine the Bayesian equilibrium of your revised model, and compare this result with a scenario that involves complete information.

8.14   Consider a contest model with sabotage as discussed in Chapter 6. Incorporate an element of asymmetric information into this basic model by selecting a parameter that would logically be subject to incomplete information. Provide examples that demonstrate the rationale for this chosen element of incomplete information. Determine the Bayesian equilibrium of your revised model, and compare this result with a scenario that involves complete information.

8.15   Fu (2006) examined endogenous timing in contests with one-sided asymmetric information. Using Fu's setup, prove the following:
(1)   In equilibrium, the informed contestant never moves first.
(2)   There exists an equilibrium where the uninformed contestant moves first.
(3)   If the probability of low-value realization is sufficiently high, there is an
      equilibrium where both contestants move simultaneously.
Give an interpretations of the results.

8.16   Münster (2009) considered a two-period repeated contest with two-sided asymmetric information. Using Münster's model prove that when effort is observable, contestants with high valuation may strategically choose to exert little effort in an early round to deceive his opponent into believing that his valuation is low.

8.17   Beccuti and Möller (2022) examined a race model featuring two contestants, with asymmetric information about a single, common-value prize. The prize is awarded to the contestant who wins two out of three matches. The paper concludes that the discouragement effect, often observed in such scenarios, may be counteracted by the encouragement effect when private information is present. This is because losing a match conveys positive news about a rival's estimation of a contested prize, giving incentives to the loser to renew efforts and increasing the probability of reaching the contest's final match, thereby providing contestants with the opportunity to exert additional efforts. Your task is to replicate this result using a simple race model with the Ratio Form CSF.

Part III

Applications

9 Contests in Other Environments: Draws, Large Contests, and Entry

In previous chapters, we have assumed a simple setup in which contestants decide effort in a contest with only two possible outcomes, either you win or you lose, where strategic considerations are paramount. But this setting abstracts key features.

In this chapter, we show how to tailor the basic model outlined in the previous chapters to new environments in which (1) the outcome of the contest may be a draw; (2) there are so many contestants that the impact of one's effort on aggregate effort is insignificant; and (3) contestants decide to enter in one out of several alternative contests. We now expand this preliminary description of the topics of the chapter.

(1) **Draws**. So far, we have assumed that someone wins and everybody else loses. But in many contests, other results are possible: It could be a tie when each contestant scores the same points on the board which determines the outcome of the contest. Or it could be a draw when the outcome has an inconclusive result. In soccer, matches during national leagues may end up in a draw when teams score the same number of goals. In chess, a draw occurs when both players agree to finish the game without a winner. A war without a clear winner, like the Korean or Iran–Iraq wars, can be considered a draw. Other examples involve prizes that can be shared, like the Nobel Prize or procurement contracts such as the one that confronted Siemens and Alstom to build Spanish high-speed trains.[1] Finally, as we remarked in Chapter 1, there are contests, like R&D contests, in which the prize might not be delivered. This can be understood as a tie with zero reward. Abusing language, we will use both draw and tie to refer to all these situations that we model jointly.

(2) **Large contests**. In the allocation of college admissions and certain grants, the number of applicants is large and the strategic interaction is, therefore, weak. In such a case, we either assume that there is a continuum of applicants or we look for an approximate equilibrium of the large but finite game. Both approaches are technically very demanding. The interested reader may take a look at the papers by Olszewski and Siegel (2016) and Bodoh-Creed and Hickman (2018). Here we take a much simpler approach which is an adaptation of the one presented in the papers by Lahkar and Mukherjee (2023) and Doğan et al. (2023).

---

[1] Prizes could be monetary and nonmonetary. Thus, the Nobel Prize award consists of a monetary prize, a diploma, and a medal. In our model, the prize melts all its components in a quantity that represents its value.

(3) **Several alternative contests.** Think of a firm deciding to locate a new plant in Taiwan or in Santa Clara County, an athlete deciding in which event to perform, a professional selecting jobs, an actor choosing where to act, or a student selecting academic institutions. In all these cases, previous to the contests, there is a stage where potential contestants choose where to perform. This is naturally modeled as a two-stage game where, as in Chapter 7, we use subgame perfection to solve this game. When there are externalities among contests – so payoffs in, say, the New York Marathon depend on the number of runners in New York and in the Chicago Marathon – equilibrium may not exist. Fortunately, when there are two contests only or more than two with no externalities, an equilibrium exists.

9.1   Contest with Draws

In this section, we develop a contest with draws and explore its implications, focusing on the basic scenario of two contestants. This simplification is chosen to streamline the analysis, as in cases involving three contestants, we would need to consider four potential draws (1 and 2, 1 and 3, 2 and 3, and 1, 2, 3). This highlights how even with a small number of participants, the analysis becomes quite involved.

To study contests with draws, the primary aspect to address is our main tool, specifically the CSF. In addition to the winning prize that we still denote by V, we introduce an award linked to the potential occurrence of a tie, denoted by T, where $V > T$.

The first paper dealing with this subject was written by Blavatskyy (2010). His contribution was followed by those of Jia (2012) and Yildizparlak (2018). We revise them in turn.

9.1.1   Blavatskyy CSF

Blavatskyy (2010) put forward the following CSF to handle contests involving draws

$$p_T(\mathbf{g}) = \frac{b}{b + g_i + g_j}; \; p_i(\mathbf{g}) = \frac{g_i}{b + g_i + g_j}, i, j \in \{1,2\}, i \neq j, \qquad (9.1)$$

where p_T is the probability of a tie between the two teams. Note that $p_1 + p_2 + p_T = 1$, and $p_1, p_2, p_T \geq 0$. This CSF is an extension of the Ratio Form CSF in which we have a new parameter, b, that measures the propensity to draw. Given that expenses[2] are bounded by prizes, when b is very large, the probability of a tie is as close to one as we wish.

Blavatskyy presented a list of properties that completely characterize this CSF; see Exercise 9.1 for a discussion of these properties. This is very satisfactory because we understand the basic postulates that underlie this particular CSF. Other not so satisfactory aspects of this CSF are the following. First, this CSF is not homogeneous

---

[2] Given that in some applications (war, litigation, R&D), efforts are monetary, we refer to them in this chapter as expenses.

of degree zero in expenses, so the units in which we count expenses matter. However, it is homogeneous of degree zero in expenses and b. The second concern is that a contestant can tie even if he makes zero effort and the rival is making an arbitrarily large effort. This may occur if an external event, like a storm or an earthquake, precludes the occurrence of the contest. The less satisfactory aspect of this CSF is that when efforts are large, the probability of a tie is small. For instance, this implies that a match between Manchester United and Manchester City is less likely to end in a draw than a match between two laggard teams in the English League. This may or may not be the case.

Having discussed the properties of this CSF, we now turn to the analysis of the properties of the equilibrium predicted with this CSF.

In this case, payoffs of a contestant can be written as

$$\pi_i(\mathbf{g}) = \frac{g_i}{b + g_i + g_j} V + \frac{b}{b + g_i + g_j} T - g_i, \ i, j \in \{1,2\}, i \neq j$$

or grouping terms,

$$\pi_i(\mathbf{g}) = \frac{g_i + \frac{bT}{V}}{b + g_i + g_j} V - g_i, i, j \in \{1,2\}, i \neq j,$$

where the terms bT/V and b can be understood as noise that affects the outcome of the contest. Note that this CSF is not identical to the one proposed by Amegashie (2006) to deal with noise that was discussed in Chapter 2 because here the term in the denominator, b, is not proportional to the number of contestants. The first-order condition of payoff maximization for contestant i is

$$\frac{g_j + b}{(b + g_i + g_j)^2} V - \frac{b}{(b + g_i + g_j)^2} T = 1, \quad j \neq i, \tag{9.2}$$

which can be written as

$$\frac{g_j V + b(V - T)}{(b + g_i + g_j)^2} = 1, \quad j \neq i. \tag{9.3}$$

We first note that the second-order condition holds because the left-hand side of (9.3) is decreasing in g_i. For the time being, let us focus on the existence of an interior Nash equilibrium. Expression (9.2) implies that if an equilibrium exists, it is symmetric. Let $g \equiv g_1^* = g_2^*$. Then, (9.3) can be written as

$$gV + bV - bT = b^2 + 4g^2 + 4bg.$$

Solving this second-degree equation, we have that

$$g = \frac{1}{8} V - \frac{1}{2} b \pm \frac{1}{8} \sqrt{8Vb - 16Tb + V^2}. \tag{9.4}$$

For the square root to have a real-number solution, we assume that $V^2 \geq 8b(2T - V)$. For instance, if V is three times T, as it happens with the points awarded in soccer leagues for winning (three points) and drawing (one point), the previous inequality holds for any value of b. This assumption is a necessary condition for the existence of a symmetric equilibrium. But it is not sufficient because at least one solution in (9.4) must yield a positive effort. Our first candidate is, of course, the solution coming from a plus sign in (9.4). And this amounts to

$$\frac{1}{8}V - \frac{1}{2}b + \frac{1}{8}\sqrt{8Vb - 16Tb + V^2} > 0,$$

which holds if and only if

$$\sqrt{8Vb - 16Tb + V^2} > 4b - V. \tag{9.5}$$

The inequality in (9.5) holds in two cases: When the right-hand side is negative, i.e., when $V > 4b$. Or if the right-hand side is positive and $8Vb - 16Tb + V^2 > (4b - V)^2$, which simplifies to $V - T > b$. In words, the difference between the prize of winning and the prize of a tie must be larger than the propensity to draw. In both cases, the propensity to draw cannot be very large.

Now focus on the solution coming from the negative sign in (9.4). This requires $V > 4b$ and $V - 4b > \sqrt{8Vb - 16Tb + V^2}$, which is equivalent to $V - T < b$. In this case, $V - T < b < V/4$.

Summarizing all we have learnt about the possibility of a symmetric Nash equilibrium with draws, we have the following.

PROPOSITION 9.1   *Assume a CSF like (9.1) and $V^2 \geq 8b(2T - V)$. There is an interior symmetric Nash equilibrium if*

(i) $b < V/4$ or $b > V/4$ and $V - T > b$ or
(ii) $V - T < b < V/4$.

Note that if part (ii) in Proposition 9.1 holds, there are two interior Nash equilibrium, see Exercise 9.2. The interior Nash equilibrium is unique if (ii) above does not hold.

Next we show that a Nash equilibrium with both players making zero effort is possible. For such a case to occur, the first-order conditions must hold with inequality at $g_1 = g_2 = 0$. This is because payoffs are concave, so the first-order conditions are necessary and sufficient. Marginal payoffs not positive at zero means that contestants would like to decrease efforts even further but they are unable by the nonnegativity constraint. This is akin to saying that 0 is a best reply to 0, i.e., that $(0,0)$ is a Nash equilibrium.

$$\frac{b}{b^2}V - \frac{b}{b^2}T - 1 \leq 0 \text{ if and only if } V - T \leq b.$$

Finally, let us show that there are no asymmetric equilibria in which one of the contestants spends zero effort. Suppose $g_2 = 0$. The best reply of contestant 1 is

$$\frac{b}{(b + g_1)^2}V - \frac{b}{(b + g_1)^2}T = 1 \text{ if and only if } b(V - T) = (b + g_1)^2$$

which yields a best reply of

$$\tilde{g}_1 = \sqrt[2]{b(V - T)} - b > 0 \text{ if and only if } V - T > b.$$

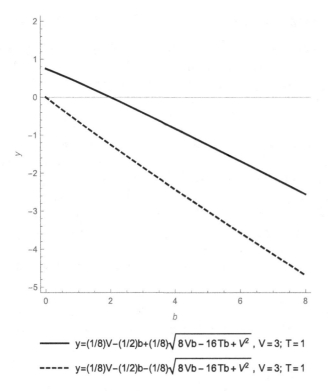

Figure 9.1 Equilibrium effort as a function of the propensity to tie

Now the first-order condition for contestant 2, when contestant 1 plays $\tilde{g}_1$, is

$$\frac{\sqrt[2]{b(V-T)}}{b(V-T)}V - \frac{b}{b(V-T)}T \le 1,$$

which holds if and only if

$$V - T \le b.$$

Thus, asymmetric Nash equilibrium is impossible in this model. Summarizing,

PROPOSITION 9.2   *Assume a CSF like (9.1).*

(i) If $V - T \le b$ there is a symmetric Nash equilibrium with $g_1^* = g_2^* = 0$.
(ii) There are no asymmetric Nash equilibrium such that $g_i^* = 0$ and $g_j^* > 0$, $i \ne j$.

Coming back to soccer ($V = 3$, $T = 1$), Figure 9.1 pictures the two roots of g in (9.4) in solid and dash. Case (i) in Proposition 9.1 arises for $b < 2$. There is an equilibrium in the intersection of the solid line with the horizontal axis. Case (ii) never holds (see the dashed line), so the Nash equilibrium is unique. For $b > 2$ according to Proposition 9.2, there is a symmetric Nash equilibrium at $g_1 = g_2 = 0$.

9.1.2   Other CSF with Draws

There are several alternative CSFs to analyze contests with draws. In this section, we consider two CSFs proposed by Jia (2012) and Yildizparlak (2018), the latter axiomatized in Vesperoni and Yildizparlak (2019). Common properties of these two CSFs are:

(1) Like Blavatskyy's, both are inspired by the Ratio Form CSF. They introduce a new parameter, the *tie-prone* parameter, that when is equal to one, makes the new CSF equal to the Ratio Form CSF. When the tie-prone parameter is very large, the probability of a tie tends to one.
(2) When efforts are identical, the probability of a tie is a positive constant irrespective of the size of efforts. When both efforts are very large and of comparable size, the probability of a tie is larger than zero.
(3) They are homogeneous of degree zero.
(4) The probability of a tie is maximized when both contestants make the same expenses.

As we can see, the above properties are postulated to deal with the less convincing properties of Blavatskyy's CSF. Let us consider first the CSF presented by Jia (2012):

$$p_T(\mathbf{g}) = \frac{(c^2 - 1)g_i^\alpha g_j^\alpha}{(g_i^\alpha + cg_j^\alpha)(g_j^\alpha + cg_i^\alpha)}; \; p_i(\mathbf{g}) = \frac{g_i^\alpha}{g_i^\alpha + cg_j^\alpha}, \, c \geq 1, i, j \in \{1, 2\}, i \neq j \tag{9.6}$$

with $\alpha \in (0, 1]$. It is easily seen that the rules of probability are fulfilled, namely $p_1 + p_2 + p_T = 1$ and $p_j \geq 0$, $j \in \{1, 2, T\}$. The tie-prone parameter is c. Clearly, p_T is increasing in c. We also see that the four properties announced just before hold in this CSF:

(1) When $c = 1$ there are no ties and the CSF is just the Ratio Form CSF. When c is very large, given efforts, $p_T \to 1$.
(2) When $g_i = g_j$,

$$p_T(\mathbf{g}) = \frac{(c^2 - 1)}{c^2 + 1 + 2c} = \frac{c - 1}{c + 1}$$

and when $c \to \infty$, $p_T \to 1$.
(3) When g_i and g_j are multiplied by λ, probabilities do not change because both the numerator and the denominator in (9.6) are multiplied by $\lambda^{2\alpha}$ and they cancel out. Thus, the CSF (9.6) is homogeneous of degree zero.
(4) To simplify the presentation, suppose $\alpha = 1$. Then $\partial p_T / \partial g_i = c(c^2 - 1)g_j(g_j^2 - g_i^2)/((g_i + cg_j)(g_j + cg_i))^2$. Thus, $\partial p_T / \partial g_i = 0$ if and only if $g_j = g_i$. Exercise 9.3 asks for a proof when α may be less than one.

Using the approach discussed in Section 4.1 of Chapter 4, this CSF can be derived from an underlying Frechet distribution of a random component (see theorem 1 in Jia, 2012). Unfortunately, the analysis of Nash equilibrium when $T > 0$ is complicated. Jia (2012) analyzes the case $T = 0$ (see Exercise 9.4). As we remarked earlier, this is the case of a Possibly Indecisive Contest like R&D in which it is possible that the discovery is never made.

Next, we consider the CSF used in Yildizparlak (2018) and axiomatized by Vesperoni and Yildizparlak (2019). First, when some effort is positive,

$$p_T(\mathbf{g}) = 1 - \frac{g_i^k + g_j^k}{(g_i + g_j)^k}; \ p_i(\mathbf{g}) = \frac{g_i^k}{(g_i + g_j)^k}, \ k \geq 1, \ i, j \in \{1, 2\}, i \neq j, \quad (9.7)$$

and when no contestant makes an effort, $p_i(\mathbf{0}) = (1/2)^k$, $k \geq 1$. Here the tie-prone parameter is k. Note that $p_1 + p_2 + p_T = 1$ and $p_j \geq 0$, $j \in \{1, 2, T\}$. Let us see that points (1) to (4) discussed at the beginning of this subsection hold too for this CSF, namely:

(1) When $k = 1$ there are no ties and the CSF (9.7) is just the Ratio Form CSF.
    When k is very large, given efforts, $p_T \to 1$.
(2) When $g_i = g_j$,

$$p_T(\mathbf{g}) = \frac{2^k - 2}{2^k}.$$

When $k > 1$, $p_T > 0$, and when $k \to \infty$, $p_T \to 1$.
(3) When g_i and g_j are multiplied by λ, probabilities do not change because both the numerator and the denominator of both expressions of (9.7) are multiplied by λ^k and they cancel out. Thus, the CSF (9.7) is homogeneous of degree zero.
(4) From the first-order condition of p_T maximization,

$$\frac{k(g_j g_i^{k-1} - g_j^k)}{(g_1 + g_2)^{k+1}} = 0.$$

Thus, $\partial p_T / \partial g_i = 0$ if and only if $g_j = g_i$.[3]

In Section 9.1.3, we show that when $k < 2$ a symmetric equilibrium exists. The proof is not difficult, but it is a little involved.

Yildizparlak (2018) applies the previous model to seven major European leagues: English Premier League, Spanish La Liga, German Bundesliga, Italian Serie A, French League 1, Turkish Super Lig, and Russian Premier Liga. Efforts are the market value of teams from a data set with 10,569 matches acquired manually from the website transfermarkt.co.uk containing club-based average market values of the lineup of teams for each match played through 12 seasons. From this data, he was able to calculate that draws occur 22–30% of the time.

An important characteristic of some sports is the Home Bias, namely that when a team play at home, its efforts count more. He finds that, on average, the probability of winning against an equal opponent goes from 27% in matches played away to 46% in matches played at home.[4] Table 9.1 shows the estimates of k in different leagues.

---

[3] The second-order condition holds locally when $g_j = g_i$, so this is a local maximum. Considering there is no alternative solution to the first-order condition, and given that $p_T(0) = p_T(g, g)$, these points are global maxima.

[4] Effects of the lockdown due to the COVID-19 pandemic on sporting outcomes have been studied by Cueva (2020). Utilizing a comprehensive dataset from 41 professional football leagues across 30

Table 9.1 Estimates of the tie-prone parameter for several European leagues

England	Spain	Italy	Germany	France	Turkey	Russia
1.475	1.408	1.512	1.467	1.533	1.463	1.505

The average value of k is 1.48, very close to the value that maximizes effort, 1.44 (see Remark 9.1). The reason for this is left to the reader's imagination.[5] Szymanski (2003) provides a comprehensive overview of contests and the economic factors influencing sports.

For an extension of the CSF to several contestants, see Exercise 9.6.

9.1.3   Advanced Material: Existence of Equilibrium in Contests with Draws

In this section, we consider the CSF used in Yildizparlak (2018) (Equation (9.7) in the previous section) and we show that an equilibrium in pure strategies exists when $k < 2$.

PROPOSITION 9.3   *Assume a CSF like (9.7), then if $k < 2$, there is a unique Nash equilibrium in pure strategies. This equilibrium is symmetric.*

Proof   We start by writing payoffs arising from (9.7)

$$\pi_i(\mathbf{g}) = \frac{g_i^k}{(g_i + g_j)^k} V + \left(1 - \frac{g_i^k + g_j^k}{(g_i + g_j)^k}\right) T - g_i$$

$$= \frac{(V - T)g_i^k - T g_j^k}{(g_i + g_j)^k} + T - g_i. \tag{9.8}$$

Note that (9.8) can be written as

$$\pi_i(\mathbf{g}) = F(g_i, g_j) + T - g_i,$$

where $F(g_i, g_j) = (V - T)g_i^k - T g_j^k/(g_i + g_j)^k$ is homogeneous of degree zero.

First note that $(0,0)$ cannot be an equilibrium since either agent has an incentive to deviate by exerting arbitrarily small effort. A situation where one contestant exerts zero effort while the other invests a positive effort cannot be an equilibrium either (see Exercise 9.7). Thus, if there is a symmetric equilibrium, it must be interior, and it must satisfy the first-order conditions of payoff maximization. Since F is homogeneous of degree zero, the symmetric interior Nash equilibrium candidate is

different countries, Cueva found significant changes when matches were played without the presence of spectators. Specifically, the home-field advantage in match outcomes decreased by approximately half. Additionally, the bias referees showed against visiting teams disappeared. These findings suggest that the social pressure exerted by home crowds, when present in the playfield, plays a significant role in influencing referee behavior and game outcomes.

[5] A beautiful tale by Jorge Luis Borges and Adolfo Bioy Casares, "Esse est percipi" (1967), advanced the idea that soccer scores (and many other things) are centrally determined. See www.lainsignia.org/2004/abril/cul_042.htm.

$$g_i^* = \frac{\partial F(1,1)}{\partial g_i}.$$

Given that

$$\frac{\partial F(g_1, g_2)}{\partial g_i} = \frac{(g_i + g_j)^k k g_i^{k-1}(V - T) - k(g_i + g_j)^{k-1}((V - T)g_i^k - Tg_j^k)}{(g_i + g_j)^{2k}} \tag{9.9}$$

then

$$g_1^* = g_2^* = \frac{kV}{2^{k+1}}, \tag{9.10}$$

which for $k = 1$ equals equilibrium efforts in the Ratio Form CSF. In a symmetric interior Nash equilibrium payoffs at $\mathbf{g}^*$ are larger than zero when

$$\frac{V}{2^k} + \frac{2^k - 2}{2^k}T - \frac{kV}{2^{k+1}} \geq 0$$

$$2V + 2(2^k - 2)T - kV \geq 0$$

$$2(2^k - 2)T \geq V(k - 2)$$

$$\frac{T}{V} \geq \frac{k - 2}{2^{k+1} - 4}. \tag{9.11}$$

Notice that when $k < 2$, condition (9.11) holds.

Let us see when the strategy vector (g_1^*, g_2^*) constitutes a pure strategy Nash equilibrium. Because of symmetry, it suffices to consider the problem faced by contestant 1. Suppose that contestant 2 exerts effort g_2^*. Notice that $\pi_1(g_1, g_2^*)$ is continuous in g_1, so it has a maximum on $[0, V]$. This maximum can only be located either in the extremes or in the first-order conditions. Contestant 1's first-order condition for an interior payoff maximum is

$$\frac{\partial \pi_1(g_1, g_2^*)}{\partial g_1} = \frac{\partial F(g_1, g_2^*)}{\partial g_1} - 1 = \frac{\partial F(\frac{g_1}{g_2^*}, 1)}{\partial g_1}\frac{1}{g_2^*} - 1. \tag{9.12}$$

Clearly, $g_1 = g_1^*$ satisfies the first-order condition. And since under condition (9.11) $\pi_1(g_1^*, g_2^*) > 0 = \pi_1(0, g_2^*)$, $g_1 = 0$ cannot be a maximum. Neither can be a maximum $g_1 = V$ because $\pi_1(V, g_2^*) < 0$. To complete the proof, let us see first under what conditions on the parameters we can assure that at $g_1 = g_1^*$ the second-order condition is negative. From (9.9)

$$\frac{\partial^2 F(g, 1)}{\partial g_1^2} = -k\frac{Tg^2 - Tg^k + Vg^k - 2Tgg^k + 2Vgg^k + Tkg^2 + Tkg^k - Vkg^k}{g^2(g + 1)^{k+2}}.$$

Simplifying,

$$\frac{\partial^2 F(g, 1)}{\partial g_1^2} = -\frac{k}{(g + 1)^{k+2}}[(1 + 2g - k)g^{k-2}(V - T) + T(1 + k)]. \tag{9.13}$$

At $g_1 = g_2^*; g = 1$,

$$\frac{\partial^2 F(1, 1)}{\partial g_1^2} = -\frac{k}{2^{k+2}}[(3 - k)(V - T) + T(1 + k)],$$

which is negative if and only if

$$\frac{T}{V} > \frac{k-3}{2(k-1)} = 1 - \frac{k+1}{2(k-1)}. \tag{9.14}$$

Again, notice that condition (9.14) holds when $k < 2$. Condition (9.14) guarantees that $g_1 = g_2^*$ is a local maximum. Let us see that there is $\bar{g}$ such that

$$\frac{\partial^2 F(g,1)}{\partial g_1^2} \begin{cases} > 0 \text{ if } g < \bar{g} \\ < 0 \text{ if } g > \bar{g} \end{cases}. \tag{9.15}$$

Recall that $\partial^2 F(g,1)/\partial g_1^2$ is given by (9.13), since the first term is always negative, let us study the second term $[(1 + 2g - k)g^{k-2}(V - T) + T(1 + k)]$. Notice that, since $k < 2$, for $g = 1$, this second term is positive. When $g \to 0$, this second term tends to minus infinity. Furthermore, since the derivative of this term is $(V - T)g^{k-3}((k - 2)(1 - k) + 2g(k - 1))$ and $1 < k < 2$, this derivative is positive and therefore, this second term is increasing. Thus, there exist a unique $\bar{g}$ such that $[(1 + 2\bar{g} - k)\bar{g}^{k-2}(V - T) + T(1 + k)] = 0$, which implies that (9.15) is proved.

Condition (9.15) implies that (9.12) has at most two solutions. We have already seen that $g_1 = g_2^*$ is a local maximum, if there is another solution, $\hat{g}$, to (9.12), it should be that $\hat{g} < \bar{g}$ and therefore cannot be a maximum. Thus, $g_1 = g_2^*$ is a global maximum. □

REMARK 9.1   *From (9.10) we see that equilibrium aggregate effort is $\frac{kV}{2^k}$. This expression is maximized at $k \simeq 1.44$. For $k \in (1,2)$ efforts are larger than in a standard contest. This is because in this region of k, T act as a second prize which encourages effort.*

9.2   Large Contests

Our analysis of contests has primarily centered on their strategic dimensions. However, there are contests where contestants decisions are closer to an individual decision problem than to a game-theoretical situation. Think of a competition for a place in public administration/college with hundreds of applicants. Or writing a proposal for a Medicaid grant where, again, competitors are aplenty. How does this scenario look into our model? Suppose that the CSF is a generalized Ratio Form with parameter ϵ. For contestant i,

$$p_i(\mathbf{g}) = \frac{g_i^\epsilon}{\sum_{j=1}^n g_j^\epsilon}, \tag{9.16}$$

whenever $\sum_{j=1}^n g_j^\epsilon \neq 0$, and $1/n$ otherwise.

A way to translate the large number of contestants hypothesis is to assume that contestant i regards the denominator of (9.16) as constant. To ensure this assumption is entirely robust, we must assume a continuum of contestants, each so insignificant that the summation symbol is replaced by an integral. In this way, each effort is just a point that does not add much to the length of the function (see Exercise 9.15). As we aim to minimize technical complexities in this book, we keep the equation determining probabilities as in (9.16). Our approach can be viewed as an approximation of a contest with a large, yet finite, number of participants.

The assumption that contestants regard the denominator of (9.16) as constant is also technically very convenient in the case in which contestants are heterogeneous. To see this, assume that costs are $c_i g_i$ (the fact that we are placing the heterogeneity in the cost function is, as we saw in Section 3.1 of Chapter 3, just a matter of convenience). Then, the first-order conditions of payoff maximization are

$$\frac{\epsilon g_i^{\epsilon-1} \sum_{j=1}^{n} g_j^{\epsilon} - \epsilon g_i^{\epsilon-1} g_i^{\epsilon}}{(\sum_{j=1}^{n} g_j^{\epsilon})^2} V = c_i, \quad i \in \{1, 2, \dots, n\}. \tag{9.17}$$

This system of equations is not easy to solve (except, of course if we assume that all individuals are identical) because of the second term in (9.17).

But what if we assume that, when deciding effort, contestants regard the denominator of (9.16) as constant?[6] In this case, variations in g_i do not affect $\sum_{j=1}^{n} g_j^{\epsilon}$. Consequently, the first-order condition for payoff maximization simplifies to

$$\frac{\epsilon g_i^{\epsilon-1}}{\sum_{j=1}^{n} g_j^{\epsilon}} V = c_i \text{ or}$$

$$g_i^{\epsilon} = \left(\frac{1}{c_i} \frac{\epsilon V}{\sum_{j=1}^{n} g_j^{\epsilon}} \right)^{\frac{\epsilon}{1-\epsilon}}. \tag{9.18}$$

For this equation to make sense, we have to assume that $\epsilon < 1$. If $\epsilon = 1$ payoffs are linear in g_i and the solution to the maximization problem typically will be a corner solution or will not exist, see Exercise 9.9. To simplify notation let $t_i \equiv (1/c_i)^{\frac{1}{1-\epsilon}}$. Thus, (9.18) becomes

$$g_i^{\epsilon} = t_i \left(\frac{\epsilon V}{\sum_{j=1}^{n} g_j^{\epsilon}} \right)^{\frac{\epsilon}{1-\epsilon}}.$$

Adding up over contestants and letting $t \equiv \sum_{i=1}^{n} t_i$, we obtain

$$\sum_{j=1}^{n} g_j^{\epsilon} = t \left(\frac{\epsilon V}{\sum_{j=1}^{n} g_j^{\epsilon}} \right)^{\frac{\epsilon}{1-\epsilon}}$$

and this equation can easily be solved to find the equilibrium value of $\sum_{j=1}^{n} g_j^{\epsilon}$, namely,

$$\sum_{j-1}^{n} g_j^{\epsilon} = (\epsilon V)^{\epsilon} t^{1-\epsilon}.$$

---

[6] This "large group" assumption has a large history in the theory of monopolistic competition. It was introduced in the 1970s by Spence and Dixit and Stiglitz. See Corchón (2001), p. 98 for a discussion and references.

With this in our hand and using (9.18), the equilibrium values of g_i^ϵ and p_i are

$$g_i^\epsilon = t_i \left(\frac{\epsilon V}{t} \right)^\epsilon, \; i \in \{1, \dots, n\}$$

$$p_i(\mathbf{g}) = \frac{g_i^\epsilon}{\sum_{j=1}^n g_j^\epsilon} = \frac{t_i}{t}, \; i \in \{1, \dots, n\}.$$

The only remaining task is to make sure that the previous variables are indeed equilibrium values. On the one hand, payoffs are concave in the decision variable so the first-order conditions yield a maximum. And since contestants have the choice of no effort and zero payoffs, this interior solution is a global maximum if payoffs are nonnegative. Indeed,

$$\pi_i(\mathbf{g}) = \frac{t_i}{t} V - c_i \frac{\epsilon V}{t} t_i^{\frac{1}{\epsilon}}$$

$$= \frac{t_i}{t} V (1 - \epsilon)$$

since $t_i \equiv (1/c_i)^{\frac{\epsilon}{1-\epsilon}}$ and therefore, $c_i t_i^{\frac{1}{\epsilon}} = t_i$. Thus, payoff are positive (recall that $\epsilon \in (0,1)$) and we have found an equilibrium.

PROPOSITION 9.4   *There is an equilibrium in large contests with a generalized Ratio Form CSF where heterogeneous contestants take aggregate impact of efforts as independent of their own action.*

We end this section by remarking that our methods here were meant to pick up a reasonable approximation to a difficult problem namely, the analysis of contests with a large number of contestants like some scientific prizes, college admissions, etc. Exercise 9.15 suggests an alternative more rigorous way. Exercise 9.16 ask to find the rent dissipation in large contests.

Finally, the reader can check that when contestants are identical, the solution to the maximization problem as we do in the rest of the book and the solution when contestants take $\sum_{j=1}^n g_j^\epsilon$ as constant are virtually identical when n is very large, see Exercise 9.10, parts (1) and (2).

9.3   Several Alternative Contests

Until now, we have concentrated on the characteristics of a single contest. However, in many situations, participants decide which contest to enter. Consider an athlete choosing between the Madrid or NY Marathon, a professional weighing job options in the public versus private sector, a building contractor deciding on a city to provide services, or researchers determining the type of problem they wish to solve. In this section, we will present a model of how contests are chosen by contestants.

Assume a given number of contests, K and a given number of contestants, N. The model we present has two main characteristics. Contestants are identical and the game is played in two stages. In the first period, contestants decide which contest to run (only one), and in the second, they exert effort. We represent the second stage by a list of K functions, one for each contest, that yield payoffs as a function of the distribution of contestants in the contests. Denote by n_i the number of contestants in contest i. As an example, if $K = 3$, Π_1 yields payoffs for a contestant in contest 1 as a function of the distribution of contestants in the three contests and thus $\Pi_1 = \Pi_1(n_1, n_2, n_3)$. The same for payoffs in contests 2 and 3. We remark that subindexes of these payoffs represent the contest and not a particular contestant. These functions assume that for any distribution of contestants, there is a symmetric equilibrium effort and consequently a payoff associated with any particular contest. As a backup, the reader may think of any of the numerous results on the existence of a symmetric equilibrium presented in Chapter 2. In general, payoffs obtained in a contest may depend on the whole allocation of contestants across contests. For instance, an increase in the number of runners in the Chicago Marathon may attract sponsors and attention to this event and decrease those at the New York Marathon, and so the runners of the latter see their payoffs wane.

Now is time to present our main equilibrium notion.

DEFINITION 9.1 *An entry equilibrium is a list of natural numbers* $\mathbf{n}^* = (n_1^*, n_2^*, \ldots, n_K^*)$ *such that they add up to N and for all contests for which $n_r^* \geq 1$,*

$$\Pi_r(n_1^*, \ldots, n_r^*, \ldots, n_s^*, \ldots, n_K^*) \geq \Pi_s(n_1^*, \ldots, n_r^*-1, \ldots, n_s^*+1, \ldots, n_K^*), r, s \in \{1, 2, \ldots, K\}. \tag{9.19}$$

In words, no agent in a contest has incentives to switch to another contest. Note that contestants are fully rational and when they calculate the consequences of jumping from a contest to another, they calculate precisely the payoffs achievable in this new contest when there is a new contestant. Exercise 9.12 asks how to reinterpret this definition when there are limitations to the number of contestants who can be accommodated in certain contests.

Let us start first with the case where there are only two contests, $K = 2$.

PROPOSITION 9.5 *When $K = 2$, there is an entry equilibrium.*

Proof We will present an algorithm that visits all possible nonnegative integers between 0 and N. Assuming that none of these integers is an equilibrium, we arrive at a contradiction. Start with $n_1 = N$ and suppose that this allocation of contestants is not equilibrium. This must be because a contestant has incentives to switch from contest 1 to contest 2, so now we are at $(N - 1, 1)$. But for $n_1 = N - 1$ to be not an equilibrium, it must be that a contestant finds it profitable to switch from contest 1 to contest 2, so we are at $(N - 2, 2)$, so on and so forth. Finally, if $n_1 = 1$ is not an equilibrium, it must be that the remaining contestant in contest 1 has incentives to switch to contest 2. But then, $(0, N)$ is an equilibrium.[7] □

Note that no condition on the $\Pi_i's$ function was imposed above. Unfortunately, this result does not survive to the consideration of more than two alternative contests; see Exercise 9.13. But this fact is not as destructive as it may seem at first glance.

---

[7] The proof of this result is reminiscent of the proof of proposition 1 in Barberá and Beviá (2002).

If we assume that payoffs in each contest depend only on the number of contestants in this contest, an assumption that does not look too bad in the examples quoted in this section, equilibrium is restored and found by means of the following algorithm.

Harvester algorithm. Consider the list of all payoffs yielded by an allocation of contestants, $\Pi_1(1), \ldots, \Pi_1(N), \Pi_2(1), \ldots, \Pi_2(N), \ldots, \Pi_K(1), \ldots, \Pi_K(N)$. At any step, our algorithm "fills" the contest which has the largest payoff achieved with the contestants that have not been allocated so far. By simplicity we describe the algorithm assuming that there are no ties among payoffs. In case of ties, they are broken arbitrarily.

(1) Start with the largest payoff; let us assume it is $\Pi_j(\hat{n}_j)$.
    Allocate $\hat{n}_j$ contestants in contest j.
(2) Consider the next largest payoff; let us assume it is $\Pi_k(\check{n}_k)$.
    If $\check{n}_k > N - \hat{n}_j$ disregard this payoff because there are not enough remaining contestants to allocate them into contest k.
    If $k = j$ and $\check{n}_k < \hat{n}_j$ disregard this payoff because a larger number of contestants are already allocated to this contest.
    If $k = j$ and $\check{n}_k > \hat{n}_j$ allocate $\check{n}_k$ contestants to this contest.
    In any other case allocate $\check{n}_k$ to the k contest.
(3) Continue allocating contestants to contests with the rules specified for the second largest payoff, namely: Disregard payoffs for contests in which either there are no remaining contestants to fill this contest or a larger number of contestants have been already allocated. If the number of contestants in this contest exceeds the number already allocated in a previous step, delete the allocation in the contest with fewer contestants.

At each stage, the Harvester algorithm visits all contests in order of profitability and allocates new contestants in contests in which (a) in a previous stage we allocated less contestants and (b) there are enough remaining contestants to be allocated there. Clearly, this algorithm, eventually, places all contestants in some contest optimizing payoffs in each stage. Let us denote such an allocation by $\hat{\boldsymbol{n}}$.

PROPOSITION 9.6   *When payoffs in each contest depend only on the number of contestants in this contest, the Harvester algorithm defines an allocation of contestants, $\hat{\boldsymbol{n}}$, that is an equilibrium.*

Proof Suppose a contestant is considering switching, say from contest j to contest k. Now in contest k there are $\hat{n}_k + 1$. But if payoffs there are larger than in contest j with $\hat{n}_j$, there should be $k + 1$ contestants allocated to this contest. Contradiction.   □

Finally, we remark that the equilibrium allocation selected by the Harvester algorithm may be dominated in terms of payoffs by another allocation that is not an equilibrium, see Exercise 9.14.

The previous discussion may give the impression that an entry equilibrium exists only when there are no externalities among contests. But lack of existence is entirely due to the requirement that the number of contestants in each contest is an integer. If we are prepared to consider that the number of players in a contest is a real number, the lack of existence of an equilibrium problem vanishes. This approach may be interpreted as an approximation or as a fraction of the time devoted by a contestant to a particular contest. The tools used to show the existence of an entry equilibrium are advanced, so we leave it as an extension in Section 9.3.1.

The model explained in this section will be used later on in Sections 11.1, in which there are two possible contests one with a socially valuable output and the other with a wasteful output, and 12.3.1 in which it is studied the optimal allocation of contestants in several contests.

An interesting application of the idea that contestants move between different contests is presented by Masera (2021). Using data at the police department level, he finds that one-fourth of the effect of militarization on violent crime is due to the displacement of violent crime to neighboring areas. Police departments overmilitarize because they do not consider this externality. These findings have significant implications for the policy debate concerning the costs and benefits of police militarization.

9.3.1 Advanced Material: Existence of an Entry Equilibrium When the Number of Contestants Is Not an Integer

We first provide a separate definition of an entry equilibrium when the number of contestants is a real number. We call this the continuous entry problem. The idea is the same as in the definition when the number of contestants must be an integer.

DEFINITION 9.2 *An entry equilibrium for the continuous entry problem is a list of real numbers* $n^* = (n_1^*, n_2^*, \ldots, n_K^*)$ *summing up* N *such that for all contests* $r, s \in \{1, 2, \ldots, K\}$, $r \neq s$,

$$\text{if} \quad n_r^*, n_s^* > 0, \quad \Pi_r(n^*) = \Pi_s(n^*),$$
$$\text{if} \quad \Pi_r(n^*) > \Pi_s(n^*), \quad n_s^* = 0.$$

When the number of contestants in a contest is a continuous variable, equilibrium requires that for each active contest (i.e., a contest with a positive number of contestants) payoffs are identical. And if a contest yields less payoffs than another, this contest must be inactive. Let $S = \{(n_1, n_2, \ldots, n_k) \mid \sum_{j=1}^{K} n_j = N\}$ be the set (actually a simplex) of allocation of contestants.

In this case, we have the following result:

PROPOSITION 9.7 *If payoff functions are continuous, there is an entry equilibrium for the continuous entry problem.*

Proof This result is proved by using a fixed-point theorem.

Let P_i be the compact set in which every payoff in the contest i is. This set exists since payoffs are continuous and the set of contestants is compact.

Let $P = \times_{i=1}^{K} P_i$ and $\Pi = (\Pi_1, \ldots, \Pi_K) \in P$. Given a vector of payoffs, let $\Pi^M(\Pi)$ be the maximum payoff in all contests. There might be several contests at which this profit is maximum. These contests are those at which contestants in contest r will migrate if $\Pi^M(\mathbf{\Pi}) > \Pi_r$. Now is the time to define our mappings.

On the one hand, we have payoff functions $\Pi\colon S \to P$.

On the other hand, consider the following maximization problem: Given a vector of payoffs, say $\bar{\mathbf{\Pi}}$, choose $\mathbf{n}$ to Maximize $\sum_{h=1}^{K} n_h(\bar{\Pi}_h - \Pi^M(\bar{\mathbf{\Pi}}))$ over S. This is the maximization of a linear function on a compact set and it has a solution for given $\tilde{\mathbf{\Pi}}$. By the maximum theorem (Berge, 1959), this maximization defines an upper hemicontinuous mapping which is convex valued $\Gamma\colon P \rightrightarrows S$. Now $\Pi \times \Gamma$ is an upper hemicontinuous and convex valued mapping from a convex, compact set into itself and by Kakutani's theorem it has a fixed point denoted by $(\tilde{n}_1, \tilde{n}_2, \ldots, \tilde{n}_K, \tilde{\Pi}_1, \tilde{\Pi}_2, \ldots, \tilde{\Pi}_K)$. At this fixed point, clearly for all s, $\tilde{n}_s(\tilde{\Pi}_s - \Pi^M(\tilde{\mathbf{\Pi}})) \le 0$. Thus, all terms in $\sum_{h=1}^{K} \tilde{n}_h(\tilde{\Pi}_h - \Pi^M(\tilde{\mathbf{\Pi}}))$ have the same sign (with zero counting as both positive and negative). Also, for those in which $\tilde{n}_r$ and $\tilde{n}_s$ are positive $\tilde{\Pi}_r = \tilde{\Pi}_s = \Pi^M(\tilde{\mathbf{\Pi}})$. Lastly, it should be noted that it is impossible that all terms in this sum are strictly negative because, at least, a contest has the maximum profits. □

9.4   Exercises

9.1   Discuss the properties that characterize Blavatskyy CSF, especially the relative homogeneity assumption. Compare these properties with those presented by Skaperdas (1996) and Clark and Riis (1998a).

9.2   Prove that there are two interior Nash equilibrium with the Blavatskyy CSF if $b = 2$, $T = 10.1$, $V = 12$. Show that $g = 0.94721$ and $g = 0.052786$ are Nash equilibrium strategies.

9.3   Show that in the Jia's CSF the probability of a tie is maximized when $g_i = g_j$.

9.4   Find the Nash equilibrium of the contests induced by Jia's CSF when $T = 0$.

9.5   Loury (1979), who discusses innovation (in which case $T = 0$), presented the following CSF:

$$p_i(\mathbf{g}) = \frac{f(g_i)}{1 + f(g_i) + f(g_j)}, \, i, j \in \{1, 2\}, \, i \ne j.$$

Discuss the similarities with other CSFs presented in this chapter.

9.6   Extend the CSF of Yildizparlak (2018) to several players (see Vesperoni and Yildizparlak, 2019).

9.7   Following Section 9.1.3, show that $(0, 0)$ cannot be an equilibrium. Prove also that an equilibrium cannot exist when one contestant exerts zero effort while the other invests a positive effort.

9.8 Suppose a CSF with draws as Blavatsky. But in case of a draw, the contest must be repeated.
(1) Find real-life examples of such a contest.
(2) Suppose that effort is time-invariant and that the contest is repeated either a finite number of times – in which in the final period the CSF is the Ratio Form – or an infinite number of times. Show that in both cases the problem collapses into the static model of a one period contest, see Franke and Metzger (2023).

9.9 Suppose that the contest is large and $\epsilon = 1$.
(1) Study the maximization problem of a typical contestant when costs are linear.
(2) Idem when costs are strictly convex.
(3) Show that the term $\epsilon g_i^{2\epsilon-1}/(\sum_{j=1}^n g_j^\epsilon)^2$ that was neglected in the payoff maximization is indeed very small when the number of contestants is large.

9.10 Assume that contestants are identical. Calculate the equilibrium values of effort when:
(1) Contestants take $\sum_{j=1}^n g_j^\epsilon$ as constant.
(2) Contestants do not take $\sum_{j=1}^n g_j^\epsilon$ as constant.

9.11 In some contests, like the UEFA Champions League in soccer or the World Series in baseball there must be a winner. When a tie occurs in such contests, a winner is selected by a tie-breaking rule.
(1) Show that in two-contestants contest where ties are possible, if the probabilities of winning and the probability of a tie are based either solely on the ratio of efforts or solely on the difference in effort, then an effort-maximizing tie-breaking rule should favor the weaker agent. Interpret this in light of what we know of the properties of best reply functions in Chapter 3.
(2) Consider random tie-breaking rules. Under which conditions these rules lead to greater expected effort than those under part (1) above.[8] See Goel and Goyal (2023).

9.12 Give examples of real-life contests where the number of contestants is limited. And sketch how this fact can be accommodated in Definition 9.1 (see the comment below definition 2 in Corchón and Torregrosa, 2022).

9.13 Show an example of inexistence of an entry equilibrium in which payoffs in each contest are decreasing in the number of contestants in this contest, see Corchón and Torregrosa (2022), example 5.

9.14 Show an example in which entry equilibrium is dominated in term of payoffs (see example 6 in Corchón and Torregrosa, 2022).

9.15 Extend the model of a large contest presented in Section 9.2 to a continuum of contestants where instead the sum of the efforts we have an integral reflecting the mass of contestants using a certain strategy. See Lahkar and Mukherjee (2023).

9.16 Find rent dissipation in large contests; see Lahkar and Sultana (2023).

---

[8] The International Football Association (FIFA) used a random tie-breaking rule in the games leading to the World Cup in Switzerland in 1954.

10 Contests in Classical Problems: Divisionalization, Monopoly Welfare Losses, Coase Theorem, Voting

Contest theory does not pretend to be just a nice theoretical construct. It is meant to be a tool to analyze real-life problems. It is a point of view that, in principle, could be applied to any economic issue. We review several classical problems in the light of what we have learnt in previous chapters. Three of these problems refer to organizations functioning in a market: The division of managers' time between rent-seeking and productive activities, the hidden costs of securing a monopolistic position, and the cost of fighting for ownership. The final application refers to the fight for the vote of the electorate. We will see that contests shed new light on each of these problems.

10.1   Divisionalized Firms

A divisionalized firm is one in which some decisions are taken by some semi-autonomous units, the divisions. These decentralized decisions usually refer to output, but they may include revamping of basic products offered by the center to make them more appealing to the local market or designing brand-new products. The center usually decides overall investments and is a source of funds for the divisions. Automobile firms like General Motors were among the first to be divisionalized, but this form has since become popular in other markets, Apple being another prominent example of this form of organization.

According to Scharfstein and Stein (2000), in divisionalized firms, the policy of the center is not characterized by allocating more funds/investments to the successful divisions, i.e., rewarding success. On the contrary, there is substantial redistribution toward less successful branches. They call this "Internal Socialism." Traditional explanations range from consumption smoothing, i.e., the center smooths over time the funds allocated to all divisions which calls for an counter-cyclical allocation of funds, to risk sharing, i.e., the center compensates unlucky divisions. These authors provide an explanation based on rent-seeking.

Consider the following model. There are two divisions, 1 and 2, each commanded by a manager. Each manager has a time endowment of L to be divided between productive (i.e., managing the division) or rent-seeking activities devoted to convince the center to allocate more funds to the division she manages. Managers differ in their marginal return of productive activities which, by simplicity, is taken to be constant and denoted by ρ_i, $i \in \{1,2\}$, with $\rho_1 > \rho_2$. In words, the manager of division 1 is more productive managing this division than the manager of division 2 managing his division. Let V be the amount of internal funds to be allocated. V is the prize that we assume is infinitely divisible. Let p_i represent the fraction of funds allocated to division $i \in \{1,2\}$. Given that their working time is fixed, managers are faithful servants of their division so they maximize the expected revenue accruing to each division. Let l_i be the time devoted by manager i to productive activities and g_i the time devoted to rent-seeking activities, with $g_i + l_i = L$. The expected revenue of division i is

$$\pi_i(\mathbf{g}) = p_i(\mathbf{g})V + \rho_i(L - g_i). \tag{10.1}$$

The following result characterizes the outcome of the rent-seeking game.

PROPOSITION 10.1 *Assume that the CSF is homogeneous of degree zero. Then, $g_2^* > g_1^*$. If additionally, the CSF is symmetric, $p_1(\mathbf{g}^*) < p_2(\mathbf{g}^*)$.*

Proof For the expected revenue of division i, given by (10.1), the second-order conditions hold (see Exercise 10.1) and the first-order conditions for each division are

$$\frac{\partial p_1(\mathbf{g}^*)}{\partial g_1}V = \rho_1 \text{ and } -\frac{\partial p_1(\mathbf{g}^*)}{\partial g_2}V = \rho_2.$$

Given that $\rho_1 > \rho_2$,

$$\frac{\partial p_1(\mathbf{g}^*)}{\partial g_1} > -\frac{\partial p_1(\mathbf{g}^*)}{\partial g_2}.$$

By homogeneity of degree zero,

$$\frac{\partial p_1(\mathbf{g}^*)}{\partial g_1}g_1^* = -\frac{\partial p_1(\mathbf{g}^*)}{\partial g_2}g_2^*,$$

therefore,

$$\frac{\partial p_1(\mathbf{g}^*)}{\partial g_1} > -\frac{\partial p_1(\mathbf{g}^*)}{\partial g_2} = \frac{\partial p_1(\mathbf{g}^*)}{\partial g_1}\frac{g_1^*}{g_2^*},$$

which implies that $g_2^* > g_1^*$.

The last part of the proposition follows directly from the symmetry assumption on the CSF. □

This result says that less productive managers devote more time to rent-seeking and, if symmetrically treated by the center, obtain more funds from it than productive managers. This is because for a productive manager, the opportunity cost of rent-seeking is higher than for an unproductive manager. Thus, more productive contestants have a larger opportunity cost of rent-seeking, devote less time to rent-seeking and are less successful in this activity.

Our model has been deliberately kept simple, but the lesson learned there can be applied to any organization in which rent-seeking affects the distribution of funds. Gustafsson, Gustavsson, and Halvarsson (2020) present a model in which entrepreneurs are free to allocate their effort between production and seeking grants.

Using a large database from Sweden's three largest grant-awarding agencies, they find evidence of a negative relation between the probability of receiving a grant and firm productivity. In a more casual way, both authors of this book have management experience in several universities and can attest to the power of this effect. If you are the chairman of a good department, you have a lot of things to do: teaching, research, PhD students, hiring new faculty, referee reports, attending and giving seminars, etc. In bad departments, the effort devoted to these issues is low, and so their chairmen have lots of time to scheme how to direct funds to their coffers. The disturbing conclusion is that in organizations where allocation of resources is made by rent-seeking, productive contestants will obtain less funds than unproductive ones.

10.2   The Fight for Monopoly Rents

This topic is one of the cornerstones of contests. It started with a paper by Gordon Tullock in 1967 that pointed out that classical theory of welfare losses under monopoly, as pioneered by Harberger (1954), is just a part of the story. In particular, the welfare loss triangles that you can find in any elementary textbook (see Tirole, 1988, chapter 1) do not exhaust the list of problems inflicted by monopolies to the society. The reliance on such welfare costs alone masks the fight for the right to be a monopolist.

Suppose there is a market with a single consumer with a utility function given by

$$U = \hat{a}x - \frac{b}{\rho + 1}x^{\rho+1} + l \text{ with } \hat{a} \geq 0, \rho b > 0 \text{ and } \rho > -1$$

and a budget constraint $px + l = M$. Where x and p are, respectively, the output and the market price of the good, M is income and l is a good that encapsulates all other goods. Plugging the budget constraint into the utility function and disregarding income – which is just a constant – we obtain

$$U = \hat{a}x - \frac{b}{\rho + 1}x^{\rho+1} - px.$$

The consumer maximizes utility taking p as given. The second-order conditions hold and the first-order conditions yield the inverse demand function $p = \hat{a} - bx^{\rho}$. This utility function is very convenient because it encapsulates two important special cases. If $b > 0$ and $\rho = 1$, the inverse demand is linear. If $\hat{a} = 0$, $b < 0$, and $\rho < 0$, the inverse demand is isoelastic. The parameter ρ is a measure of the degree of concavity of demand because ρ equals the elasticity of the derivative of inverse demand plus one.

The good is supplied by a single firm, i.e., a monopolist which produces the good at a constant marginal cost, denoted by k. Let $a \equiv \hat{a} - k$. The monopolist profit function is

$$\pi = (\hat{a} - bx^{\rho})x - kx = (a - bx^{\rho})x.$$

The reader can check that the second-order conditions hold and that the first-order conditions yield

$$x^* = \left(\frac{a}{b(1+\rho)}\right)^{\frac{1}{\rho}} \text{ and } \pi^* = \left(\frac{a}{b(\rho+1)}\right)^{\frac{1}{\rho}} \frac{a\rho}{\rho+1}.$$

Next, we compute the socially optimal allocation which is the one that maximizes the sum of consumer and producer surpluses, i.e.,

$$W = U + \pi = \hat{a}x - \frac{b}{\rho+1}x^{\rho+1} - kx = ax - \frac{b}{\rho+1}x^{\rho+1}.$$

Again, the second-order conditions hold and the first-order conditions yield

$$x^O = \left(\frac{a}{b}\right)^{\frac{1}{\rho}}.$$

Plugging the values of output into the formula for social welfare, we obtain social welfare in the optimum (W^O) and under monopoly (W^*), namely,

$$W^O = \left(\frac{a}{b}\right)^{\frac{1}{\rho}} \frac{a\rho}{1+\rho} \text{ and } W^* = \left(\frac{a}{b(1+\rho)}\right)^{\frac{1}{\rho}} \frac{a\rho(2+\rho)}{(1+\rho)^2}.$$

We now calculate the welfare loss of monopoly that under linear demand is the standard triangle mentioned above. It is customary to divide welfare losses by the optimal social welfare in order to obtain a measure of inefficiency that does not depend on the size of the market. In other words, large markets may have huge welfare losses just because a small friction occurs in each transaction (i.e., a transportation cost). Dividing welfare losses by the value of social welfare at the optimum gets rid of the effect of the volume of transactions.

Denoting by RM the standard relative welfare loss due to misallocation in the market of the good, we have that

$$RM \equiv \frac{W^O - W^*}{W^O} = 1 - \left(\frac{1}{1+\rho}\right)^{\frac{1}{\rho}} \frac{2+\rho}{1+\rho}.$$

It is remarkable that the percentage of welfare losses only depend on ρ, the degree of concavity of demand. Under linear demand $\rho = 1$ and $RM = 0.25$. This exhaust the classical theory of welfare losses under monopoly.

It is now time to ask how this firm came to be a monopoly. There are several possibilities. Perhaps the firm markets an invention for which there are only poor substitutes. Perhaps there is a large fixed cost (that does not interfere with the calculations above because it is sunk at the time the monopolist is deciding output) that makes entry into this market unprofitable. Another view is presented by Parente and Prescott in their book *Barriers to Riches* (2000). "Differences in international incomes are the consequences of different knowledge. These differences are the primary result of country-specific policies that result in constraints on work practices and better production methods. Many of these barriers are put in place to protect the interests of groups." See also Parente and Prescott (1999). According to this view, monopoly is protected by a legal cover-up. But this fact unveils that behind the curtain there has been a process of allocating monopoly rights. To make things simple, suppose that the rent is completely dissipated, i.e., the value of the prize (the monopoly profits π^*) equals expenses in

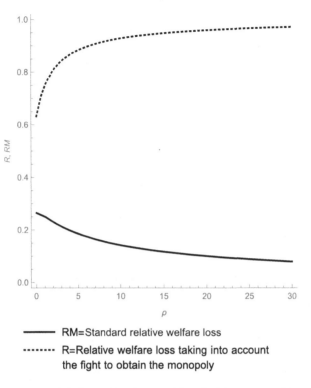

RM=Standard relative welfare loss

R=Relative welfare loss taking into account the fight to obtain the monopoly

Figure 10.1 Relative welfare losses with and without rent-seeking

the contest. With the All Pay Auction, this occurs with two contestants with identical valuations, and with the Ratio Form CSF when the number of contestants is very large.

We assume that expenses are a complete waste from a social point of view. You can think of lawyers and bureaucrats filling endless papers or time spent visiting the allocating unit (ministry, royal court, etc.). Under these, admittedly extreme, assumptions total welfare losses are $W^O - W^E + \pi^*$ and relative welfare losses are

$$R = \frac{W^O - W^E + \pi^*}{W^O} = 1 - \left(\frac{1}{1+\rho}\right)^{\frac{1}{\rho}} \frac{2+\rho}{1+\rho} + \left(\frac{1}{\rho+1}\right)^{\frac{1}{\rho}}.$$

Now it is time to see the role of ρ. Note that $\lim_{\rho \to \infty}(1/(1+\rho))^{\frac{1}{\rho}}(2+\rho)/(1+\rho) = 1$, $\lim_{\rho \to \infty}(1/(1+\rho))^{\frac{1}{\rho}} = 1$. Thus,

$$\lim_{\rho \to \infty} RM = 0, \text{ and } \lim_{\rho \to \infty} R = 1.$$

In words, when ρ is very large, classical welfare losses are zero but welfare losses due to the cost of allocating monopoly rights are 100%. The explanation of this will come in a moment. For the time being, take a look at Figure 10.1 representing RM (solid line) and R (dotted line).

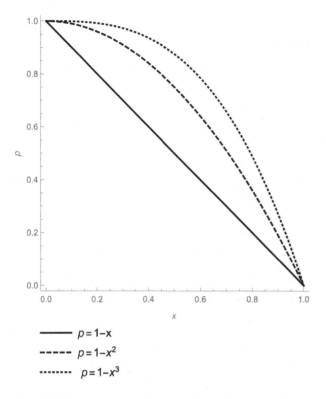

Figure 10.2 Inverse demand when $\rho = 1$, $\rho = 2$, and $\rho = 3$

For $\rho = 1$ or $\rho = -0.5$ welfare loss becomes, respectively, three times or twice the magnitude predicted by the classical theory. When $\rho \to \infty$, relative welfare loss approaches one but the relative welfare loss due to misallocation of resources approaches zero! How is that? Well, when $\rho \to \infty$ there is no allocative distortion, but all consumer surplus is captured by the monopolist. Figure 10.2 illustrates this by picturing the special case in which inverse demand is $1 - x$ (solid), $1 - x^2$ (dash), $1 - x^3$ (dots). In the limit, inverse demand approaches a square of the north and east boundaries of $[0, 1]^2$. Market price and output converge to 1. And the whole surplus is captured by the monopolist. But this surplus is entirely wasted during the rent-seeking process of allocating monopoly rights.

We end this section by cautioning the reader that our calculations rely on extreme assumptions and are only made to illustrate that the classical theory may underestimate the magnitude of welfare losses. See Hillman and Katz (1984) for an extension to risk-averse firms.

10.3   The Coase Theorem with a Previous Contest

The reader surely remembers from her intermediate microeconomics course the first fundamental theorem of welfare economics: Perfectly competitive equilibrium is

Pareto-efficient. The reader also remembers several important caveats to this result. In particular, the theorem fails when

1. Markets are imperfect because some firms have market power or markets are incomplete.
2. There are externalities or public goods.
3. There are asymmetries of information due to hidden actions (moral hazard) or to hidden characteristics (adverse selection).[1]

Economists have devised mechanisms to overcome these points. One of the most famous is Pigouvian taxes/subsidies that equalize social and private costs by taxing those firms producing negative externalities and subsidizing those that yield positive externalities. Another is to subsidize firms to incentive them to produce more than in oligopolistic equilibrium. Another is Lindahl equilibrium in which different consumers are charged different prices for the consumption of the public good. These models do not explain how these taxes, subsidies, and prices are found in practice. They rely on the use of information that, with a high probability, is just in the hands of firms and not in the hands of those in charge of setting taxes, subsidies, or personalized prices.[2]

A completely new approach to the question of the relationship between free market and Pareto efficiency was pioneered by Ronald Coase (1910–2013) in his famous 1960 paper. Here comes a statement of the renowned Coase theorem. "With well defined property rights and zero transaction costs, private and social costs will be equal" (Coase, 1988, p. 158). This theorem, which some term a tautology, says that any Pareto improving allocation will be realized by those agents that profit from it. But the interest of this theorem lies in the fact that, of course, transaction costs are never zero: Contracts are incomplete because they cannot forecast all possible circumstances (i.e., states of the world) and they are costly to write and to enforce because justice is imperfect. And the information to make these contracts workable is sometimes in private hands with no clear incentives for the contestants holding this information to disclose it truthfully. The important lesson to be learned from this theorem is that any public policy aimed to correct market failure will face similar constraints to the ones faced by the market. Thus, if an externality problem has been caused by the inability of the agents to contract because justice is corrupt, a law is not going to solve this problem. Or if the cause of this inability is that some information is private, this constraint will be faced by the public authority too. Summing up, the planner will have to deal with the transaction costs that prevent the private contestants to attain an efficient allocation of resources.

But there is also another important assumption of the Coase theorem – that property rights are well defined. But, are they? Rather than telling the never-ending story of countries fighting for a piece of land or a resource, let us focus on a nicer, real-life

---

[1] A different kind of failure occurs when the theorem is an empty statement because perfectly competitive equilibrium does not exist. A particularly important source of nonexistence is economies of scale arising from increasing returns or fixed costs in the production of some goods.

[2] Implementation theory was created to address this issue, see, e.g., Corchón (2009) for a survey.

Figure 10.3 Sue, the Tyrannosaurus rex in the Chicago's Field Museum of Natural History

story. Sue is one of the largest complete skeletons of a *Tyrannosaurus rex* in the world. It was found in native American territory by a private company. The Native Americans and the company fought a protracted legal battle that, after wasting several million dollars, ended with the skeleton in the hands of the native Americans. The skeleton was auctioned, and the best bid was made by a consortium of Chicago personalities and institutions. Thus, it ended up in the Chicago's Field Museum of Natural History where one of us pictured it, see Figure 10.3.[3]

This example serves to prepare the field for our analysis of the Coase theorem when property rights are in conflict. We will see that the cost of the conflict can be dear.

Suppose two contestants fighting for the ownership of a prize that they value in V_1 and V_2 with $V_1 \geq V_2$. In the case of Sue, both contestants were interested just in the money value of the skeleton, so it is likely that both valuations were close.

After property rights have been allocated, assume that contestants may trade if they wish. Thus, finally, the object ends in the hand of the agent that values it the most. Because trade benefits both contestants, this part represents the traditional gains from trade.

There are two possible outcomes of the rent-seeking process:

(1) Agent 1 gets the property right and no trade results: Payoffs from this outcome for contestants 1 and 2 are $(V_1, 0)$.
(2) Agent 2 gets the property right and sells the object to agent 1. Assume that trade occurs at a price which is the average of the valuations of both contestants, i.e., $(V_1 + V_2)/2$. Expected payoffs of this outcome are $((V_1 - V_2)/2, (V_1 + V_2)/2)$.

Agents can influence the allocation of the property right by incurring expenses g_1 and g_2. Letting p_1 be probability that agent 1 ends up owning the property right after the contest, total payoffs are

---

[3] Here is the complete story: https://en.wikipedia.org/wiki/Sue_(dinosaur).

$$\pi_1(\mathbf{g}) = p_1 V_1 + (1 - p_1)\frac{V_1 - V_2}{2} - g_1,$$

$$\pi_2(\mathbf{g}) = (1 - p_1)\left(\frac{V_1 + V_2}{2}\right) - g_2.$$

To simplify notation, let $V \equiv (V_1 + V_2)/2$. Thus, total payoffs become

$$\pi_1(\mathbf{g}) = p_1 V + \frac{V_1 - V_2}{2} - g_1,$$

$$\pi_2(\mathbf{g}) = (1 - p_1)V - g_2.$$

These are the standard formulae for payoffs with the only difference that agent 1 has a fixed plus $(V_1 - V_2)/2$ which reflects her superior valuation of the contested good. Since this is constant, it does not affect the maximization of agent 1. Assuming a Ratio Form CSF, in the unique Nash equilibrium,

$$g_i^* = \frac{V}{4} \text{ and } p_i^* = \frac{1}{2}, \ i \in \{1, 2\}.$$

If expenses are wasteful, the losses due to the conflict are $V/2$, which in terms of the original valuations amounts to $(V_1 + V_2)/4$. To obtain a relative measure of welfare loss, denoted by WL, we divide by V_1 and obtain

$$WL = \frac{V_1 + V_2}{4V_1}.$$

When valuations are very close, the fight for the ownership of the object may dissipate as much as half of the total value of the object. In the best case, when $V_2 = 0$, a quarter of the value dissipates. See Exercise 10.2 when trade is not certain due to transaction costs.

10.4   Contests and Voting

Some contests are settled by the voting of a certain constituency. Examples are elections, awarding grants by a committee, location of public events like Olympic games or FIFA world championship, corporate firms policies, and congress voting. Our analysis will unveil what is behind these decisions by focusing on how the necessary votes are obtained.

We present the simplest case of two contestants and simultaneous elections. Two contestants fight for a single prize that they value in V_A and V_B, respectively. Assume $V_A \geq V_B$. The prize is awarded by voting by a group of voters. Voters are divided into *friends* with n_i voters always voting for contestant $i \in \{A, B\}$ and n *undecided* voters that are influenceable by means of some expenses, (g_A, g_B), with $g_i \in [0, V_i]$, $i \in \{A, B\}$. These expenses could be advertising, expenses in the region of undecided voters or vote buying.

Voters are not strategic players. Either they vote for a given candidate no matter what (friends) or they have a certain probability to vote for a candidate (undecided).

The probability that an undecided voter votes for contestant i is given by a Ratio Form,[4]

$$p(g_i, g_j) = \begin{cases} \frac{g_i}{g_i + g_j} & \text{if} \quad g_i + g_j \neq 0 \\ \frac{1}{2} & \text{if} \quad g_i + g_j = 0 \end{cases}. \tag{10.2}$$

Note that (10.2) is not a CSF because votes of friends and undecided count equally. We call it a persuasion function. Undecided voters behave randomly like in the models of probabilistic voting (see Coughlin and Nitzan, 1981 and Lindbeck and Weibull, 1987). The difference here is that this unpredictability can be steered by the expenses made by the contestants.

Let $t = n_A - n_B$ be the net number of friends of A. When t is positive, contestant A has more friends than B, otherwise t is negative. To avoid the case of a tie vote, we assume that n is odd and t is even. Contestant A wins if a majority of voters, i.e., $(n_A + n_B + n + 1)/2$, vote for A. Given that n_A voters will vote for A independently of g_A, A will need at least $(n - t + 1)/2$ votes among the undecided voters. To make the problem not completely determined by friends, we assume that $n \geq |t| + 1$.

Let $f_{n,t}(p)$ denote the probability that A wins. This probability is not (10.2) because this equation gives us the probability that an undecided voter votes for contestant i. We require combinatorial mathematics to determine $f_{n,t}(p)$. We address these calculations in Section 10.5.

Payoffs of A and B are

$$\pi_A = f_{n,t}(p)V_A - g_A;$$
$$\pi_B = (1 - f_{n,t}(p))V_B - g_B.$$

The necessary and sufficient condition for the existence of a Nash equilibrium in pure strategies depends on the elasticity of A (resp. of B) winning the contest with respect to the changes in the probability that an undecided voter votes for A (resp. for B). Formally, let

$$E_{n,t}^A(p) = \frac{\partial f_{n,t}(p)}{\partial p} \frac{p}{f_{n,t}(p)}$$

be the elasticity of the probability that A wins with respect to the probability that an undecided voter votes for A. And

$$E_{n,t}^B(p) = -\frac{\partial f_{n,t}(p)}{\partial p} \frac{p}{1 - f_{n,t}(p)}$$

be the corresponding elasticity for B.

PROPOSITION 10.2   *Let* $\gamma = V_A/V_B$. *A Nash equilibrium in pure strategies exists if and only if*

$$\gamma + 1 \geq \max \left\{ E_{n,t}^A \left(\frac{\gamma}{1 + \gamma} \right), -E_{n,t}^B \left(\frac{\gamma}{1 + \gamma} \right) \right\}. \tag{10.3}$$

---

[4] Skaperdas and Vaidya (2012) analyze a persuasion contest in which a single jury can be persuaded by making expenses and find that the form (10.2) arises under some assumptions on the structure of information.

Proof   The first-order conditions of payoff maximization are

$$\frac{\partial f_{n,t}(p)}{\partial p}\frac{\partial p}{\partial g_A}V_A = 1 \quad \text{and} \quad -\frac{\partial f_{n,t}(p)}{\partial p}\frac{\partial p}{\partial g_B}V_B = 1.$$

Since p is of the Ratio Form,

$$\frac{\partial f_{n,t}(p)}{\partial p}\frac{g_B}{(g_A + g_B)^2}V_A = 1 \quad \text{and} \quad \frac{\partial f_{n,t}(p)}{\partial p}\frac{g_A}{(g_A + g_B)^2}V_B = 1. \tag{10.4}$$

Dividing one equation by the other, we obtain that

$$g_A = g_B\frac{V_A}{V_B}.$$

Having obtained that, if a Nash equilibrium in pure strategies exists,

$$p^* = \frac{V_A}{V_A + V_B}.$$

From (10.4) we obtain the values of expenses in the candidate equilibrium

$$g_A^* = \frac{\partial f_{n,t}\left(\frac{V_A}{V_A+V_B}\right)}{\partial p}\frac{V_A^2 V_B}{(V_A + V_B)^2}; \quad g_B^* = \frac{\partial f_{n,t}\left(\frac{V_A}{V_A+V_B}\right)}{\partial p}\frac{V_A V_B^2}{(V_A + V_B)^2}.$$

Contestant A (resp. B) chooses g_A (resp. g_B) in $[0, V_A]$ (resp. $[0, V_B]$) to maximize payoffs taking g_B^* (resp g_A^*) as given. Since payoffs are continuous and the opportunity set is compact, given g_B^* (resp g_A^*) the maximum exist. The first-order condition yields an equilibrium whenever payoffs are nonnegative there and payoffs at the extremes of $[0, V_A]$ (resp. $[0, V_B]$) are nonpositive. Note that, in equilibrium, an agent will never use effort equal to V_i because no matter the effort of the other agent, choosing V_i always gives a nonpositive payoff. Effort equal to zero for some agent and a positive effort for the other agent cannot be part of a pure strategy equilibrium either. The agent that chooses a positive effort can always be better off by slightly reducing effort. Finally, both contestants choosing zero effort cannot be an equilibrium either. Because an agent, by slightly increasing his effort, will win with probability one and will have positive payoff. Thus, a Nash equilibrium in pure strategies exists if and only if payoffs, evaluated at expenses obtained from the first-order conditions – g_A^* and g_B^* – are nonnegative. This is the case if and only if

$$f_{n,t}\left(\frac{V_A}{V_A + V_B}\right) \geq \frac{\partial f_{n,t}\left(\frac{V_A}{V_A+V_B}\right)}{\partial p}\frac{V_A V_B}{(V_A + V_B)^2} \quad \text{and} \tag{10.5}$$

$$1 - f_{n,t}\left(\frac{V_A}{V_A + V_B}\right) \geq \frac{\partial f_{n,t}\left(\frac{V_A}{V_A+V_B}\right)}{\partial p}\frac{V_A V_B}{(V_A + V_B)^2} \tag{10.6}$$

Given that $\gamma = V_A/V_B$, inequalities (10.5) and (10.6) can be written as

$$\gamma + 1 \geq E_{n,t}^A\left(\frac{\gamma}{1 + \gamma}\right);$$

$$\gamma + 1 \geq -E_{n,t}^B\left(\frac{\gamma}{1 + \gamma}\right).$$

Or equivalently,

$$\gamma + 1 \geq \max \left\{ E_{n,t}^A \left(\frac{\gamma}{1+\gamma} \right), - E_{n,t}^B \left(\frac{\gamma}{1+\gamma} \right) \right\},$$

as we wanted to prove.   □

The necessary and sufficient condition (10.3) says that, for a Nash equilibrium to exist, the probability of winning should not be "too much" responsive to the probability of convincing an undecided voter, p. If this were not the case, contestants will have incentives to go beyond the expenses recommended by the first-order conditions of payoff maximization to reap undecided voters from the other contestant.

It is remarkable that p only depends on valuations and not on the number of voters/friends. In particular, if valuations are identical, this probability is 0.5 no matter how many friends or voters are in the contest. This comes from the fact that p only depends on relative expenses which, in turn, only depend on relative valuations. This implies that contestants who are disadvantaged in terms of friends exert an extra effort which exactly offsets this disadvantage.

Note that when $\gamma \geq 1$, and $t \geq 0$,

$$f_{n,t}(\gamma/(1+\gamma)) \geq 1 - f_{n,t}(\gamma/(1+\gamma)),$$

and therefore

$$-E_{n,t}^B(\gamma/(1+\gamma)) > E_{n,t}^A(\gamma/(1+\gamma)).$$

Exercise 10.4 asks you to prove that $-E_{n,t}^B(\gamma/(1+\gamma))$ is increasing in n (the result in Exercise 10.3 will help).

The previous result can be worked out in the more general case in which the persuasion function is just homogeneous of degree zero (see Exercise 10.5).

Further properties of Nash equilibrium in pure strategies can be obtained in the case in which both contestants have the same number of supporters, i.e., when $t = 0$. Using Proposition 10.2 and the result in Exercise 10.4, it is not difficult to prove the following:

PROPOSITION 10.3   *Let $t = 0$*

(i) If $n \geq 7$, there is no Nash equilibrium in pure strategies.
(ii) If $n = 3$, a Nash equilibrium in pure strategies exists if and only if $\gamma \leq 1.5486$.
(iii) If $n = 5$, a Nash equilibrium in pure strategies exists if and only if $\gamma \leq 1.073$.

This proposition illustrates that to predict the prizes awarded by committees is a tricky business (as common experience tells us!). Our main equilibrium tool, Nash equilibrium in pure strategies exists, fails in important cases to give a prediction on outcomes that we can expect from such scenario. You are asked to try your hand and prove this result in Exercise 10.6.

Exercise 10.7 asks you to prove that maximal effort when $t = 0$, and $\gamma \leq 1.073$ is obtained when $n = 5$. If the society wants to maximize effort, five-person juries are optimal. Examples of this type of jury in the real world are the Scotiabank Giller

Prize, the group of experts in Eurovision contests, the Pritzker Prize (where the independent jury of experts ranges from five to nine members), Indiana juries (except in serious felonies), the Pulitzer Prize both in journalism (1964–1999) and in books, Parsi divorce, the Cherokee Nation Tribal Court, the Tribeca X Award in storytelling, and the old system in Spain for awarding PhD's or deciding a chair.[5]

When the number of friends is not identical between A and B, it can be shown that $E_{n,t}^B(\gamma/1 + \gamma)$ decreases with t, the net number of friends of A. In other words the elasticity that B wins with respect to p decreases with t, the net number of friends of A. The intuition is that the fewer friends of B, the harder for B to find a majority. With this result in hand, when $t > 0$, chances that a Nash equilibrium in pure strategies exists are slim. However, when $t < 0$, there are cases in which the net number of friends of B compensate for B's disadvantage in terms of valuations. For an analysis of the general case when the number of friends of A and B may be different and covering the existence of a Nash equilibrium in mixed strategies, the interested reader can consult the paper by Klumpp and Polborn (2006).

10.5   Derivation of the Winning Probabilities

In this section, we derive $f_{n,t}(p)$ mathematically as a function of p. First, A needs at least $(n - t + 1)/2$ votes among the undecided voters to win. Therefore, the probability that A wins is the probability that at least $(n - t + 1)/2$ undecided voters vote by A. Given an arbitrary subset of k undecided voters, the probability that all vote for A is $p^k(1 - p)^{n-k}$ where p^k is the probability that all k voters vote by A and $(1 - p)^{n-k}$ is the probability that the rest of undecided voters vote for B. We have $\binom{n}{k}$ groups of k voters, so the probability that a group of k undecided voters vote for A is $\binom{n}{k}p^k(1 - p)^{n-k}$. Finally, the probability that A wins is the sum of all the events in which a group of $(n - t + 1)/2$ undecided voters vote for A plus the probability that $(n - t + 1)/2 + 1$ undecided voters vote for A, and so on and so forth until we reach the whole group of undecided voters. Thus, the probability that A wins is

$$f_{n,t}(p) = \sum_{k=\frac{n-t+1}{2}}^{n} \binom{n}{k} p^k (1 - p)^{n-k}.$$

The probability that B wins is $1 - f_{n,t}(p)$, or equivalently

$$1 - f_{n,t}(p) = \sum_{k=\frac{n+t+1}{2}}^{n} \binom{n}{k} (1 - p)^k p^{n-k}.$$

---

[5] According to some sources, the number of juries in most Anglo-Saxon countries is 12, which comes from the number of apostles, see the heading "Jury" in the *Encyclopædia Britannica* (1911) (online).

10.6   Exercises

10.1 Calculate the second-order conditions of the manager maximization problem described in Section 10.1.

10.2 In the model described in the Section 10.3, assume that trade only occurs with probability r. Calculate the Nash equilibrium and explore its characteristics (see section 5.2 in Corchón, 2007). Complement this result with the discussion of the effects of transaction costs described in Jung et al. (1995).

10.3 Show that

$$\frac{\partial f_{n,t}(\gamma(1+\gamma))}{\partial p} = \frac{1}{(1+\gamma)^{n-1}} \sum_{k=\frac{n-t+1}{2}}^{n} \binom{n}{k}(k\gamma^{k-1} - (n-k)\gamma^k),$$

which is reduced to the following expression

$$\frac{\partial f_{n,t}(\gamma(1+\gamma))}{\partial p} = \frac{1}{(1+\gamma)^{n-1}} \binom{n}{\frac{n-t+1}{2}}\left(\frac{n-t+1}{2}\right)\gamma^{\frac{n-t-1}{2}}.$$

10.4 Use the result in Exercise 10.3 to prove that $-E_{n,t}^B(\gamma/(1+\gamma))$ is increasing in n.

10.5 Suppose that the persuasion function is just homogeneous of degree zero.
1. Show that if a Nash equilibrium in pure strategies exists, the ratio of expenses equals the ratio of valuations.
2. Show that nonnegativity of payoffs amounts to

$$1 \geq E_{n,t}^A\left(\frac{\gamma}{1+\gamma}\right)E_{g_A}^P(\gamma).$$

3. Check that this formula generalizes the one in the text because, when the persuasion function is of the Ratio Form,

$$E_{g_A}^P(\gamma) = \frac{1}{1+\gamma}.$$

10.6 Prove Proposition 10.3

10.7 Show that if $t = 0$, and $\gamma \leq 1.073$, maximal effort is obtained when $n = 5$.

10.8 Suppose that two contestants are fighting to obtain a contract of a value V. A jury with three members has to make the decision by majority voting on who gets the contract. Contestants have to make effort to convince the members of the jury. The probability of obtaining the vote of one member of the jury is given by the Ratio Form CSF.
(1) Write the probability of obtaining the contract.
(2) Suppose that the marginal cost of effort is constant and equal to 1. Write the payoffs.

(3)   Discuss the existence of a Nash equilibrium in pure strategies. Find the equilibrium.

(4)   Suppose now that one member of the jury will always vote in favor of contestant 1 no matter what. Write the probability of obtaining the contract in this case. Discuss the existence of a Nash equilibrium in pure strategies in this case.

11 Contests, Institutions, Wars, and Economic Success

This chapter primarily focuses on history, highlighting the significant role of rent-seeking in restraining economic growth. Section 11.1 presents a model that shows the basic trade-off between productive and unproductive (rent-seeking) activities. Section 11.2 explores how institutions can be undermined by rent-seeking activities that bias decision-making toward suboptimal alternatives and consume valuable resources. Furthermore, this erosion of institutions leads to a decline, or at best stagnation, in the standard of living of the society by diverting a significant portion of productive forces. Finally, Section 11.3 studies why armed conflicts occur and the way to prevent them. Two models of war are presented in which the armed conflict is produced by resource inequality, and recommendations are offered on how to prevent them. Specifically, a one-sided transfer of resources from wealthy to less developed countries may provide incentives for peace even in the absence of enforceable agreements.

11.1 Rent-Seeking and Economic Performance: The Basic Trade-off

In this section, we study the relationship between unproductive (rent-seeking) and productive activities. We start with a stylized model to highlight the basic principles. This model is a special case of the model explained in Section 9.3; several alternative contests, of Chapter 9.

Suppose that N identical agents have the opportunity to enter either a productive activity or a rent-seeking activity as in Krueger (1974) and Usher (1989). This implies that these agents do not need any special skill prior to entering any of these two activities. Let n^R be the number of agents choosing to rent-seek and $n^P = N - n^R$ the number of agents in productive activities. Once they have chosen roles, they have to compete with the other agents that have chosen the same activity. We are not going to be specific about this competition, but just to assume that agents in the productive activity obtain a payoff of U^P each. And rent-seeking agents obtain U^R. We are implicitly assuming that in the competition stage, there is a unique symmetric equilibrium yielding a unique payoff. Now assume that payoffs depend negatively on the number of agents inside each activity. We have seen that this happens with many CSFs. In fact, in Chapter 2 we saw a related property, rent-dissipation. Here we do not assume that payoffs go to zero when the number of contestants goes to infinity but that $U^R = R(n^R)$, where R is a strictly decreasing function. The reader can check that this

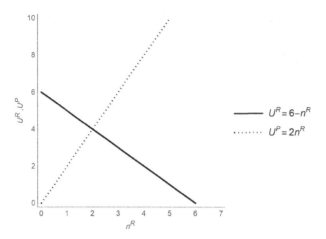

Figure 11.1 Payoffs of productive and rent-seeking agents

happens in most of the CSFs discussed in Chapter 2, see Exercise 11.1. Analogously, in the productive sector, we assume that $U^P = P(n^P) = P(N - n^R)$, where P is a strictly decreasing function. In models of oligopolistic competition, this property is called *Quasi-competitiveness* (for an explanation, see figure 2 and the subsequent comments in Corchón, 2021). Since P is strictly decreasing on $N - n^R$, P is strictly increasing in n^R, i.e., the larger rent-seekers are, the smaller the competition in the productive sector and the larger payoffs there. We assume free entry in both activities. For agents in the rent-seeking sector to be happy with their choice, it must be that $R(n^R) \geq P(N - n^R + 1)$, i.e., what they obtain by rent-seeking yields no less that what they can obtain by switching to productive activities. The same holds for agents in productive activities, namely $P(N - n^R) \geq R(n^R + 1)$. Forgetting for a moment that n^R is a natural number and assuming that n^R could be a real number, we have two equations $R(n^R)$, decreasing in n^R, and $P(N - n^R)$, increasing in n^R. There is an equilibrium when they intersect. In Figure 11.1, $U^R = 6 - n^R$ and $U^P = 2n^R$. Hence, in equilibrium $n^R = 2$ and $n^P = 4$. This is exactly as supply and demand match.

Once we have understood the basics, it is time to ask some questions. What if $U^P = 8 + 2n^R$? In this case, no agent would be a rent seeker, since to be productive yields more payoff than the alternative for all values of n^R. What if $U^P = \max\{0, -20 + 2n^R\}$? This case is the opposite; to be a productive agent does not pay, no matter what.[1] Another possible problem arises when the curves meet at a value of n^R larger than N, e.g., if $U^P = n^R$ the intersection is at $n^R = 3$, but $N = 2$. In this case, equilibrium is again in the boundary and at $n^R = 2$ with no one in the productive sector. When we insist in n^R being a natural, not a real number, we have a ladder going

---

[1] These two alternatives correspond in the case of supply and demand to an equilibrium with zero transactions and an equilibrium with zero price, respectively.

up and another ladder going down instead of continuous curves. Their intersection is the equilibrium whose existence was proved in Proposition 9.5.[2]

What we take home from here is that rent-seeking and productive activities are substitutes. And that a strong rent-seeking sector is not only a waste by itself, but the opportunity cost of rent-seeking can be very high indeed. We will delve into this topic in the next section.

To end this section, we invite the reader to solve Exercises 11.3 and 11.4 that present basic models of rent-seeking versus productive activities. In Exercise 11.3 the productive activity yields a constant return, for instance determined internationally. In Exercise 11.4 payoffs in the productive sector depend positively on n^P.

11.2   Why Some Countries Succeed While Others Do not

The United Kingdom was the dominant power on earth in much of the nineteenth century and the first three decades of the twentieth century. It is indisputable that this dominance was due to the fact that England was the nation that initiated the Industrial Revolution starting in the mid-eighteenth century. The question is why such a paramount event occurred in a relatively remote island and not in India or China that at this time were wealthier countries than England, or in other European colonial powers.

In a famous article, North and Weingast (1989) offered an answer. They compared the English monarchy after and before the Glorious Revolution in 1688. Recall that this revolution abolished the absolute monarchy and started a parliamentary monarchy.[3] They characterized the former in not very flattering terms: Under absolute monarchy "the sovereign will alter property rights for his ... own benefit" (North and Weingast, 1989, p. 803). In particular, the sovereign levied taxes unapproved by the Parliament, unpaid some loans, conferred monopoly and peerage (for a price, of course), and used purveyance at will.[4] In brief, theft all over the place. And problems did not end there. The actions of the king fostered rent-seeking activities that, as we have seen, diverted potentially useful talents away from productive business. Under the Parliament rule established in 1680, dominated by "wealth holders, its increased role markedly reduced the king's ability to renege" (p. 804). On the contrary, other countries "faced no such constraint, such as early modern Spain, created economic conditions that retarded long-run economic growth" (p. 808). You can add to the latter category Portugal and the Ottoman Empire, among the wealthiest nations in 1500 but not in 1700.

The contribution by North and Weingast (1989) has been immensely influential because it motivated economists to think about the role of institutions in the develop-

---

[2] Many papers implicitly or explicitly assume that N is very large and dismiss the integer problem, since the real number found at the intersection of the curves is a good approximation for a natural number.

[3] Parliaments existed during the late Middle Ages, starting in 1188 in the Kingdom of Leon, Spain.

[4] Purveyance was the right of the monarch to buy equipment (carriages, ships, food, etc.) from the private sector at prices set by the sovereign.

ment of nations. Acemoglu and Robinson have published a number of very influential papers on this topic that expanded and qualify these early conjectures (see Acemoglu, 2009). For instance, when Europeans colonized territories, they faced a choice between establishing permanent settlements or extracting wherever natural resources they possibly could.[5] Establishing settlements involved the creation of robust institutions, whereas extraction did not require such infrastructure. This decision was influenced by the prevalence of diseases that Europeans had little resistance to, leading them to settle and build strong institutions in areas with lower disease risks. Acemoglu, Johnson, and Robinson (2001) found that, after controlling for the impact of institutions, countries in Africa located near the equator, which were more susceptible to epidemic diseases and therefore more likely to have been subjected to extractive practices, did not have lower per capita incomes than other regions.

Another example that illustrates the importance of institutions is Korea, which was a relatively homogenous and impoverished country before being divided into North and South. Currently, the North is governed by a communist elite and remains one of the poorest countries on the planet, while the South, which is a parliamentary democracy, has become one of the wealthiest (Acemoglu and Robinson, 2012).

An identical observation can be made about Cuba and Spain, the former being richer than Spain until its government was taken over by the communist party.[6] Today, Spanish per capita GDP is almost three times that of Cuba.[7]

Acemoglu and Johnson (2005) distinguish between "property rights institutions," which protect citizens against indiscriminate expropriation, and "contracting institutions," which enable private contracts between citizens. Their empirical analysis shows that the former play a more important role than the latter.

Given that institutions are ruled by laws enacted by parliaments (democratically elected or not), it seems sensible to study how parliaments work and who populate them. Recall that, according to North and Weingast (1989), the dividing line between the old and the new England was drawn by the 1688 revolution, which established the preeminence of a parliament dominated by wealth holders over the unrestricted wishes of the king.

A natural question to ask is why the Parliament would not proceed to act just like the king. Would the removal of a corrupt leader have cleansing effects? It is possible, but there are other answers. Ekelund and Tollinson (1981) point out that the English parliament was composed of about 210 members and that coordination among them to push the actions that will bring the desired rents became hard. We will come back to this point at the end of this section. Tullock (1988) points out that those in charge of implementing the law, judges, were elected from among prominent local people who

---

[5] The latter gives rise to the curse of natural resources, namely weak and corrupt institutions and long-run stagnation, see Ploeg (2011).

[6] One of the authors of this book endured childhood in Spain (1950s) very different from the country that it is now. He recalls his mother – a high school teacher – making soap at home because it was not easy to obtain this good in the market. About the same time, the brother of a colleague suffered a permanent disability from a shot of impure penicillin obtained by his father – a high-ranking military – in the black market.

[7] But a sizable part of Korean and Spanish growth was achieved under military dictatorships.

had little incentive to punish those locals who defied monopoly laws selling goods at cheaper prices. So, it was not the parliament, but the implementation of the policies enacted by the parliament the item that prevented rent-seeking.

Buchanan and Tullock (1962) and Olson (1982) qualify the North and Weingast argument.[8] The former contribution describes all sorts of tricks by means of which representatives lumber the American tax payer with useless projects. Famous is the concept of "logrolling," where a coalition of politicians team up to construct a bill – that mixes a bridge in a state in the Pacific coast with an airport in the Midwest and a tunnel in an Atlantic city. Such a mixture satisfies a decisive majority of congressmen … and disappoint the taxpayer. Olson (1982), as we explained in Chapter 4, put the blame of the relative stagnation of the winners of World War II – especially Britain – with respect to the losers – Germany and Japan – to the fact that their rent-seeking rings were not disbanded after the war. Losers of war, especially Germany and Japan, disbanded such rings so that they were less affected by rent-seeking and thus grew faster.[9]

At this point, it may be useful to bring to the field the two most powerful weapons in our arsenal: data and economic theory. Let us start with data on taxes. Did parliaments under democracy set lower taxes than under previous absolutist regimes? The answer is, not at all. "Panel regressions indicate that centralized and limited regimes were associated with significant increases in per capita revenues relative to fragmented and absolutist ones" (see Dincecco, 2009, p. 48). This study covers France, England, Austria-Hungary, Prussia, and Spain. In particular, per capita public revenue in Britain multiplied by 4 between 1680 and 1780. The fact that taxes were more democratically voted in 1780 than in 1680 is of no consolation if the argument against absolute monarchy was based on the size of taxation.

Glaezer, et al. (2004) review the existing empirical evidence and note the low impact of institutions per se, but the high impact of policies. They propose a triad "Education→Policies→Institutions" that, according to their study, fit the data better. So, first countries become educated, then they implement successful economic policies and, finally, they build strong institutions. Examples of the link between economic policies and growth abound. A capitalist nondemocratic country, Spain (1940–1959 vs. 1960–1974), a socialist democratic country, India (1950–1992 vs. 1993–2015), and a socialist nondemocratic country, China, (1950–1975 vs. 1976–2015), experienced no institutional change but dramatically altered their growth rates when markets became liberalized. In these three cases, the *policies* pursued in the contrasting periods were very different but the basic institutions remained the same.

---

[8] After all, it can be argued that because absolute kings are the sole owners of everybody and everything in a country, they have clear incentives to maintain it in good shape. Of course, there are all sorts of reasons why this argument fails – informational problems, impossibility to micromanage a large kingdom, etc.

[9] But this argument cannot explain why two countries with notoriously bad institutions like Germany and Japan, before World War II, were able to develop a high-quality industry whose military output was of the finest quality.

The previous discussion suggests that the relationship between institutions, policies, and economic performance is not as direct as North and Weingast (1989) thought.[10] Let us now see what the theory may suggest to us.[11]

Suppose N agents who can be either rent-seekers or entrepreneurs. There is a king, later a parliament, who decides the tax rate on the output of productive agents. Taxes raised will be used entirely to create a prize that will attract rent-seekers. You can think of a duchy that will be awarded to one of the rent-seekers. The game has three stages. First, agents decide occupation, then the king/parliament decides the tax rate and finally production and rent-seeking take place.

The productive sector produces corn that will be consumed entirely by workers. Workers supply labor – assumed to be the numeraire – to produce corn. The representative worker has a utility function $U = Ax - x^2/2 + l$ where x is the consumption of corn and l is leisure. His budget constraint is $(p + t)x + l = L$ where p is the price of corn, t is the tax rate on corn, and L is the labor endowment. Plugging the budget constraint into the utility function we obtain $U = Ax - x^2/2 + L - (p+t)x$. Since the second-order conditions hold, the first-order conditions of utility maximization yield the inverse demand function

$$p = A - t - x.$$

Suppose that m agents become producers (the value of m will be determined in equilibrium). The marginal cost of producing corn is constant and denoted by c. We can think of an economy in which land is abundant and freely accessible. Letting $a \equiv A - c$ each producer has a profit function

$$\pi_i = (a - t - x)x_i.$$

In a Cournot equilibrium,

$$x^* = \frac{(a-t)m}{m+1}; \quad \pi_i^* = \left(\frac{a-t}{m+1}\right)^2.$$

Profits are spent in labor services.

The king provides a duchy that is valued by n rent seekers at V. The prize is produced from taxes collected, i.e., $V = tx$. Each rent-seeker supply favors, g_i, with unit marginal cost. Payoffs of rent-seekers are

$$\frac{g_i}{\sum_{j=1}^n g_j} V - g_i.$$

In equilibrium, each rent-seeker gets V/n^2, and total expenses are $g = \sum_{j=1}^n g_j = V(n-1)/n$.

---

[10] In this discussion, we have set aside other factors that influence economic performance, like military strength and religion, the latter being emphasized by Max Weber (1864–1920).

[11] This model is a simplification of Corchón (2008). Other models in this vein are Acemoglu (1995), Gradstein (2004), Grossman (1991), Hausken (2005), and Murphy, Shleifer, and Vishny (1991).

Finally, the king chooses t to maximize rent-seekers expenses, g, subject to $V = tx$. Which is equivalent to the king maximizing tx, i.e.,

$$t \frac{(a - t)m}{m + 1}$$

which yields $t^* = a/2$. We plug the value of this "optimal" tax into V and profits of producers to find the corresponding values.

Let us find equilibrium under absolute monarchy. Equalization of payoffs between rent-seekers and producers yields

$$\left(\frac{a - t}{m + 1} \right)^2 = \frac{V}{n^2} = \frac{tx}{n^2}. \tag{11.1}$$

Solving this equation for $t^* = a/2$, we obtain the equilibrium number of rent-seekers.

$$n^* = \frac{N^2 + N}{2N + 1}.$$

Check that $n^* < N$ and $n^* > N/2$. The later inequality will be recalled later on. See Exercise 11.5 for the consideration of n as a natural number.

Next, let us find equilibria under parliament rule. We assume that parliament is composed of producers and rent-seekers or their representatives. They vote on the tax rate. There is always an equilibrium with $n^* = 0$, so nobody is a rent-seeker and the parliament votes $t = 0$ because taxes in this model only finance rent-seeking expenses. But, as we saw in (11.1), $n^* > N/2$, thus, there is another equilibrium in which rent-seekers command a majority in the parliament and they vote a tax rate identical to the one under absolute monarchy and ... "to the winner the spoils."

This simple model warns us against the belief that democratic institutions will take care of rent-seeking and they will foster a healthy economy. Democratic institutions appear more like a necessary rather than a sufficient condition for rent-seeking to be kept to a minimum and for a good economic performance.[12] And they might explain why certain countries like the United Kingdom or France are still strong after losing their empires but others like Spain or Turkey did not (another factor might be that empires of the United Kingdom and France lasted less than the empires of Spain and Turkey). Finally, there is ample evidence of "failed democracies" around the world.

Moreover, the recent rise of China as an economic superpower spreads doubts on such necessity.[13] Milanovic (2019) presents a group of 11 countries (including China, Vietnam, and others) which in the period 1990–2016 were one-party regimes with high levels of corruption (that in our model may be identified with rent-seeking) but produced 21% of world output in 2016 while the same countries produced 5.5% of world output in 1990 (see Milanovic, 2019, pp. 96–97).

What to take home from this section? First, thanks to the contributions of the authors quoted above we now understand much better the process of development

---

[12] Income is also an important determinant of corruption in democracies, see Jetter, Agudelo, and Hassan (2015).

[13] Especially if we compare China's performance in the first two decades of the twenty-first century with neighboring democratic India.

that took the world extreme poverty from a 76% in 1820 to a 10% in 2018 (Moatsos, 2021). Second, we agree on the basic causes of such development: Good democratic institutions, good public policies, education, and peace (see Section 11.3). Third, we disagree on the weights of these factors. More research is necessary!

11.3   War

Historically, war, other than a big calamity, has been the greatest land and resource allocator.[14] Countries have been shaped by their performance in the battlefields, expanding and contracting along with each success and failure of their respective armies.[15] Wars have long-term consequences. Prados de la Escosura and Rodríguez-Caballero (2022) find that pandemics and twentieth-century World Wars are the most influential structural breaks that conditioned long-run growth in European history. Milanovic (2019) writes, "The Great War significantly changed the trajectory of world history.... It caused the communist revolution ... produced ... in its continuation WWII, the rise of the US to a position of global hegemony and accelerated the process of decolonization." With respect to the latter, Arteaga (2022) finds the roots of political fragmentation of the eighteenth-century Spanish empire in the disruption of sea communications caused by the rising power of the Royal Navy.

In this section, we will study several models of war and will be attentive to the lessons provided by these models. How to stop war will be our primary concern.

First of all, let us define our subject. By war we mean a violent conflict, and it includes civil war, revolutions, etc. War has been analyzed both in the East and in the West by distinguished scholars like Sun Tzu (about sixth or fifth century BC) and Machiavelli (1469–1527), among many others. Special mention is due to a Prussian officer Carl von Clausewitz (1780–1831), who defined war as "A mere continuation of policy by other means" (Clausewitz, 1832).[16] He acknowledged the game-theoretical nature of war, "war is akin to a card game" (Chapter 1). In modern parlance, war is a risky, but potentially very profitable, asset. But the reader is warned that the reasons for war are many: religion, revenge, ethnic cleansing, or simply human nature (see Jackson and Morelli, 2011). By focusing on rational agents and keeping away emotions, as we do here, we are simplifying the picture, perhaps too much, see Exercise 11.6.[17]

---

[14] War also has played an important role in fostering new technology; see Hoffman (2012).

[15] But as a source of country prosperity, war has consistently shown a lack of success. Thus, Italy, Japan, and Germany are now richer than envisioned in their wildest dreams by their authoritarian leaders in the 1930s. And this was achieved without any invasion, colony, or dominant political status, but thanks to the ingenuity and hard work of Italian, Japanese, and German people working in a democratic environment.

[16] The book was posthumously edited, corrected, and taken to the print by his widow Marie von Brühl, a well-educated Prussian aristocrat. More details on Clausewicz's life are provided in Beviá and Corchón (2009).

[17] Wars also occur in the animal kingdom. Jane Goodall (2010) was dismayed when she watched a war between two tribes of chimpanzees. And ants and fungi play arms races, see www.science.org/content/article/arms-race-between-ants-and-fungi-has-echoes-last-us.

Given the highly destructive nature of war, the immediate question is why rational actors do not settle on a resource distribution that avoids war costs and benefits both parties. One initial response is that the resource in question might be indivisible. While a lottery could offer a potential solution in such cases, it remains uncertain whether the losing party would accept an unfavorable draw. Consequently, we turn our attention to the traditional reasons for the failure of the Coase theorem.

Failures of the Coase theorem are clustered under the portmanteau of "transaction costs" but can be divided into, basically, two categories: information asymmetries and commitment problems (see Fearon, 1995).

For the first count, Myerson and Satterthwaite (1983) showed that there is no trading mechanism that yields outcomes that are efficient, individually rational, and compatible with the incentives of agents when they are only probabilistically informed on each other's preferences. A result with a similar flavor related to war was provided by Brito and Intriligator (1985) and Corchón and Yildizparlak (2013).

Commitment problems arise when there is no guarantee that the agreed-upon outcome, although signed, will be respected by the contestants. This is especially relevant in international conflicts in which, despite the efforts of the United Nations, lack of enforcement plays an important role. The same can be said about revolutions.

In this section, we will focus attention on wars caused by the impossibility of writing a binding contract among the interested (and greedy) parties. See Baliga and Sjöström (2023) for a thorough survey on the causes of war that, in addition to the previously mentioned reasons, includes coalitions.

Jackson and Morelli (2007) worked out a simple model of no commitment in which those suffering war are not necessarily those deciding about it. They called this situation political bias. Suppose two identical countries with military resources w each. These resources are completely spent in case of war. These countries might (or not) fight about a resource of value V. If there is war, each country wins with 0.5 probability. Thus, the expected payoff for a country in war is $0.5V - w$. Under peace, they get w each. For war to be the best option, it must be that $0.5V - w \geq w$, or $V \geq 4w$. In this case, war can arise if the value of the resource is sufficiently large. Now suppose that war is decided by a clique for whom costs and benefits of war are different from those considered before. Decision-making agents can secure a fraction α of the spoils of war but have to pay a fraction β of the cost of the military resource. Then, war arises if and only if

$$0.5V\alpha - \beta w > \beta w \Leftrightarrow 5\alpha V > 2\beta w \Leftrightarrow V > 4w\frac{\beta}{\alpha}.$$

And now war is possible for relatively small values of the contested resource whenever β is small. The interested reader can find variations and extensions of this result in the original paper. In Exercise 11.7, we present another simple model of war in which dispossessing a third agent of her belongings might trigger war.

Having shown that war is indeed a theoretical possibility, let us consider more thorough models.

11.3.1   War as a Contest

The model presented above makes a number of simplifications to make the point. One of those is assuming that resources for war are given. It is true that at the moment when war is declared, armies are what they are, but unless the war ends very quickly, new armies can be raised, and in general, it is not a good assumption to assume that a country with a small or depleted army will not raise new resources. In 1941 the armies of the USSR and the United States were relatively small and ineffective, but both countries overcame initial defeats and managed to crush their enemies by numbers (and technology). So let us start with a model in which resources poured into war are a decision variable.

We face the following paradox. Suppose both countries choose peace. Then there is no need to have an army. But if one of the agents raises a small army, it can conquer the contended resource! Modeling war as a one-shot contest yields too much power to countries initiating war. This suggests that war must be modeled as a game with several stages.

Suppose that in the first stage, agents can declare war or not. To declare war is not necessarily a formal declaration of such. But it must be understood as an act that, as the famous line says, "of course you realize that this means war." It could be an invasion, like the Nazi invasion of the USSR; an attack, like the infamous Pearl Harbor bombing; or the killing of a leader, like the assassination of the Archduke Franz Ferdinand of Austria and his wife, which triggered World War I.[18] The recent war in Ukraine is another example of what we mean here. If just one of the agents declares war, in the second period, agents rise armies (make efforts) and there is war. If both choose peace, peace prevails in the second period. By simplicity, war is modeled as a canonical contest in which just one side wins. A more complete scenario would allow for the possibility of a draw like the Korean War (1950–1953) or the Iran–Iraq War (1980–1988).

Suppose that two agents – countries, social classes – may fight for a resource of value V of which they initially own εV and $(1 - \varepsilon)V$, respectively. If peace prevails in the second period, they end up with their initial resources. The CSF is the weighted Ratio Form,

$$p_1(\mathbf{g}) = \frac{g_1}{g_1 + \theta g_2} \quad \text{and} \quad p_2(\mathbf{g}) = \frac{\theta g_2}{g_1 + \theta g_2},$$

where $\theta \in (0, \infty)$ is the relative efficiency of country 2 in war. This may be caused by previous investment of contestants that we take as given (see Schaller and Skaperdas, 2020 for a model of how these investments are chosen). Both countries are risk-neutral. In case of war, their payoffs are

$$\pi_1(\mathbf{g}) = \frac{g_1}{g_1 + \theta g_2}V - g_1 \quad \text{and} \quad \pi_2(\mathbf{g}) = \frac{\theta g_2}{g_1 + \theta g_2}V - g_2, \qquad (11.2)$$

---

[18] These acts were preceded by a general animosity and arms races of the countries concerned. These can be understood as the stored explosives and the actual attacks as lighting the wick that caused the subsequent explosion.

the first-order conditions of payoff maximization yield

$$\frac{\partial \pi_1}{\partial g_1} = \frac{\theta g_2}{(g_1 + \theta g_2)^2} V - 1 = 0 = \frac{\theta g_1}{(g_1 + \theta g_2)^2} V - 1 = \frac{\partial \pi_2}{\partial g_2}. \qquad (11.3)$$

As usual, these conditions are also sufficient. Note that (11.3) implies

$$g_1 = g_2,$$

and equilibrium war efforts are

$$g_1^W = \frac{V\theta}{(1+\theta)^2} = g_2^W. \qquad (11.4)$$

This model assumes that war resources are not constrained. For a model in which war resources are constrained, see Exercise 11.8. Substituting expressions (11.4) in (11.2), we obtain the equilibrium payoff for each country in case of war:

$$\pi_1(\mathbf{g}^W) = \frac{V}{(1+\theta)^2} \; ; \; \pi_2(\mathbf{g}^W) = \frac{V\theta^2}{(1+\theta)^2}.$$

For country 1 to be peaceful, it must be that

$$\pi_1(\mathbf{g}^W) = \frac{1}{(1+\theta)^2} V \leq \varepsilon V \Leftrightarrow \frac{1}{(1+\theta)^2} \leq \varepsilon. \qquad (11.5)$$

Performing a similar calculation for the second country,

$$\varepsilon \leq \frac{1+2\theta}{(1+\theta)^2}. \qquad (11.6)$$

Then, peace is achieved if

$$\frac{1}{(1+\theta)^2} \leq \varepsilon \leq \frac{1+2\theta}{(1+\theta)^2}.$$

So we have the following result.

PROPOSITION 11.1 *Under complete information, there is always a set of initial divisions of the resource where peace is the unique equilibrium. In particular, equal division yields peace.*

In Figure 11.2, the area between the two curves is the area in which peace prevails. We see for any given θ, there is an ε that yields peace. And that asymmetries, either in initial endowments or in war efficiency, are bad for peace. In particular, if ε is small, the poor country 1 will find war appealing. And if ε is close to one, country 2 – now the poor one – will face the same choice. This reminds one of the famous dictum "proletarians got nothing to lose except their chains" (Marx and Engels, 1848). Another implication is that poor agents may use conflict to increase their share. This was first pointed out by Hirshleifer (1991) who termed it "The Paradox of Power."

Now consider that, before the game is played, the rich country might make a transfer to the poor one. This transfer is unilateral and does not imply any agreement

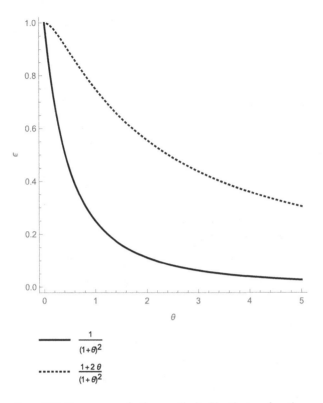

Figure 11.2 Peace occurs in the area limited by the two functions

between parties. The idea is that by making the rich less rich and the poor less poor, incentives for the latter to start a war wane. On the one hand, if the poor loses the war, they will end up with much less than under peace. And if they wins, the spoils of war will be less than before because a part of the riches was already transferred to the poor. Thus, by transferring part of its resources, the rich country induces the peaceful behavior of the poor country; see Jackson and Morelli (2007). Beviá and Corchón (2010) document historical instances of this mechanism.[19] Let us see how it works.

Let T be the net transfer paid by country 1 and received by country 2. From (11.5) and (11.6), we obtain that

$$\frac{V}{(1+\theta)^2} \leq \varepsilon V - T \; ; \; \frac{\theta^2 V}{(1+\theta)^2} \leq (1-\varepsilon)V + T.$$

Solving for T

$$\frac{\theta^2 V}{(1+\theta)^2} - (1-\varepsilon)V \leq T \leq \varepsilon V - \frac{V}{(1+\theta)^2}. \qquad (11.7)$$

---

[19] For instance, Bismarck introduced social security in Germany with the goal of achieving peace with trade unions.

To find the suitable transfer, all we need is that the left-hand side be less than the right-hand side in (11.7), or equivalently,

$$\frac{\theta^2 + 1}{(1 + \theta)^2} \leq 1,$$

which is always true! Thus, peace can always be achieved. To see that this is a happy coincidence because there are models in which peace cannot be achieved when the poor are very poor, see Exercise 11.8. Another interesting robustness exercise looks at this problem when the order of moves is reversed and war may be more or less destructive, see Exercise 11.11.

We end this section by sketching how asymmetric information may trigger war. It is based on Corchón and Yildizparlak (2013). Suppose that strength θ can be high or low. Contestant 2 is informed of his own strength, but contestant 1 has just a probability distribution on the strength of its rival. In a pooling equilibrium (see Fudenberg and Tirole, 1991, chapter 8), the low type fakes the high type and demands a big share of the pie. But if he is a low type, with high probability the uninformed contestant might prefer war. This reasoning might help to explain apparently irrational war declarations like bombing Pearl Harbor or the Nazi attack on USSR. In both cases, aggressors thought that the other country had too many resources and too little army to defend them. But despite their belief that the United States was ravaged by the great depression and USSR by Stalinist purges, both countries retained a strong industrial and technological basis that allowed them to win the war.

11.3.2 War on Several Fronts

The previous model hides the fact that, often, war involves several fronts. Thus, in both World Wars, Germany had to fight east and west. And in World War II, the United States fought on the European and the Pacific front. In these circumstances, success in war depends on success on the fronts. The mathematician Èmile Borel (1871–1956) introduced as early as 1921 a game (later called Colonel Blotto) in which two players with a fixed resource place it in several locations interpreted as fronts.[20] He assumed that within each battlefield the player that allocates the higher resource wins the battlefield, i.e., what we call the All Pay Auction. Borel proved that any symmetric two-person zero-sum game where each player has three undominated strategies has an equilibrium in mixed strategies.[21] Roberson (2006) solved the game for the general case and provided a survey of the literature. When the endowment is allocated in expectation, we have Colonel Lotto games; see Kovenock and Roberson (2020). And when the result of each battle is decided by the relative forces allocated in each battlefield, there is an equilibrium in pure strategies; see Li and Zheng (2022).

It is clear that no equilibrium exists in pure strategies because of the All Pay Auction nature of the local battles. The characterization of the equilibrium probability

---

[20] Borel was motivated by the belief that understanding the causes of war would avoid conflicts like World War I. We share his belief and this section is written in this spirit.

[21] For a history of the origins of game theory, see Myerson (2021).

distribution is very technical and outside the scope of this book. Friedman (1958) solved the game with a Ratio Form CSF with asymmetric valuations on winning local battles but symmetric between contestants, while Li and Zheng (2022) considered fully asymmetric valuations and heterogeneous rules for different contests. They also provided a survey of this literature, see table 1 in their paper.

Equilibrium predictions fare well in experiments: "In the auction treatment ... disadvantaged players use a 'guerilla warfare' strategy that stochastically allocates zero resources to a subset of battlefields. Advantaged players employ a 'stochastic complete coverage' strategy, allocating random, but positive, resource levels across the battlefields. In the lottery (ratio) treatment, both players divide their resources equally across all battlefields" (Chowdhury, Kovenock, and Sheremeta, 2013, p. 997). The assumption that one more unit wins the battle in its front is, of course, extreme in the war application. But it is well grounded when each front is interpreted as an electoral district.

A different approach was taken by Franke and Öztürk (2015). They assume a network structure with local conflicts. They show that if a conflict network is star-shaped, a peaceful resolution of a local conflict leads to a decrease in the overall level of conflict in the network. Unfortunately, this result is not true in general conflict networks, see Exercise 11.9. This is because if a conflict is solved, for instance in World War I Russia sued for peace with Germany in 1918, the resources spent in the defunct conflict can be used to revitalize other conflicts as imperial Germany did with the 1918 spring offensive in the western front. And this may trigger more war expenses for other contestants.

Another branch of the literature distinguishes between attack and defence. This literature and the experimental evidence is summarized in Chowdhury (2019), see Exercise 11.10. A general survey on war and conflict using experiments and data broadly confirms the predictions of the theory (see Kimbrough, Laughren, and Sheremeta, 2015).

11.3.3   A Dynamic Model of War

The order of moves that we assume can be criticized because it presumes that once countries have not declared war they cannot perform a surprise attack in the second stage. For instance, Garfinkel and Skaperdas (2000) assume that in the first stage agents decide the army size and in the second they decide if they wage war or not.[22] This kind of models are reviewed in Baliga and Sjöström (2013). In this section, we develop an infinite horizon model in which an attack can be anticipated at any moment.

Suppose there are two contestants that live forever. Both discount the future at a rate $\delta \in (0,1)$. Under peace, they enjoy utilities of V_i, $i \in \{1,2\}$, in each period. So perpetual peace yields discounted utilities of $V_i/(1-\delta)$, $i \in \{1,2\}$.

---

[22] And that once this period is over, agents play again in the future. This model also emphasizes the importance of the future when making decisions about war or peace.

At the beginning of every period, one of the countries (or both) may start a war that lasts one period and determines an owner of aggregate resources forever, i.e., $V_1 + V_2 \equiv V$. The loser gets zero forever. Instead of modeling war, we will simply assume that contestant 1 wins with probability q. Thus contestant 2 wins with probability $1 - q$. During war, contestants obtain utilities of W_i, $i \in \{1, 2\}$. These numbers may be derived from the models solved in previous chapters. The losing nation disappears.

War yields the following expected payoffs

$$W_1 + \delta \frac{qV}{1-\delta} \quad \text{and} \quad W_2 + \delta \frac{(1-q)V}{1-\delta}.$$

Perpetual peace can be achieved if no contestant has incentives to go to war, namely

$$\frac{V_1}{1-\delta} \geq W_1 + \delta \frac{qV}{1-\delta};$$
$$\frac{V_2}{1-\delta} \geq W_2 + \delta \frac{(1-q)V}{1-\delta}.$$

Multiplying by $1 - \delta$, the previous inequalities are

$$V_1 \geq W_1(1 - \delta) + \delta qV; \tag{11.8}$$
$$V_2 \geq W_2(1 - \delta) + \delta(1 - q)V. \tag{11.9}$$

When δ is close to one, what happens during war is irrelevant because it is overwhelmed by the infinity stream of utility. Then, inequalities (11.8) and (11.9) become

$$V_1 \geq \frac{qV_2}{1-q};$$
$$V_2 \geq \frac{(1-q)V_1}{q}.$$

Hence, we have that perpetual peace can be achieved if and only if

$$\frac{1-q}{q} \geq \frac{V_2}{V_1} \geq \frac{1-q}{q}. \tag{11.10}$$

In this case, peace is practically impossible except when the ratio of one-period utilities under peace equals the ratio of winning probabilities.

To explore further possibilities when δ is not close to one, assume that $W_i = \alpha V_i$, i.e., utilities during war are a fraction of utilities during peace. And let $\beta = V_2/V_1$. Then (11.8) and (11.9) can be written as

$$1 \geq \alpha(1 - \delta) + \delta q(1 + \beta);$$
$$1 \geq \alpha(1 - \delta) + \delta(1 - q)\left(1 + \frac{1}{\beta}\right).$$

We will see that the main insights of the previous section are still valid.

Under Tullock CSF, $q = 1/(1 + \beta)$, and in this case, incentives to war are identical to both contestants.

Also rearranging these two equations, we obtain

$$\frac{1 - \alpha(1 - \delta) - \delta q}{\delta q} \geq \beta \geq \frac{\delta(1 - q)}{1 - \alpha(1 - \delta) - \delta(1 - q)}. \tag{11.11}$$

Peace requires certain bounds in the distribution of initial resources. For instance, suppose $\alpha = 0$ (i.e., war is very destructive) and $\delta = q = 0.5$; in this case, (11.11) requires $3 \geq \beta \geq 1/3$. Again we see that inequality in resources is bad for peace.

11.4   Exercises

11.1   Check that all the CSFs presented in Chapter 2 except the All Pay Auction yield games in which Nash equilibrium payoffs are strictly decreasing in the number of contestants.

11.2   Suppose N contestants can enter into one of two contests with prizes V_1 and V_2, yielding payoffs of V_i / n_i^2, where n_i is the number of contestants in contest $i \in \{1, 2\}$ and V_i is the prize in contest i. Construct the interval in which the equilibrium number of contestants must lie.

11.3   In the framework of Section 11.1, suppose the productive activity yields a constant return of ρ. The rent-seeking contest is played with contestants facing a Ratio Form CSF.
(1)   Find the number of contestants for which payoffs in each activity are identical.
(2)   Derive and interpret the conditions under which this number is larger than one and less than N.
(3)   Suppose the productive activity consists in the extraction of a natural resource. Check that if a positive shock increases the supply of the natural resource, rent-seeking is fostered. This is a simple model of the "Dutch disease"(see Baland and Francoise, 2000; Torvik, 2002).

11.4   In the framework of Section 11.1, suppose that the rent-seeking contest is played with a Ratio Form CSF. The productive sector is composed of agents that take the market price as given and extract a unit of a natural resource which is sold to in the market. The inverse demand function is $p = A/(N - n)$, where $N - n$ represents supply.
(1)   Show that the number of rent-seekers that equalizes returns is

$$n^* = \frac{-V + \sqrt{V^2 + 4AVN}}{2A}.$$

(2)   Show that n^* depends positively on V and N and negatively on A.
(3)   Show that $n \in [1, N - 1]$ if and only if $N - 1 \geq \max\{A/V, \sqrt{V/A}\}$.

11.5 In the framework of Section 11.2, find the equilibrium number of rent-seekers under absolute monarchy when this number is bound to be an integer.

11.6 Discuss the economic reasons behind the following wars: Punic Wars (264–146 BC), Germanic invasions of Roman Empire (400–476), Opium War (1839–1842), US Civil War (1861–1865), World Wars I (1914–1918) and II (1939–1945).

11.7 (Based on Rosenberg, 2020) There are three agents: Local Government (LA), Opposition (guerrilla) (OG), and a Foreign actor (FA). The latter could be a multinational or a foreign power. They fight for a resource valued in V. Suppose that LA and FA bargain about how to share the resource. The outcome of the bargaining is V_L and V_F, with $V_L + V_F = V$ (this outcome becomes the status quo). Now OG has the opportunity to start a guerrilla war and obtain αV_L at a total cost of C. Derive conditions under which OG will start a guerrilla war if and only if FA is kicked out of the country and its share is now bargained between LA and OG. Discuss the applicability of this idea when FA are former European powers. Similarly when FA is a multinational firm owned by a foreign country.

11.8 Consider a model in which agents have a maximum amount of resources that they can pour into war, like in Beviá and Corchón (2010). Show that if the country with less resources is really poor, there are no transfers stopping war.

11.9 Give an example of a conflict network in which the resolution of a local conflict yields an increase in the overall level of conflict in the network (see example 2 in Franke and Öztürk, 2015).

11.10 In the Attack-Defence game in Chowdhury (2019), table 1, if you were the defender, would you choose the (mixed strategy) Nash equilibrium of this game or would you choose a more conservative strategy?

11.11 Consider a model where decisions about arming and the choice between war and peace are made simultaneously.
(1) Discuss the incentives for peace in such a model in relationship with the model explained in the main text.
(2) Discuss how the introduction of a different assumption on the destructiveness of war may reverse the incentives discussed in point 1 above. (See Garfinkel and Syropoulos, 2021.)

11.12 Discuss how feelings of revenge may cause peace (see Amegashie and Runkel, 2012). Discuss also how the intervention of an idealistic third party with peace as a goal may alter the outcomes under revenge and under no revenge. (See Mukherjee and Munshi, 2022.)

11.13 The Scramble for Africa was the invasion, annexation, and colonization of Africa by seven Western European powers between 1833 and 1914. This episode was in full swing by 1870, where 10% of Africa was under European control, with almost 90% by 1914. Assume that the conquest costs C and yields a constant return of I

for T periods. Assuming a constant discount of δ, find the condition under which imperialistic countries profited from such invasions.

11.14 Give historical examples in which an external threat has contributed significantly to the creation of social capital (see section 2 in Jennings and Sanchez-Pages, 2017).

12 Contests: Social Welfare and Public Policy

Economists have a dual vision of competitive systems. On the one hand, we look at the surface in which there is blood and tears of competing agents. On the other hand, we regard competitive systems as a way in which the desires of participants are – or are not – satisfied and to what extent. The first approach is equilibrium analysis where we study equilibrium and its properties. The second is welfare economics where we delve deeper to see how competition affects the welfare of competing individuals. After all, the goal of competitive systems is to fulfill the needs of the participants.

In this final chapter, we look at this issue from several angles. Are there contests that are "better" than others? And what is "better"? Can we design a contest that is optimal from the point of view of the welfare of the contestants? Or from the point of view of the welfare of a contest organizer? Or given a limited choice, say, among several alternative ways to run a contest, which one is better from a social point of view? And, can we say something about the policies that are currently implemented, such as compulsory education or affirmative action? These are the issues that we will address in subsequent sections.

12.1 Social Valuation of Contests

In the preceding chapters, we have assumed a given contest and explored its properties. The question that some contests may be more socially valuable than others arises naturally. This point of view requires a careful consideration of, at least, three issues.

(1) Do we consider efforts socially valuable?
(2) How do we compare two – or several – contests?
(3) How can we influence contests to make them more socially worthy?

Recall that, in the beginning, contests started by analyzing rent-seeking. Efforts there are pure waste. The same happens with other contests like war. If efforts are not socially valuable, the best would be to restrain the occurrence and the magnitude of such contests to a minimum. But in other cases, efforts can be valuable. Think of firms doing R&D, individuals fighting for a prize/contract, political parties competing for office, sports or architectural bureaus preparing original designs, etc. In all these cases, we like agents to exert effort because effort increases the quality of the project and/or the performance at the contest. In this chapter, we will assume that effort is valuable, which takes us to point 2.

There are several reasonable ways to ascertain the social value of efforts. The simplest would be to maximize total effort. Or if social merit is a function of effort – like in the Logit CSF in Chapter 2 – to maximize total merit. In sports you may appraise the efforts of all competitors because this yields a more enjoyable show. We call these kind of contests *Aggregate Merit* contests. Or perhaps society just cares about the average merit. We call these kinds of contests *Average Merit* contests. Another possibility would be to consider just the merit of the (expected) winner. In architectural contests or in R&D you mainly care about the winning project. We call these kind of contests *Quality* contests. These three criteria require a separate analysis that we will perform duly.

The third point restricts the kind of contests that we can consider. Social control on a war or a scientific discovery is very limited. However, other contests, such as awarding contracts or prizes, are totally under the grip of organizing institutions. For example, when electing a host city for the Olympic Games, the Olympic Committee controls, to some extent, the form of the contest success function by determining the number of contestants and designing how the winning candidacy is selected.

A last issue is that we regard the design of a contest as done previously to the actual performance of contestants. We will consider two-stage games in which in the first stage a contest is put in place and in the second stage the contest is actually played.[1]

Having cleared the basic issues, we plunge into the analysis.[2]

12.2   Properties of Socially Optimal Contests

12.2.1   Aggregate Merit Contests

In these contests, social objectives are represented by the overall merit produced by the contests. Let ϕ_i be a function that measures the excellency or the quality of contestant i. We assume that it is strictly increasing, differentiable, and concave in g_i. Social welfare, denoted by W, is defined as

$$W(\mathbf{g}) = \sum_{i=1}^{n} \phi_i(g_i). \tag{12.1}$$

When $\phi_i(g_i) = g_i$, social welfare is just the sum of efforts. In this case, efforts might be the money spent in the contest and collected by the society.

Let us start with the simplest case, namely, one in which all contestants are identical and the CSF is the Logit with $\phi(g_i)$ being the impact of g_i in the contest.

To find the socially optimal contest, given the number of contestants, the planner chooses ϕ to maximize (12.1) with the restriction that efforts are those made in the

---

[1] For the case in which the planner cannot commit, see Section 4.3 in Chapter 4.
[2] A complementary source of information on optimal contests is the survey by Fu and Wu (2019).

subsequent Nash equilibrium of the contest. Under symmetry, maximizing (12.1) is identical to maximizing $n\phi(g_i)$ which is identical to maximizing $\phi(g_i)$. This would involve a maximization in a functional space which is a complicated task. To make the problem simple, suppose that the impact function ϕ is parametrized by a real number $\gamma \in [\underline{\gamma}, \bar{\gamma}]$. Hence, the function ϕ depends now on g_i, and the parameter γ, and choosing the best CSF reduces to choosing the γ maximizing (12.1). We assume that γ affects ϕ in the following way:

$$\frac{\partial \phi(g_i; \gamma)}{\partial g_i} \frac{g_i}{\phi(g_i; \gamma)} \text{ is increasing in } \gamma \text{ for given } g_i. \tag{12.2}$$

Condition (12.2) means that γ raises the elasticity of ϕ with respect to g_i. For instance, if ϕ has a constant elasticity, $\phi(g_i; \gamma) = g_i^\gamma$, $\underline{\gamma} = 0$ and $\bar{\gamma}$ is the maximum elasticity that allows an equilibrium in pure strategies, namely $n/(n-1)$. The parameter γ can be interpreted as a measure of meritocracy in the sense that rewards efforts.

PROPOSITION 12.1   *With a Logit CSF fulfilling (12.2), the optimal Logit CSF is given by the choice of $\gamma = \bar{\gamma}$.*

Proof   From the first-order condition of payoff maximization of a contestant i,

$$\frac{\partial \phi(g_i^*; \gamma)}{\partial g_i} \frac{V(n-1)}{\phi(g_i^*; \gamma)n^2} = 1, \tag{12.3}$$

$$\frac{\partial \phi(g_i^*; \gamma)}{\partial g_i} \frac{1}{\phi(g_i^*; \gamma)} = \frac{n^2}{(n-1)V}. \tag{12.4}$$

The left-hand side of (12.4) is decreasing in g_i^*, given that ϕ is increasing and concave in g_i, and it is increasing in γ (by (12.2)). Thus, total and individual effort are maximized with the highest value of γ.   □

The intuition behind Proposition 12.1 is that if $\phi(g_i; \gamma) = g_i^\gamma$, γ measures how the probability of getting the prize responds to efforts. To encourage agents to make the greatest effort possible, we must choose the highest γ. In other words, the contest must be as competitive as possible. See Dasgupta and Nti (1998) for this and more results in this vein.

A corollary of the previous result is that if a planner could split the prize into several smaller prizes $V^1, V^2, \ldots, V^k$, allowing contestants to contest for every prize but maintaining the total amount awarded equal to V, the optimal prize is a single prize for the contest with the largest γ. This is because elasticities measure how the probability of getting the prize responds to efforts: If the planner wants to give incentives to agents to exert effort, she should choose the contest with the largest elasticity. See Exercise 12.1 for details. A general analysis is provided by Moldovanu and Sela (2001) in the case of an All Pay Auction under incomplete information. Liu and Lu (2023) extend this analysis to allow negative prizes and find that they may arise in the optimal aggregate effort-maximizing policy.

We now turn to the determination of the socially optimal number of contestants.[3] The scenario is one in which we have a large number of potential entrants and the institution organizing the contest can limit entry into it. Without any restriction on the CSF, it is difficult to arrive at any conclusion. But it is not difficult to show that with identical agents and the Logit CSF with constant elasticity impact function, in order to maximize total effort, the planner should not restrict the number of contestants (see Exercise 12.2).

If agents have different valuations, Baye, Kovenock, and de Vries (1993) showed that in the All Pay Auction it might pay off to exclude high valuation contestants who discourage the effort of other contestant. However, Fang (2002) showed that this does not happen with the Ratio Form CSF. To illustrate this last point, recall that in a Nash equilibrium total effort denoted by g^* is

$$g^* = \frac{n-1}{\sum_{j=1}^{n} \frac{1}{V_j}}.$$

Remember also that only agents with a valuation $V_k > (n-1)/\sum_{j=1}^{n} \frac{1}{V_j}$ exert a positive effort. We concentrate on agents who meet this criterion.

PROPOSITION 12.2   *With the Ratio Form CSF, if the planner wants to maximize total effort, he should never eliminate a contestant who exerts positive effort.*

Proof   Suppose the planner eliminates contestant k, prevents any other contestant from entering and this yields more aggregate effort. That is,

$$\frac{n-1}{\sum_{j \neq k} \frac{1}{V_j} + \frac{1}{V_k}} < \frac{n-2}{\sum_{j \neq k} \frac{1}{V_j}},$$

or equivalently,

$$n \sum_{j \neq k} \frac{1}{V_j} - \sum_{j \neq k} \frac{1}{V_j} < n \sum_{j \neq k} \frac{1}{V_j} - 2 \sum_{j \neq k} \frac{1}{V_j} + \frac{n-2}{V_k}.$$

Upon simplification, this yields

$$\sum_{j=1}^{n} \frac{1}{V_j} < \frac{n-1}{V_k}.$$

This contradicts the initial assumption that $V_k > (n-1)/\sum_{j=1}^{n} \frac{1}{V_j}$.   □

To conclude this section, we ask the reader to compare the aggregate effort in a two-person contest using both the Ratio Form CSF and the All Pay Auction (see Exercise 12.3). And to examine the implications of leveling the playing field, i.e., helping weak competitors (see Exercise 12.4). This exploration requires revisiting the shape of best replies, as discussed in Chapter 3.

---

[3] This is not always possible. Some contests, by law, are open to any citizen holding certain qualifications.

12.2.2   Average Merit Contests

In some cases, e.g., when watching a sports final on TV, spectators not rooting for one of the teams may be interested in the average quality of the game. Fans will watch the game anyway, so a planner wishing to maximize the audience would be interested in maximizing the average quality of the game. Social welfare is now

$$W(\mathbf{g}) = \frac{1}{n} \sum_{i=1}^{n} \phi_i(g_i).$$

The problem of choosing the CSF given n in aggregate and average merit contests is identical. So let us focus on how to choose the socially optimal number of contestants. Assume that the CSF is Logit and all contestants are identical. Then we have the following result:

PROPOSITION 12.3   *With a Logit CSF and identical contestants, the number of contestants that maximizes average merit is two.*

Proof   First, note that when contestants are identical, their equilibrium efforts are the same. Thus, average merit simplifies to $\phi(g_i^*)$. From the first-order condition of payoff maximization of a contestant i,

$$\frac{\partial \phi(g_i^*)}{\partial g_i} \frac{V(n-1)}{\phi(g_i^*)n^2} = 1. \tag{12.5}$$

The left-hand side of (12.5) is decreasing in g_i^* and n. Thus, g_i^* and $\phi(g_i^*)$ decrease with n as long as $n > 1$.   ☐

This result indicates that in average merit contests, competition adversely affects social welfare. An increase in competition does not enhance social welfare, even if the expenses are considered valuable. This result can easily be adapted to contests where contestants have different valuations. In such situations, only the two contestants projected to exert the highest effort should participate in the contest (see Exercise 12.5). A similar finding can be seen in the work of Fullerton and McAfee (1999). This result resembles those in the industrial organization, showing that an increase in competition harms the sum of consumer and producer surpluses. In the latter, the causes are very different, namely (a) economies of scale (von Weizsäcker, 1980), (b) asymmetric firms (Lahiri and Ono, 1988), and (c) moral hazard (Scharfstein, 1988).

This result may explain why many sports finals are played by two teams. Or why US defence selected two firms to compete in the Joint Strike Fighter. Shapiro and Varian (1999, p. 124) name "Dual Sourcing" as a common practice among firms, where they opt for two potential suppliers.[4]

---

[4] Risk aversion plays, no doubt about it, an important role in these examples.

12.2.3   Quality Contests

In certain contests, the primary concern is the quality of the winner, as seen, e.g., in architectural projects. In these cases, social welfare is measured as the expected winner's effort which reflects expected winner quality,

$$W(\mathbf{g}) = \sum_{i=1}^{m} p_i(\mathbf{g}) g_i \qquad (12.6)$$

(see Drugov and Ryvkin, 2017; Serena, 2017). When agents are identical, social welfare in quality contests collapses into average merit contests with $\phi(g_i) = g_i$. We focus on the case in which agents are not identical.

To simplify the analysis in this part, consider the case of two contestants. The marginal cost of effort for contestant 1 is c_1, and the marginal cost of contestant 2 is $c_2 = 1$. We assume that contestant 1 is the disadvantaged one, so $c_1 > 1$. We restrict the analysis to the following family of weighted Ratio Form CSFs:

$$p_1(\mathbf{g}) = \frac{\alpha_1 g_1}{\alpha_1 g_1 + g_2}; \quad p_2(\mathbf{g}) = \frac{g_2}{\alpha_1 g_1 + g_2}.$$

The problem boils down to choosing α_1 in order to maximize the expected winner's effort.

At this point, we may ask the following question. If agents are differently weighted in the CSF, why are these weights not used when computing welfare? The answer is that the weights are there to counter the handicap in the cost function of player 1, and not to give an advantage per se to this player. Let us give an example. In a city architectural contest, the mayor wants the best project to be implemented so she can use it as a showcase in the next election. Suppose that the quality of a project is proportional to the hours devoted by the corresponding team. The mayor's office, being aware that certain projects are prepared by a handicapped social group, designs the contest in a way that this handicap is, somehow, compensated, i.e., they give extra points to projects prepared by this group so it can compete more fairly with the others. But the target is to have the best project, not to help the handicapped group. This is shown in the following result:

PROPOSITION 12.4   *In a two-person quality contests, the optimal weight of the disadvantaged agent, α_1, is less than c_1.*

Proof   Consider the maximization of (12.6) with the restriction that efforts are a Nash equilibrium given α_1. This is equivalent to

$$\max \frac{V \alpha_1^2 + c_1^2 \alpha_1 V}{(\alpha_1 + c_1)^3}. \qquad (12.7)$$

From the first-order condition of the maximization program (12.7), we obtain

$$\frac{c_1^3 - 2\alpha_1 c_1^2 - \alpha_1^2 + 2\alpha_1 c_1}{(\alpha_1 + c_1)^4} = 0.$$

The second-order condition holds, so the first-order condition above gives a maximum. Solving for α_1,

$$\alpha_1 = -c_1(c_1 - 1) + c_1\sqrt[2]{c_1^2 - c_1 + 1}.$$

We see that $\alpha_1 < c_1$ when $c_1 > 1$.   □

Note that this weight is less than the one obtained under aggregate effort maximization (see Section 12.4.1 on affirmative action). Therefore, in quality contests, there may be less redistribution than under effort maximization. This is due to the fact that we care only about the effort of the (expected) winner.

With respect to the number of contestants, when all are identical, $\sum_{i=1}^{n} g_i^* p_i^* = (n-1)V/n^2$ which is decreasing in n so in this case, quality and average contests coincide and the less competition the better.

12.3   Choosing Contests

In this section, we consider two examples in which the options of the society to reform contests are severely limited. In the first example, there are several contests with different prizes and agents are allowed to enter just one of them. This scenario is a specific instance of the model presented in Section 9.3 of Chapter 9. A planner can reshuffle contestants into contests to maximize aggregate social welfare. In the second example, society must choose between having several small local contests, each with a modest prize, or a single large contest with a prize that is the sum of all the local prizes.

12.3.1   Free Entry and Social Welfare

Suppose there are K contests with prizes V^i, $i \in \{1, 2, \ldots, k\}$. There are N identical agents that can participate at most in a single contest. Let n_j be the number of agents in contest j. The CSF is the Ratio Form. In a Nash equilibrium, the payoff of an agent in contest j is V^j/n_j^2. If agents can move among different contests ex ante and, for simplicity, if the number of agents in each contest can be considered as a real number, the entry equilibrium is characterized by

$$\frac{V^1}{n_1^2} = \frac{V^2}{n_2^2} = \cdots = \frac{V^k}{n_k^2}. \tag{12.8}$$

Consider a planner who can allocate contestants in contests and wants to maximize aggregate effort. This planner maximizes the following Lagrangian,

$$L = \sum_{j=1}^{k} \frac{n_j - 1}{n_j} V^j - \lambda\left(\sum_{j=1}^{k} n_j - N\right),$$

where λ is the Lagrange multiplier associated with the restriction $\sum_{j=1}^{n} n_j = N$. The first-order conditions are

$$\frac{V^j}{n_j^2} = \lambda, \; j \in \{1, \ldots, k\}.$$

The second-order conditions hold because $\partial^2 L / \partial n_j^2 < 0$ and $\partial^2 L / \partial n_j n_r = 0$. The previous equation and Equation (12.8) are identical and demonstrate the following result (see Bernergård and Wärneryd, 2017):

PROPOSITION 12.5   *When the CSF is Ratio, in K mutually exclusive contests, free entry maximizes aggregate effort.*

12.3.2   Centralization or Decentralization?

Is it preferable to centralize all rent-seeking in one location, like Washington DC or Brussels, making it accessible to all citizens, rather than dispersing it throughout the United States/EU where it is only available to locals? Similarly, should research funds for, say, economics be allocated through a single large contest open to everyone, or should they be distributed in several smaller contests exclusive to local participants?

The impact of breaking down a large contest into several smaller ones on aggregate effort is not immediately clear. Nonetheless, there are two opposing effects at play. On the one hand, there is the *Competitive Effect*: In smaller contests, there are fewer competitors, leading to increased individual efforts. On the other hand, the diminished prize size in these smaller contests could reduce the incentive to exert effort. This is termed the *Prize Effect*. Wärneryd (2001) and Beviá and Corchón (2015) have studied this issue.[5] Formally, we consider the following two scenarios.

- **Decentralized contests** where there are k independent, identical contests, each with n identical contestants, and a prize valued at V
- **Centralized contests** where there is a single contest with kn participants and a prize valued at kV.

We use the relative difference CSF introduced in Section 2.5 of Chapter 2, where the probability of winning is linear on the relative difference between an agent's effort and the average of other agents' efforts weighted by a positive number s. The parameter s can be interpreted as a measure of how competitive the contest is. This CSF is well suited to study how the socially optimal contest depends on how competitive these contests are. Recall that the notional relative difference CSF with m contestants is

---

[5] For more references on this problem, see Brookins and Jindapon (2022).

$$f_i(\mathbf{g}) = \alpha + \beta \frac{g_i - s\frac{\sum_{j \neq i} g_j}{m-1}}{\sum_{j=1}^m g_j}, \text{ if } \sum_{j=1}^m g_j \neq 0,\ \alpha \in [0,1],\ \beta \geq 0,$$

$$f_i(\mathbf{g}) = \frac{1}{m} \text{ if } \sum_{j=1}^m g_j = 0, i \in \{1,\ldots,m\}$$

with $m\alpha + \beta(1 - s)) = 1$. Recall that we can work safely with this notional CSF disregarding the nonnegativity constraints and that when $\alpha = s = 0$ and $\beta = 1$, we go back to the Ratio CSF.

Existence of a Nash equilibrium when all players have identical valuations is guaranteed when

$$m \geq \beta(m + s - 1) > 0.$$

Recall that the Nash equilibrium actions and payoffs are

$$g_i^* = \beta W \frac{m + s - 1}{m^2}, i \in \{1,\ldots,m\},$$

$$\pi_i^* = \frac{W}{m^2}(m - \beta(m + s - 1))$$

where W is the prize. Setting $m = n$ and $W = V$ we have the equilibrium for a decentralized contest. And setting $W = kV$ and $m = kn$ we have the centralized contest. Now we have the following result

PROPOSITION 12.6   *Suppose $\beta \neq 0$. Aggregate effort is larger in the centralized contest if and only if $s < 1$.*

Proof   Aggregate effort is larger in the centralized contest if and only if

$$\frac{kV}{kn}(kn - \beta(kn + s - 1)) > k\frac{V}{n}(n - \beta(n + s - 1)).$$

Which is equivalent to

$$\beta(1 - s) > \beta k(1 - s).$$

The above inequality holds if and only if $s < 1$.   □

The rationale for this outcome is as follows: when $s < 1$, the contest is less competitive. Thus, the prize effect outweighs the competition effect, leading to greater efforts in the centralized contest compared to the decentralized ones. Conversely, when $s > 1$, the contest is highly competitive, resulting in the opposite effect.

Table 12.1 shows which contest to choose based on the degree of competitiveness and whether efforts are socially valuable or not.

If $s < 1$ rent-seeking and lobbying activities – where efforts are pure waste- should be kept locally. But sports and R&D should be made at a central place. When $s > 1$ the opposite occurs.

As an illustration, consider the case of Spain. Until 1978 Spain was a centralized country, very much like France. Today, Spain is one of the most decentralized countries in Europe, closer to Germany (which is a federal state) or even to the United

Table 12.1 Selection of contest type based on competitiveness and social value of effort

	Effort socially bad	Effort socially good
$s < 1$	Decentralized	Centralized
$s > 1$	Centralized	Decentralized

States. The consequences have been twofold. On the one hand, rent-seeking, traditionally concentrated in Madrid – has spread to all regions with the deleterious effects that we already discussed in Chapter 11. And Madrid, partially liberated from this burden, has grown to be the economic center of Spain, traditionally located in Catalonia. But Catalonia has put in good use part of the money that it received and is now an important European hub in science.

Exercise 12.6 requests an extension of the prior analysis to situations where agents are heterogeneous and then to derive conclusions regarding which agents prefer which type of contest.

12.4   Effects of Policy on Contests

In this final section, we will study how two paramount policies affect the outcomes of contests. First, we will consider *Affirmative Action*, a policy whose name comes from an Executive Order signed by President John F. Kennedy on March 6, 1961. It refers to a set of policies seeking to increase the chances of underrepresented groups to get certain jobs or achieve higher educational levels. The second policy considered here is *Compulsory Education.* This kind of education has its European root in the classical Greek and Roman periods and was retaken in the second part of the eighteenth century as part of the Age of Enlightenment. As we have seen in Section 11.2 of Chapter 11, education has been seen as one – may be the main – engine of growth (see Jamison, Jamison, and Hanushek, 2007).[6] Policies aimed at good deeds do not necessarily achieve the intended objectives. Careful design of policies is important.

12.4.1   Affirmative Action

The goal of affirmative action is to favor members of a group who suffer (or suffered) from discrimination. Discrimination can arise from past actions that impeded the education of a particular group or because the jury of the contest is biased toward a particular group.[7] This policy seems agreeable to many people from the point of view of fairness. But some people object to affirmative action from the point of view of efficiency. They point out potential disincentives with respect to effort provision.

---

[6] Exercise 2.15 considers the effect of taxes in a contest model.

[7] For instance, Watts (2022) finds evidence of gender bias in the judges of a culinary competition.

Franke (2012a) presented a specific theoretical model in which affirmative action is modeled as a contest. Consider the two contestant case. Contestant 1 is disadvantaged. Her marginal cost of effort is $c_1 > 1$. The marginal cost of effort for contestant 2 is $c_2 = 1$. Suppose that the planner can affect how the effort of the disadvantaged contestant counts. For instance, the planner may add points for gender or for belonging to a minority. We will study the effect of this policy in a moment. For the time being, we focus on a different way of affecting the CSF assuming that points are added proportionally to the current effort. Thus, if effort are citations in the Social Science Citation Index, the effort of the disadvantaged that counts in the CSF is her citations times a number α_1 larger than one. The CSF is the weighted Ratio Form,

$$p_1(\mathbf{g}) = \frac{\alpha_1 g_1}{\alpha_1 g_1 + g_2} \; ; \quad p_2(\mathbf{g}) = \frac{g_2}{\alpha_1 g_1 + g_2} \; ; \quad p_i(0,0) = 0.5.$$

The first-order conditions yield

$$g_1^* = \frac{V \alpha_1}{(\alpha_1 + c_1)^2} \; ; \quad g_2^* = \frac{\alpha_1 c_1 V}{(\alpha_1 + c_1)^2}.$$

We see here that a policy aimed to equalize efforts of both contestants is fruitless because $g_2^* > g_1^*$. Exercise 12.7 asks the reader to perform a generalization of this result. But given that

$$p_1(\mathbf{g}^*) = \frac{\alpha_1}{\alpha_1 + c_1},$$

setting $\alpha_1 = c_1$ yields an equal probability to both contestants to obtain the prize. This is not only fair if the disadvantage was not contestant 1's fault, but it maximizes aggregate effort. Indeed

$$g_1^* + g_2^* = \frac{V \alpha_1}{(\alpha_1 + c_1)^2}(1 + c_1)$$

$$\frac{\partial (g_1^* + g_2^*)}{\partial \alpha_1} = (1 + c_1)\frac{(c_1 - \alpha_1)}{(\alpha_1 + c_1)^3} = 0 \text{ if and only if } c_1 = \alpha_1.$$

Summarizing:

PROPOSITION 12.7 *Setting $\alpha_1 = c_1$ equalizes the probabilities that both contestants obtain the prize and maximizes aggregate effort.*

This contrast with the finding that in quality contests α_1 should be kept below c_1. This hints at a possible trade-off between finding the best (excellency) and affirmative action. In Exercise 12.8 we ask the reader to draw the best replies of both contestants and to provide a graphical complement to the proof of Proposition 12.7.

There is empirical literature showing that affirmative action policies indeed promote effort. For example, Brown (2011) shows how large skill gaps reduce efforts by studying the impact of the presence of Tiger Woods in the outcomes of golf games. Franke (2012b) shows that leveling the play field in amateur golf tournaments increases performance. And Calsamiglia, Franke, and Rey-Biel (2013) conducted tournaments between pairs of children from two similar schools who systematically differed in how much training they received ex ante. Affirmative action enhanced the performance for a large group of participants. Moreover, affirmative action resulted in a more equitable tournament winner pool where half of the selected tournament winners came from the originally disadvantaged group.

A different way to give a push to the disadvantaged agent is to give her γ_1 extra points. The CSF is now

$$p_1(\mathbf{g}) = \frac{\gamma_1 + g_1}{\gamma_1 + g_1 + g_2} \ ; \quad p_2(\mathbf{g}) = \frac{g_2}{\gamma_1 + g_1 + g_2},$$

where the effective effort of the disadvantaged agent is $\gamma_1 + g_1$. In this case, the first-order conditions associated to the maximization of payoffs give

$$g_1^* = \frac{V}{(1 + c_1)^2} - \gamma_1; \ g_2^* = \frac{c_1 V}{(1 + c_1)^2}.$$

This policy disincentives the effort of the disadvantaged agent and does not change the effort of the competitor. Furthermore, it does not affect the probability of winning.

$$p_1(\mathbf{g}^*) = \frac{1}{1 + c_1}; \ p_2(\mathbf{g}^*) = \frac{c_1}{1 + c_1}.$$

We see that this policy increases the payoff of the disadvantaged agent but it achieves nothing in terms of efforts or how the prize is awarded. Exercise 12.9 asks the reader to generalize this result.

The results here are only meant to boost your appetite for this question whose importance will just grow in the foreseeable future.[8] The interested reader could do no better than to immerse themselves in the lecture of the surveys by Mealem and Nitzan (2016) and Chowdhury, Esteve-Gonzalez, and Mukherjee (2023) for a full discussion of the models, issues, and experiments related to this fascinating topic.

12.4.2   Compulsory Education

Consider a very simple two-person contest in which g_i is the education chosen by i. V is the output, which, by simplicity we take as constant. In this simple model, education is just a signal. Agent 1 is poor and agent 2 is rich. Because of the educational advantages of the rich, the marginal cost of effort of the poor, c_1, is larger than one, and the marginal cost of effort of the rich is just 1. Again, let $\alpha_1 \geq 1$ be the discrimination in favor of the poor (often $\alpha_1 = 1$).

In a Nash equilibrium in which agents choose freely education

$$g_1^* = \frac{V \alpha_1}{(\alpha_1 + c_1)^2} \ ; \quad g_2^* = \frac{c_1 V \alpha_1}{(\alpha_1 + c_1)^2}.$$

---

[8] The introduction and removal of AA policies affect the behavior of the participants in a nontrivial way. Chowdhury, Danilov, and Kocher (2023) examine these questions in a laboratory experiment and find less sabotage under AA when the tournament started directly with the AA regime. But the removal of AA policies intensifies sabotage.

Suppose now that the government introduces a minimum level of compulsory education, $\underline{g}$, that yields a new Nash equilibrium. There are three possibilities:

(1) If $\underline{g} \leq g_1^*$, this policy has no consequences because the required educational policy is already attained.
(2) If $\underline{g} \geq V/4\alpha_1$ (which is the maximal education for 2 in the Nash equilibrium without minimal compulsory education), both choose $\underline{g}$.
(3) If $\underline{g} \in (g_1^*, V/4\alpha_1)$, then, the new equilibrium effort, g_i^{**}, increases for both agents, but $g_1^{**} < g_2^{**}$. This is because the Nash equilibrium without minimal compulsory education occurs in the increasing part of 2's best reply.

The interesting case is the one described in point 3, in which as a consequence of the poor becoming better educated, the rich become better educated too. In other words, minimal compulsory education has a multiplicative effect on the quantity of education chosen by the more fortunate. The explanation is that once everybody has graduated, college becomes important, and once a large majority has a college degree, a Master's degree becomes a must, so on and so forth.

12.5   Exercises

12.1   Prove that if a prize of value V can be divided into k prizes, $V_1, V_2, \ldots, V_k$ such that $\Sigma V_{i=i}^k = V$ and agents are allowed to contend for all prizes with the same effort, the contest that maximizes aggregate effort is the one with the largest elasticity.

12.2   Suppose agents are identical and the CSF is Logit with constant elasticity impact function ϕ. Show that, in order to maximize total effort, the number of contestants should not be restricted.

12.3   Show that if $n = 2$, a symmetric Ratio Form CSF yields larger aggregate effort than All Pay Auction. But if weights can be chosen, then efforts in both are identical (see Epstein, Mealem, and Nitzan, 2013). Show that when $n > 2$, the All Pay Auction – with suitable weights – dominates a contest with a weighted Ratio Form CSF (see Franke et al., 2014).

12.4   Show that the optimal policy in aggregate merit contests implies leveling the playing field by encouraging weak contestants, but not up the point in which contestants' chances are equalized (see Franke et al., 2013).

12.5   Show that when agents are different and the CSF is the Ratio Form, the optimal policy in an Average Merit Contest is to exclude all but the two best contestants.

12.6   In the decentralized and centralized contests defined in Section 12.3.2, suppose that prize valuations are different across agents. Compute the Nash equilibrium for both kinds of contests. Analyze the parameters that determine the preference of a contestant for decentralized or centralized contests (see Beviá and Corchón, 2015).

12.7 Following Section 12.4.1, assume that the CSF is homogeneous of degree zero. Show that contestant 1's effort is less than contestant 2's effort.

12.8 Draw the best replies of contestants in the game induced by affirmative action and show the Nash equilibrium with $\alpha_1 = 1$ and with $\alpha_1 > 1$.

12.9 Suppose that a subset of agents, N_1, are given extra points for their effort. The effective effort for $j \in N_1$ is $g_j + \gamma_j$. Let $\pi_i(g_i, g_{-i})$ be the payoff function of a contestant. When extra points are zero, we have a Nash equilibrium $(g_1^b, g_2^b, \dots, g_n^b)$ (b denotes before affirmative action). Let $(g_1^a, g_2^a, \dots, g_n^a)$ be the equilibrium with extra points (a denotes after affirmative action). Show that for any contestant, say j, in N_1, $g_j^a = g_j^b - \gamma_i$ and for those not in N_1, say k, $g_k^a = g_k^b$ (see Fu and Wu, 2020).

12.10 Show that by introducing preliminary contests to select the finalists to contest in a final stage, an increase in the sensitivity of the CSF to efforts might result in a decrease in total expenses (see Amegashie, 1999b).

12.11 Give examples in which a conflict yields a better allocation of resources. See Nugent and Sanchez (1989) for the case of Spanish cattle rising versus agriculture and Sanchez-Pages (2006) for a theoretical model.

12.12 Compare the total effort of simultaneous versus (partially and completely) sequential contests with three players with asymmetric valuations. Show that with the Ratio Form CSF total effort is always maximized by the fully sequential contest, where the strongest player moves first, the second, strongest second, and the weakest third. On the other hand, the total effort is minimized when the players move in the opposite direction (weakest first, strongest last). (See Xu, Zhang, and Zhang, 2020.)

12.13 Would penalties with or without an exit option be equivalent to prizes? Work out the case of the Ratio Form CSF (see Sela, 2020).

12.14 Suppose there is a contest with two contestants in which the winner must reimburse the loser for his expenses of the contest. Assuming a Ratio Form CSF, payoffs for contestant i are

$$\pi_i(\mathbf{g}) = V - g_i - g_j \quad \text{with probability} \quad \frac{g_i}{g_i + g_j}.$$

$$\pi_i(\mathbf{g}) = 0 \qquad\qquad \text{with probability} \quad \frac{g_j}{g_i + g_j}.$$

Show that in a symmetric Nash equilibrium, efforts and payoffs are identical to those obtained under the rule that each contestant pays her own expenses. (See Chowdhury and Sheremeta, 2015.)

12.15 The supply side of the simplest macroeconomic model assumes that a price taker firm with decreasing returns produces the private consumption and the investment of the whole economy. If the supply side were modeled as a contest, it could be as follows:

The economy is composed of a single artisan who, from the scratch, can bake a delicious pie and n workers who only know how to take care of a plot of land owned by the artisan. The effort of the artisan is denoted by g_0 and the effort of workers by $g_i, i = 1, 2, \ldots, n$. The proportion of the pie received by a worker is her proportion of effort in total effort. The quantity of the pie, denoted by V, depends on the effort of the artisan as follows $V = dg_0^\alpha$ where $\alpha \in (0, 1)$. The artisan does not like the pie. The game is played in two stages. First, the artisan bakes the pie. Once the pie is completed and shown to the workers, they labor in the land. Their labor is meticulously controlled by the artisan who distributes the pie. The artisan consumes the produce of the land who is just $e \sum_{i=1}^{n} g_i$.

(1) Assuming that all agents are risk neutral and have payoffs that are additively separable between consumption and effort, write payoffs and find the subgame perfect Nash equilibrium of the game.

(2) Suppose that a planner is just interested in aggregate effort, i.e., $g_0 + \sum_{i=1}^{n} g_i$. Study how this magnitude depends on the parameters of the economy: productivity (d and e) and the number of workers.

(3) Introduce a tax on V that is used to redistribute income in favor of workers. What is the effect of t on aggregate effort?

Summary: The Lost Continent – A Tale of Discovery

Economics is the study of resource allocation mechanisms. The first mechanism that called our attention was the market, the most visible resource allocator. The study of markets devoted the best energies of classical and neoclassical economists from 1776 onward. In the 1930s, with the Great Depression looming, some economists began to suggest alternative ways of allocating resources; for instance by a well-informed and benevolent planner. This viewpoint, admittedly unrealistic but appealing, produced in the last three decades of the twentieth century the economics of information and its sister, the study of optimal mechanisms under informational constraints. In parallel, resource allocation by voting called the attention of many economists and other social scientists.[9] Thus, we arrive at the twenty-first century with the trilogy of markets, authority, and voting as the only mechanisms of resource allocation. A geographical analogy would be that Africa, Asia, and Europe were the only continents on earth.

In retrospect, it is surprising that it took so long to focus research on contests as a resource allocator. Civil servants are not selected by the market, authority, or voting but by a public examination that requires a lot of effort to prepare. Sport trophies are allocated by points or rankings that are achieved on the field. The same about Michelin stars and college admissions! Countries engage in costly affairs to procure territories. In some unlucky cases, people end up in a courtroom litigating for fame and property. Firms spend plentiful resources to steer – legally or otherwise – the direction of public policies like subsidies, regulations, or laws. Advertising pursues the same ends in a more civil manner. Publication of papers or books requires a tremendous effort that may be rewarded or not. And the same about patents.

All examples above share common features. Participants must incur expenses – money, effort – to achieve something that from their point of view is guided by rules that are partially random. This is what we call a contest, the lost continent in the previous analogy. As in this analogy, at the beginning, different people were discovering parts of land that were thought to be unrelated. But at some point it was realized that all these different bits must be understood as part of a new continent.[10]

Who discovered America? In the case of contests, there are many earlier contributors whose work is summarized in Chapter 1. But what is really important is that this new field (continent) allows us to have a better understanding of what economics (geography) is about. This is the takeaway of this book.

---

[9] These new approaches would have been impossible without the concepts developed by game theorists in the 1940s and 1950s.

[10] The first map in which this was acknowledged was made by the Spanish cartographer Juan de la Cosa; see https://en.wikipedia.org/wiki/Map_of_Juan_de_la_Cosa.

References

Acemoglu, D. "Rewards structures and the allocation of talent." *European Economic Review*, 39, 1, 17–33, 1995.

Acemoglu, D. *Introduction to Modern Economic Growth*. Princeton University Press, 2009.

Acemoglu, D., and S. Johnson. "Unbundling institutions." *Journal of Political Economy*, 113, 5, 949–995, 2005.

Acemoglu, D., S. Johnson, and J. A. Robinson. "The colonial origins of comparative development: An empirical investigation." *American Economic Review*, 91, 5, 1369–1401, 2001.

Acemoglu, D., and J. A. Robinson. *Why Nations Fail: The Origins of Power, Prosperity and Poverty.* Crown, 2012.

Aiche, A., E. Einy, O. Haimanko, D. Moreno, A. Sela, and B. Shitovitz. "Tullock contests reward information advantages." *Economics Letters*, 172, 34–36, 2018.

Aiche, A., E. Einy, O. Haimanko, D. Moreno, A. Sela, and B. Shitovitz. "Information in Tullock contests." *Theory and Decision*, 86, 3, 303–323, 2019.

Alcalde, J., and M. Dahm. "Tullock and Hirshleifer: A meeting of the minds." *Review of Economic Design*, 11, 2, 101–124, 2007.

Alcalde, J., and M. Dahm. "Rent seeking and rent dissipation: A neutrality result." *Journal of Public Economics*, 94, 1–2, 1–7, 2010.

Amegashie, J. A. "The number of rent-seekers and aggregate rent-seeking expenditures: An unpleasant result." *Public Choice*, 99, 1, 57–62, 1999a.

Amegashie, J. A. "The design of rent-seeking competitions: Committees, preliminary and final contests." *Public Choice*, 99, 1, 63–76, 1999b.

Amegashie, J. A. "A contest success function with a tractable noise parameter." *Public Choice*, 126, 1–2, 135–144, 2006.

Amegashie, J. A. "Productive versus destructive efforts in contests." *European Journal of Political Economy*, 28, 4, 461–468, 2012.

Amegashie, J. A., and M. Runkel. "Sabotaging potential rivals." *Social Choice and Welfare*, 28, 1, 143–162, 2007.

Amegashie, A., and M. Runkel. "The paradox of revenge in conflicts." *The Journal of Conflict Resolution,* 56, 2, 313–330, 2012.

Anbarci, N., S. Skaperdas, and C. Syropoulos. "Comparing bargaining solutions in the shadow of conflict." *Journal of Economic Theory*, 106, 1, 1–16, 2002.

Apesteguia, J., and I. Palacios-Huerta. "Psychological pressure in competitive environments: Evidence from a randomized natural experiment." *American Economic Review*, 100, 5, 2548–2564, 2010.

Arbatskaya, M., and H. Mialon. "Multi-activity contests." *Economic Theory,* 43, 1, 23–43, 2010.

Arteaga, F. "The merchant guilds and the political economy of the Spanish Empire on the eve of independence." *Journal of Historical Political Economy*, 2, 2, 299–331, 2022.

Arve, M., and M. Serena. "Level-k models and overspending in contests." *Games*, 13, 3, 2022.

Baik, K. H. "Effort levels in contests: The public-good prize case." *Economics Letters*, 41, 4, 363–367, 1993.

Baik, K. H. "Difference-form contest success functions and effort level in contests." *European Journal of Political Economy*, 14, 4, 685–701, 1998.

Baik, K. H., and J. F. Shogren. "Strategic behavior in contests: Comment." *American Economic Review*, 82, 1, 359–362, 1992.

Baland, J.-M., and P. Francoise. "Rent-seeking and resource booms." *Journal of Development Economics*, 61, 2, 527–542, 2000.

Balard, P., S. Flamand, and O. Troumpounis. "Strategic choice of sharing rules in collective contests." *Social Choice and Welfare*, 46, 2, 239–262, 2015.

Baliga, S., and T. Sjöström. "The strategy of manipulating conflict." *American Economic Review*, 102, 6, 2897–2922, 2012.

Baliga, S., and T. Sjöström. "Bargaining and war: A review of some formal models." *Korean Economic Review*, 29, 2, 235–266, 2013.

Baliga, S., and T. Sjöström. "The causes of war." In O. Dube, M. Morelli, D. Ray, and T. Sjöström (eds.), *Handbook of the Economics of Conflict*, vol. 2. North Holland, forthcoming 2023.

Barberà, S., and C. Bevia. "Self-selection consistent functions." *Journal of Economic Theory*, 105, 2, 263–277, 2002.

Barbieri, S., and M. Serena. "Winners' efforts in multi-battle team contests." Working paper of the Max Planck Institute for Tax Law and Public Finance No. 2019-03, 2019.

Baye, M., and H. Hoppe. "The strategic equivalence of rent-seeking, innovation, and patent-race games." *Games and Economic Behavior*, 44, 2, 217–226, 2003.

Baye, M., D. Kovenock, and C. de Vries. "Rigging the lobbying process: An application of the all-pay auction." *American Economic Review*, 83, 1, 289–294, 1993.

Baye, M., D. Kovenock, and C. de Vries. "The solution to the Tullock rent-seeking game when $R > 2$: Mixed-strategy equilibria and mean dissipation rates." *Public Choice*, 81, 3, 363–380, 1994.

Baye, M., D. Kovenock, and C. de Vries. "The all-pay auction with complete information." *Economic Theory*, 8, 2, 291–305, 1996.

Beccuti, J., and M. Möller. "Fighting for lemons: The encouragement effect in dynamic competition with private information." Discussion papers, No. 20-17, Department of Economics, University of Bern, Bern, 2020.

Becker, G. "A theory of competition among pressure groups for political influence." *The Quarterly Journal of Economics*, 98, 3, 371–400, 1983.

Berge, C. *Espaces topologiques, fonctions multivoques*. 1959. English translation *Topological Spaces: Including a Treatment of Multi-Valued Functions, Vector Spaces and Convexity*, Dover Books, 2010.

Bernergård, A., and K. Wärneryd. "Self-allocation in contests." CESifo working paper, No. 6636, Center for Economic Studies and Ifo Institute (CESifo), Munich, 2017.

Beviá, C., and L. Corchón. "Rational sabotage in cooperative production with heterogeneous agents." *The B.E. Journal of Theoretical Economics: Topics*, 6, 1–27, 2006.

Beviá, C., and L. Corchón. "War or peace." In E. Aragonés, C. Beviá, H. Llavador, and N. Schofield (eds.), *The Political Economy of Democracy*. Fundación BBVA, 2009.

Beviá, C., and L. Corchón. "Peace agreements without commitment." *Games and Economic Behavior*, 68, 2, 469–487, 2010.

Beviá, C., and L. Corchón. "Endogenous strength in conflicts." *International Journal of Industrial Organization*, 31, 3, 297–306, 2013.

Beviá, C., and L. Corchón. "Centralized vs decentralized contests." *Economics Letters*, 137, 32–35, 2015.

Beviá, C., and L. Corchón. "Dynamic contests with bankruptcy: The despair effect." *The B.E. Journal of Theoretical Economics*, 16, 1, 217–241, 2016.

Beviá, C., and L. Corchón. "Meritocracy, efficiency, incentives and voting." *Annals of Public and Cooperative Economics*, 89, 1, 87–108, 2018.

Beviá, C., and L. Corchón. "Contests with dominant strategies." *Economic Theory*, 74, 4, 1–19, 2022.

Binmore, K. *Fun and Games: A Text on Game Theory*. D. C. Heath and Company, 1991.

Blavatskyy, P. R. "Contest success function with the possibility of a draw: Axiomatization." *Journal of Mathematical Economics*, 46, 2, 267–276, 2010.

Bodoh-Creed, A., and B. Hickman. "College assignment as a large contest." *Journal of Economic Theory*, 175, 344–375, 2018.

Borel, E. "La théorie du jeu et les équations intégrales à noyau symétrique." *Comptes rendus de l'Académie des Sciences*, 173, 1304–1308, 1921. English translation by Leonard J. Savage, *Econometrica*, 21, 97–100, 1953.

Brams, S. J., and D. Kilgour. "The truel." *Mathematics Magazine*, 70, 5, 315–326, 1997.

Brito, D. L., and M. D. Intriligator. "Conflict, war, and redistribution." *The American Political Science Review*, 79, 4, 943–957, 1985.

Brookins, P., and P. Jindapon. "Contest divisioning." *Review of Economic Design*, forthcoming 2022. https://doi.org/10.1007/s10058-022-00311-9

Brown, A., and S. M. Chowdhury. "The hidden perils of affirmative action: Sabotage in handicap contests." *Journal of Economic Behavior & Organization*, 133, 273–284, 2017.

Brown, J. "Quitters never win: The (adverse) incentive effects of competing with superstars." *Journal of Political Economy*, 119, 5, 982–1013, 2011.

Buchanan, J., and G. Tullock. *The Calculus of Consent: Logical Foundations of Constitutional Democracy*. University of Michigan Press, 1962.

Bulow, J., J. Geanakoplos, and P. Klemperer. "Multimarket oligopoly: Strategic substitutes and complements." *Journal of Political Economy*, 93, 3, 488–511, 1985.

Calsamiglia, C., J. Franke, and P. Rey-Biel. "The incentive effects of affirmative action in a real-effort tournament." *Journal of Public Economics*, 98, 15–31, 2013.

Chamberlin, E. "An experimental imperfect market." *Journal of Political Economy*, 56, 2, 95–108, 1948.

Che, Y.-K., and I. Gale. "Difference-form contests and the robustness of all-pay auctions." *Games and Economic Behavior*, 30, 1, 22–43, 2000.

Chen, K.-P. "Sabotage in promotion tournaments." *Journal of Law, Economics, & Organization*, 19, 1, 119–140, 2003.

Chowdhury, S. M. "The attack and defense mechanisms: Perspectives from behavioral economics and game theory." *Behavioral and Brain Sciences*, 42, e121, 2019.

Chowdhury, S. M., P. Esteve-Gonzalez, and A. Mukherjee. "Hetereogeneity, leveling the playing field, and affirmative action in contests." *Southern Economic Journal*, 89, 3, 924–974, 2023.

Chowdhury, S. M., A. Danilov, and M. Kocher. "The lifecycle of affirmative action policies and its effect on effort and sabotage behavior." CESifo working paper No. 10501, June 14, 2023.

Chowdhury, S. M., and O. Gürtler. "Sabotage in contests: A survey." *Public Choice*, 164, 1, 135–155, 2015.

Chowdhury, S. M., D. Kovenock, and R. M. Sheremeta. "An experimental investigation of Colonel Blotto games." *Economic Theory*, 52, 3, 833–861, 2013.

Chowdhury, S. M., D. Lee, and R. M. Sheremeta. "Top guns may not fire: Best-shot group contests with group-specific public good prizes." *Journal of Economic Behavior and Organization*, 92, 94–103, 2013.

Chowdhury, S. M., and R. M. Sheremeta. "Strategically equivalent contests." *Theory and Decision*, 78, 4, 587–601, 2015.

Chung, T. Y. "Rent-seeking contest when the prize increases with aggregate efforts." *Public Choice*, 87, 1/2, 55–66, 1996.

Clark, D. J., and K. Konrad. "Contests with multi-tasking." *Scandinavian Journal of Economics*, 109, 2, 303–319, 2007.

Clark, D. J., and T. Nilssen. "Learning by doing in contests." *Public Choice*, 156, 1/2, 329–343, 2013.

Clark, D. J., T. Nilssen, and J. Y. Sand. "Gaining advantage by winning contests." *Review of Economic Design*, 24, 1, 23–38, 2020.

Clark, D. J., and C. Riis. "A multiple-winner nested rent-seeking contest." *Public Choice*, 87, 1/2, 177–184, 1996.

Clark, D. J., and C. Riis. "Contest success functions: An extension." *Economic Theory*, 11, 1, 201–204, 1998a.

Clark, D. J., and C. Riis. "Influence and the discretionary allocation of several prizes." *European Journal of Political Economy*, 14, 4, 605–625, 1998b.

von Clausewitz, C. *On War*. 1832. Princeton University Press, 2008.

Coase, R. H. "The problem of social cost." *The Journal of Law and Economics*, 3, 1–44, 1960.

Coase, R. H. "The institutional structure of production." *University of Chicago Law Occasional Paper* 28, 1992.

Cohen, C., and S. Nitzan. "Advantageous defensive efforts in contests." *Economics Bulletin*, 41, 3, 2147–2157, 2021.

Corchón, L. "Comparative statics for aggregative games: The strong concavity case." *Mathematical Social Sciences*, 28, 3, 151–165, 1994.

Corchón, L. "On the allocative effects of rent-seeking." *Journal of Public Economic Theory*, 2, 4, 483–491, 2000.

Corchón, L. *Theories of Imperfectly Competitive Markets*, 2nd ed. Springer, 2001.

Corchón, L. "The theory of contests: A survey." *Review of Economic Design*, 11, 2, 69–100, 2007.

Corchón, L. "Forms of governance and the size of rent-seeking." *Social Choice and Welfare*, 30, 2, 197–210, 2008.

Corchón, L. "The theory of implementation: What did we learn?" In R. A. Meyers (ed.), *Encyclopedia of Complexity and Systems*. Springer, 2009.

Corchón, L. "Aggregative games." *SERIEs. Journal of the Spanish Economic Association*, 12, 1, 49–71, 2021.

Corchón, L., and M. Dahm. "Foundations for contest success functions." *Economic Theory*, 43, 1, 81–98, 2010.

Corchón, L., and M. Dahm. "Welfare maximizing contest success functions when the planner cannot commit." *Journal of Mathematical Economics*, 47, 3, 309–317, 2011.

Corchón, L., and M. Serena. "Properties of contests: Constructing CSF from best responses." *Journal of Dynamics and Games*, 9, 2, 151–163, 2022.

Corchón, L., and R. Torregrosa. "Entry across markets and contests and some related problems." https://ssrn.com/abstract=4080919, November 12, 2022.

Corchón, L., and A. Yildizparlak. "Give peace a chance: The effect of ownership and asymmetric information on peace." *Journal of Economic Behavior & Organization*, 92, 116–126, 2013.

Cornes, R., and R. Hartley. "Asymmetric contests with general technologies." *Economic Theory*, 26, 4, 923–946, 2005.

del Corral, J., J. Prieto-Rodríguez, and R. Simmons. "The effect of incentives on sabotage: The case of Spanish football." *Journal of Sports Economics*, 11, 3, 243–260, 2010.

Coughlin, P., and S. Nitzan. "Electoral outcomes with probabilistic voting and Nash social welfare maxima." *Journal of Public Economics*, 15, 1, 113–121, 1981.

Cubel, M., and S. Sanchez-Pages. "An axiomatization of difference-form contest success functions." *Journal of Economic Behavior and Organization*, 132, Part A, 92–105, 2016.

Cueva, C. "Animal spirits in the beautiful game: Testing social pressure in professional football during the COVID-19 lockdown." OSF Preprints. doi:10.31219/osf.io/hczkj, September 11, 2020.

Dagan, N., and O. Volij. "The bankruptcy problem: A cooperative bargaining approach." *Mathematical Social Sciences*, 26, 3, 287–297, 1993.

Dasgupta, A., and K. O. Nti. "Designing an optimal contest." *European Journal of Political Economy*, 14, 4, 587–603, 1998.

Dasgupta, P., and E. Maskin. "The existence of equilibrium in discontinuous economic games, I: Theory." *Review of Economic Studies*, 53, 1, 1–26, 1986.

Davis, D., and R. Reilly. "Rent seeking with non-identical sharing rules: An equilibrium rescued." *Public Choice*, 100, 1–2, 31–38, 1999.

Dechenaux, E., D. Kovenock, and R. M. Sheremeta. "A survey of experimental research on contests, all-pay auctions and tournaments." *Experimental Economics* 18, 4, 609–669, 2015.

Dickson, A., I. MacKenzie, and P. Sekeris. "Rent dissipation in simple Tullock contests." *Games*, 13, 6, 83, 2022.

Dincecco, M. "Fiscal centralization, limited government, and public revenues in Europe, 1650–1913." *The Journal of Economic History*, 69, 1, 48–103, 2009.

Dixit, A. "Strategic behavior in contests." *American Economic Review*, 77, 5, 891–898, 1987.

Doğan, S., E. Karagözoğlu, K. Keskin, and Ç. Sağlam. "Large Tullock contests." *Journal of Economics*, 140, 2, 169–179, 2023.

Doğan, S., K. Keskin, and Ç. Sağlam. "Sabotage in team contests." *Public Choice*, 180, 3/4, 383–405, 2019.

Drugov, M., and D. Ryvkin. "Biased contests for symmetric players." *Games and Economic Behavior*, 103, 116–144, 2017.

Ehrenberg, R. G., and M. L. Bognanno. "Do tournaments have incentive effects?" *Journal of Political Economy*, 98, 6, 1307–1324, 1990a.

Ehrenberg, R. G., and M. L. Bognanno. "The incentive effects of tournaments revisited: Evidence from the European PGA Tour." *Industrial and Labor Relations Review*, 43, 3, 74-S–88-S, 1990b.

Einy, E., O. Haimanko, D. Moreno, A. Sela, and B. Shitovitz. "Equilibrium existence in Tullock contests with incomplete information." *Journal of Mathematical Economics,* 61, 241–245, 2015.

Einy, E., D. Moreno, and A. Sela. "Continuity and robustness of Bayesian equilibria in Tullock contests." *Economic Theory Bulletin,* 8, 2, 333–345,2020.

Ekelund, R. B., D. R. Street, and R. D. Tollinson. "Rent-seeking and property rights' assignment as a process: The Mesta Cartel of Medieval-Mercantile Spain." *Journal of European Economic History,* 1, 9–35, 1997.

Ekelund, R. B., and R. D. Tollinson. *Mercantilism as a Rent-Seeking Society.* College Station, Texas A&M University Press, 1981.

Epstein, G. S., Y. Mealem, and S. Nitzan. "Lotteries vs. all-pay auctions in fair and biased contests." *Economics and Politics,* 25, 1, 48–60, 2013.

Epstein, G. S., and S. Nitzan. "The politics of randomness." *Social Choice and Welfare,* 27, 2, 423–443, 2006.

Epstein, G. S., and S. Nitzan. *Endogenous Public Policy and Contests.* Springer, 2007.

Esteban-Marquillas, J., and D. Ray. "Collective action and the group paradox." *American Political Science Review,* 95, 3, 663–672, 2001.

Ewerhart, C. "Unique equilibrium in rent-seeking contests with a continuum of types." *Economics Letters,* 125, 1, 115–118, 2014.

Ewerhart, C. "Mixed equilibria in Tullock contests." *Economic Theory,* 60, 1, 59–71, 2015.

Ewerhart, C. "Contests with small noise and the robustness of the all-pay auction." *Games and Economic Behavior,* 105, 195–211, 2017.

Ewerhart, C., and F. Quartieri. "Unique equilibrium in contests with incomplete information." *Economic Theory,* 70, 1, 243–271, 2020.

Ewerhart, C., and M. Serena. " On the (im-)possibility of representing probability distributions as a difference of I.I.D. noise terms." Working Paper Series, Department of Economics, University of Zurich. www.zora.uzh.ch/id/eprint/231569/1/econwp428.pdf, 2023.

Falcone, S., and M. Rosenberg. "Agricultural modernization and land conflict." Mimeo, 2023.

Ewerhart, C., and G. Z. Sun. "The n-player Hirshleifer contest." Working paper, No. 361, Department of Economics, University of Zurich, Zurich, https://doi.org/10.5167/uzh-189517, 2022.

Fang, H. "Lottery versus all-pay auction models of lobbying." *Public Choice,* 112, 3/4, 351–371, 2002.

Faria, J., F. G. Mixon Jr, S. B. Caudill, and S. J. Wineke. "Two-dimensional effort in patent-race games and rent-seeking contests: The case of telephony." *Games,* 5, 2, 116–126, 2014.

Farmer, A., and P. Pecorino. "Legal expenditure as a rent-seeking game." *Public Choice,* 100, 3/4, 271–288, 1999.

Fearon, J. D. "Rationalist explanations for war." *International Organization,* 49, 3, 379–414, 1995.

Flamand, S., and O. Troumpounis. "Prize-sharing rules in collective rent seeking." In R. D. Congleton and A. L. Hillman (eds.), *Companion to the Political Economy of Rent Seeking.* Edward Elgar, 2015.

Franke, J. "The incentive effects of levelling the playing field – An empirical analysis of amateur golf tournaments." *Applied Economics,* 44, 9, 1193–1200, 2012a.

Franke, J. "Affirmative action in contest games." *European Journal of Political Economy,* 28, 1, 105–118, 2012b.

Franke, J., C. Kanzow, W. Leininger, and A. Schwartz. "Effort maximization in asymmetric contest games with heterogeneous contestants." *Economic Theory*, 52, 2, 589–630, 2013.

Franke, J., C. Kanzow, W. Leininger, and A. Schwartz. "Lottery versus all-pay auction contests: A revenue dominance theorem." *Games and Economic Behavior* 83, 116–126, 2014.

Franke, J., and L. Metzger. "Repeated contests with draws." Ruhr economic papers No. 1016, 2023.

Franke, J., and T. Öztürk. "Conflict networks." *Journal of Public Economics*, 126, 104–113, 2015.

Friedman, J. "A noncooperative equilibrium for supergames." *Review of Economic Studies*, 38, 1, 1–12, 1971.

Friedman, L. "Game theory models in the allocation of advertising expenditures." *Operations Research*, 6, 5, 699–709, 1958.

Fu, Q. "Endogeneous timing of contest with asymmetric information." *Public Choice*, 129, 1/2, 1–23. 2006.

Fu, Q., and J. Lu. "Micro foundations of multi-prize lottery contests: A perspective of noisy performance ranking." *Social Choice and Welfare*, 38, 3, 497–517, 2012a.

Fu, Q., and J. Lu. "The optimal multi-stage contests." *Economics Theory*, 51, 2, 351–382, 2012b.

Fu, Q., J. Lu, and Y. Pan. "Team contests with multiple pairwise battles." *American Economic Review*, 105, 7, 2120–2140, 2015.

Fu, Q., and W. Wu. "Contests theory and topics, a survey on theoretical studies of contests." In *Oxford Research Encyclopedia of Economics*, 2019.

Fu, Q., and W. Wu. "On the optimal design of biased contests." *Theoretical Economics*, 15, 4, 1435–1470, 2020.

Fudenberg, D., and J. Tirole. *Game Theory*. The MIT Press, 1991.

Fullerton, R. L., and R. P. McAfee. "Auctioning entry into tournaments." *Journal of Political Economy*, 107, 3, 573–605, 1999.

Gao, L., J. Lu, and Z. Wang. "Equilibria in two-player sequential Tullock contests." https://ssrn.com/abstract=4322145, January 4, 2023.

Garfinkel, M. R., and S. Skaperdas. "Conflict without misperceptions or incomplete information: How the future matters." *The Journal of Conflict Resolution*, 44, 6, 793–807, 2000.

Garfinkel, M. R., and C. Syropoulos. "Self-enforcing peace agreements that preserve the status quo." *Games and Economic Behavior,* 130, 148–178, 2021.

Gelder, A., and D. Kovenock. "Dynamic behavior and player types in majoritarian multi-battle contests." *Games and Economic Behavior*, 104, 444–455, 2017.

Gilsdorf, K., and V. Sukhatme. "Testing Rosen's sequential: Elimination tournament model incentives and player performance in professional tennis." *Journal of Sports Economics*, 9, 3, 287-303, 2008.

Glaezer, E., R. La Porta, F. López de Silanes, and A. Shleifer. "Do institutions cause growth?" *Journal of Economic Growth*, 9, 3, 271–303, 2004.

Glazer, A., and R. Hassin. "Sequential rent seeking." *Public Choice*, 102, 3/4, 219–228, 2000.

Goel, S., and A. Goyal. "Optimal tie-breaking rules." *Journal of Mathematical Economics,* 108, 2023, https://doi.org/10.1016/j.jmateco.2023.102872.

Goodall, J. *Through a Window: My Thirty Years with the Chimpanzees of Gombe*. Mariner Books, 2010.

Gradstein, M. "Intensity of competition: Entry and entry deterrence in rent-seeking contests." *Economics and Politics*, 7, 1, 79–91, 1995.

Gradstein, M. "Governance and growth." *Journal of Development Economics*, 73, 2, 505–518, 2004.

Grossman, H. "A general equilibrium model of insurrections." *American Economic Review*, 81, 4, 912–921, 1991.

Grossman, G., and E. Helpman. *Interest Groups and Trade Policy*. Princeton University Press, 2002.

Gürtler, O. "On sabotage in collective tournaments." *Journal of Mathematical Economics* 44, 3–4, 383–393, 2008.

Gürtler, O., and J. Münster. "Sabotage in dynamic tournaments." *Journal of Mathematical Economics*, 46, 2, 179–190, 2010.

Gürtler, O., J. Münster, and P. Nieken. "Information policy in tournaments with sabotage." *Scandinavian Journal of Economics*, 115, 3, 932–966, 2013.

Gustafsson, A., P. Gustavsson, and D. Halvarsson. "Subsidy entrepreneurs: An inquiry into firms seeking public grants." *Journal of Industry, Competition & Trade,* 20, 3, 439–478, 2020.

Hamilton, J. M., and S. M. Slutsky. "Endogenous timing in duopoly games: Stackelberg or Cournot equilibria." *Games and Economic Behavior,* 2, 1, 29–46, 1990.

Harberger, A. "Monopoly and resource allocation." *American Economic Review, Papers and Proceedings*, 44, 2, 77–87, 1954.

Hardy, I. C. W., and M. Briffa. *Animal Contests*. Cambridge University Press, 2013.

Harsanyi, J. C. "Games with incomplete information played by Bayesian players, I–III." *Management Science*, 14, 3, 159–183 (Part I); 14, 5, 320–334 (Part II); 14, 7, 486–502 (Part III), 1967–1968.

Hausken, K. "Production and conflict models versus rent-seeking models." *Public Choice*, 123, 1/2, 59–93, 2005.

Hentschel, F. "Third-party intervention in secessions." *Economics of Governance*, 23, 1, 65–82, 2022.

Hillman, A., and E. Katz. "Risk-averse rent seekers and the social cost of monopoly power." *The Economic Journal*, 94, 373, 104–110, 1984.

Hillman, A., and J. Riley. "Politically contestable rents and transfers." *Economics and Politics*, 1, 1, 17–39, 1989.

Hinnosaar, T. "Optimal sequential contests." Forthcoming in *Theoretical Economics*, 2023.

Hirshleifer, J. "Conflict and rent-seeking success functions: Ratio vs. difference models of relative success." *Public Choice*, 63, 2, 101–112, 1989.

Hirshleifer, J. "The paradox of power." *Economics and Politics*, 3, 3, 177–200, 1991.

Hirshleifer, J. "The dark side of the force." *Economic Inquiry*, 32, 1, 1–10, 1994.

Hoffman, P. "Why was it Europeans who conquered the world?" *The Journal of Economic History*, 72, 3, 601–633, 2012.

Hoffmann, M., and G. Rota-Graziosi. "Endogenous timing in general rent-seeking and conflict models." *Games and Economic Behavior*, 75, 1, 168–184, 2012.

Hoffmann, M., and G. Rota-Graziosi. "Endogenous timing in contest." In L. Corchón and M. Marini (eds.) *Handbook of Game Theory and Industrial Organization*. Edward Elgar, 2018, 147–174.

Hurley, T., and J. Shogren. "Asymmetric information contests." *European Journal of Political Economy*, 14, 4, 645–665, 1998.

Hwang, S.-H. "Technology of military conflict, military spending, and war." *Journal of Public Economics*, 96, 1/2, 226–236, 2012.

Jackson, M., and M. Morelli. "Political bias and war." *American Economic Review*, 97, 4, 1353–1373, 2007.

Jackson, M., and M. Morelli. "The reasons for wars – An updated survey." In C. Coyne (ed.), *Handbook on the Political Economy of War*. Elgar Publishing, 2011, 34–57.

Jamison, E., D. Jamison, and E. Hanushek. "The effects of education quality on mortality decline and income growth." *Economics of Education Review*, 26, 2, 772–789, 2007.

Jennings, C., and S. Sanchez-Pages. "Social capital, conflict and welfare." *Journal of Development Economics*, 124, 157–167, 2017.

Jetter, M., A. Agudelo, and A. Hassan. "The effect of democracy on corruption: Income is key." *World Development*, 74, 286–304, 2015.

Jia, H. "A stochastic derivation of the Ratio Form of contest success functions." *Public Choice*, 135, 3/4, 125–130, 2008.

Jia, H. "Contests with the probability of a draw: A stochastic foundation." *The Economic Record*, 88, 282, 391–406, 2012.

Jia, H., S. Skaperdas, and S. Vaidya. "Contest functions: Theoretical foundations and issues in estimation." *International Journal of Industrial Organization*, 31, 3, 211–222, 2013.

Jung, C., K. Krutilla, W. K. Viscusi, and R. Boyd. "The Coase theorem in a rent-seeking society." *International Review of Law and Economics*, 15, 3, 259–268, 1995.

Kahana, N., and D. Klunover. "Sequential lottery contests with multiple participants." *Economics Letters*, 163, 126–129, 2018.

Kahneman, D., and A. Tversky. "Prospect theory: An analysis of decisions under risk." *Econometrica*, 47, 2, 313–327, 1979.

Katz, E., S. Nitzan, and J. Rosenberg. "Rent-seeking for pure public goods." *Public Choice*, 65, 1, 49–60, 1990.

Kennedy, P. *The Rise and Fall of the Great Powers*. Penguin Random House, 1987.

Kimbrough, E. O., K. Laughren, and R. Sheremeta. "War and conflict in economics: Theories, applications, and recent trends." *Journal of Economic Behavior & Organization,* 178, 998–1013, 2020.

Kirkegaard, R. "Favoritism in asymmetric contests: Head starts and handicaps." *Games and Economic Behavior,* 76, 1, 226–248, 2012.

Klumpp, T., and M. K. Polborn. "Primaries and the New Hampshire effect." *Journal of Public Economics*, 90, 6–7, 1073–1114, 2006.

Klunover, D. "Punishment for sabotage in dynamic tournaments." *Journal of Mathematical Economics*, 106, May, 2023.

Kolmar, M., and H. Rommeswinkel. "Contests with group-specific public goods and complementarities in efforts." *Journal of Economic Behavior and Organization*, 89, 9–22, 2013.

Konrad, K. "Sabotage in rent-seeking contests." *Journal of Law, Economics and Organization*, 16, 1, 155–165, 2000.

Konrad, K. *Strategy and Dynamics in Contests*. Oxford University Press, 2009.

Konrad, K., and D. Kovenock. "Multi-battle contests." *Games and Economic Behavior*, 66, 1, 256–274, 2009.

Konrad, K., and D. Kovenock. "Equilibrium and efficiency in the tug-of-war." CESifo working paper series No. 1564, 2005.

Kovenock, D., and B. Roberson. "Generalizations of the General Lotto and Colonel Blotto games." *Economic Theory*, 71, 3, 997–1032, 2021.

Krueger, A. "The political economy of the rent-seeking society." *American Economic Review*, 64, 3, 291–303, 1974.

Krumer, A., and M. Lechner. "First in first win: Evidence on schedule effects in round-robin tournaments in mega-events." *European Economic Review*, 100, 412–427, 2017.

Lahiri, S., and Y. Ono. "Helping minor firms reduces welfare." *The Economic Journal*, 98, 393, 1199–1202, 1988.

Lahkar, R., and S. Mukherjee. "Optimal large population Tullock contests." *Oxford Open Economics*, 2, 1–11, 2023.

Lahkar, R., and R. Sultana. "Rent dissipation in large population Tullock contests." *Public Choice*, https://doi.org/10.1007/s11127-023-01103-72, 2023.

Lanchester, F. W. "Mathematics in warfare." In J. Newman (ed.), *The World of Mathematics*, Simon & Shusterin, vol.4, 2138–2157, 1956; anthologized from Aircraft in Warfare Constable and Co. Ltd. 1916.

Lazear, E. P. "Pay equality and industrial politics." *Journal of Political Economy*, 97, 3, 561–580. 1989.

Lazear, E. P., and S. Rosen. "Rank-order tournaments as optimum labor contracts." *Journal of Political Economy*, 89, 5, 841–864, 1981.

Lee, D. "Weakest-link contests with group-specific public good prizes." *European Journal of Political Economy*, 28, 2, 238–248, 2012.

Lee, S. "Endogenous sharing rules in collective-group rent seeking." *Public Choice*, 85, 1–2, 31–44, 1995.

Lee, I. K., and K. Hahn. "Bid-rigging in auctions for Korean public-works contracts and potential damage." *Review of Industrial Organization*, 21, 1, 73–88, 2002.

Leininger, W. "More efficient rent seeking – A Munchausen solution." *Public Choice*, 75, 1, 43–62, 1993.

Leininger, W., and C.-L. Yang. "Dynamic rent-seeking games." *Games and Economic Behavior*, 7, 3, 406–427, 1994.

Li, X., and J. Zheng. "Pure strategy Nash equilibrium in 2-contestant generalized lottery Colonel Blotto games." *Journal of Mathematical Economics*, 103, December 2022. https://doi.org/10.1016/j.jmateco.2022.102771.

Lindbeck, A., and J. W. Weibull. "Balanced-budget redistribution as the outcome of political competition." *Public Choice*, 52, 3, 273–297, 1987.

Liu, B., and J. Lu. "Optimal orchestration of rewards and punishments in rank-order contests." *Journal of Economic Theory*, 208, 105594, 2023. https://doi.org/10.1016/j.jet.2022.105594.

Liu, H., J. Lu and A. Salvo. "Willingness to fight on: Environmental quality in dynamic contests." *The Rand Journal of Economics*, 54, 2, 189–239, 2023.

Loury, G. C. "Market structure and innovation." *The Quarterly Journal of Economics*, 93, 3, 395–410, 1979.

Luo, Z., and X. Xin. "A model of rivalries with endogenous prize and strength." *Journal of Economic Behavior & Organization*, 152, 215–223, 2018.

Machiavelli, N. *Il Principe*. Antonio Blado d'Asola, 1532.

Maci, M. "Private enforcement in bid-rigging cases in the European union." *European Competition Journal*. 8, 1, 211–227, 2012.

Malueg, D., and A. Yates. "Rent seeking with private values." *Public Choice*, 119, 1/2, 161–178, 2004.

Malueg, D., and A. Yates. "Equilibria in rent-seeking contests with homogeneous success functions." *Economic Theory*, 27, 3, 719–727, 2006.

Marx, K., and F. Engels. *Manifesto of the Communist Party*. London 1848. www.marxists.org/archive/marx/works/1848/communist-manifesto/index.htm

Marx, K. *Das Kapital.* Edited by Otto Meissner. Hamburg, 1867.

Masera, F. "Violent crime and the overmilitarization of US policing." *The Journal of Law, Economics, and Organization*, 37, 3, 479–511, 2021.

Matthews, P. H., P. M. Sommers, and F. J. Peschiera. "Incentives and superstars on the LPGA tour." *Applied Economics*, 39, 1, 87–94, 2007.

Mayer, W. (ed.). *The Making of the Presidential Candidates.* Rowman and Littlefield, 2004.

Mayoral, L., and D. Ray. "Groups in conflict: Private and public prizes." *Journal of Development Economics*, 154, Article 102759, 2022.

McFadden, D. "The measurement of urban travel demand." *Journal of Public Economics*, 3, 4, 303–328, 1974.

McKinsey & Company. "And the winner is … Capturing the promise of philanthropic prizes." www.mckinsey.com/industries/social-sector/our-insights/and-the-winner-is-philanthropists-and-governments-make-prizes-count?cid=eml-web, May 2009.

Mealem, Y., and S. Nitzan. "Discrimination in contests: A survey." *Review of Economic Design*, 20, 2, 145–172, 2016.

Merton, R. K. "The Matthew effect in science." *Science*, 159, 3810, 56–63, 1968.

Milanovic, B. *Capitalism Alone.* Harvard University Press, 2019.

Mildenberger, C. D., and A. Pietri. "How does size matter for military success? Evidence from virtual worlds." *Journal of Economic Behavior & Organization*, 154, 137–155, 2018.

Minchuk, Y., B. Keren, and Y. Hadad. "Sabotaging in contests with monitoring efforts." *Managerial and Decision Economics*, 39, 6, 674–681, 2018.

Moatsos, M. "Global extreme poverty: Present and past since 1820." In *How Was Life? Volume II: New Perspectives on Well-Being and Global Inequality since 1820.* OECD, 2021.

Moldovanu, B., and A. Sela. "The optimal allocation of prizes in contests." *American Economic Review*, 91, 3, 542–558, 2001.

Möller, M. "Incentives versus competitive balance." *Economics Letters*, 117, 2, 505–508, 2012.

Mukherjee, P., and S. Munshi. "Conflict with third-party intervention and revenge: A game-theoretic exploration." *Defence and Peace Economics*, 2022, doi: 10.1080/10242694.2022.2065187.

Münster, J. "Simultaneous inter- and intra-group conflicts." *Economic Theory*, 32, 2, 333–352, 2007a.

Münster, J. "Selection tournaments, sabotage, and participation." *Journal of Economics and Management Strategy*, 16, 4, 943–970, 2007b.

Münster, J. "Contests with investment." *Managerial and Decision Economics*, 28, 8, 849–862, 2007c.

Münster, J. "Repeated contests with asymmetric information." *Journal of Public Economic Theory*, 11, 1, 89–118, 2009.

Murphy, K. M., A. Shleifer, and R. W. Vishny. "The allocation of talent: Implications for growth." *Quarterly Journal of Economics*, 106, 2, 503–530, 1991.

Myerson, R. B. "Emile Borel and the foundations of game theory." Prepared for Nobel Symposium "One Hundred Years of Game Theory." https://home.uchicago.edu/\char126\relaxrmyerson/research/boreltalk.pdf, 2021.

Myerson, R. B., and M. A. Satterthwaite. "Efficient mechanisms for bilateral trading." *Journal of Economic Theory*, 29, 2, 265–281, 1983.

Nalebuff, B., and J. E. Stiglitz. "Prizes and incentives: Towards a general theory of compensation and competition." *The Bell Journal of Economics*, 14, 1, 21–43, 1983.

Nash, J. F. "Equilibrium points in N-person games." *Proceedings of the National Academy of Sciences*, 36, 1, 48–49, 1950a.

Nash, J. F. "The bargaining problem." *Econometrica*, 18, 2, 155–162, 1950b.

Neary, H. "A comparison of rent-seeking models and economic models of conflict." *Public Choice*, 93, 3–4, 373–388, 1997.

Neugart, M., and M. Richiardi. "Sequential teamwork in competitive environments: Theory and evidence from swimming data." *European Economic Review*, 63(C), 186–205, 2013.

Nitzan, S. "Collective rent dissipation." *The Economic Journal*, 101, 409, 1522–1534, 1991a.

Nitzan, S. "Rent seeking with non-identical sharing rules." *Public Choice*, 71, 1–2, 43–50, 1991b.

Nitzan, S. "Modelling rent-seeking contests." *European Journal of Political Economy*, 10, 1, 41–60, 1994.

Nitzan, S., and K. Ueda. "Prize sharing in collective contests." *European Economic Review*, 55, 5, 678–687, 2011.

North, D., and B. Weingast. "Constitutions and commitment: The evolution of institutions governing public choice in seventeenth-century England." *The Journal of Economic History*, XLIX, 4, 1989.

Nti, K. O. "Comparative statics of contests and rent-seeking games." *International Economic Review*, 38, 1, 43–59, 1997.

Nti, K. O. "Effort and performance in group contests." *European Journal of Political Economy*, 14, 4, 769–781, 1998.

Nugent, J. B., and N. Sanchez. "The efficiency of the Mesta: A parable." *Explorations in Economic History*, 26, 3, 261–284, 1989.

Olson, M. *The Logic of Collective Action*. Harvard University Press, 1965.

Olson, M. *The Rise and Decline of Nations*. Yale University Press, 1982.

Olszewski, W., and R. Siegel. "Large contests." *Econometrica*, 84, 2, 835–854, 2016.

Osborne, M., and A. Rubinstein. *A Course in Game Theory*. The MIT Press, 1994.

Osipov, M. "The influence of the number of combatants on their losses." *Military Collection*, 1915. Translated by RL Helmbold, AS Rehm at *Naval Research Logistics* 42, 435–490, 1995.

Parente, S. L., and E. C. Prescott. "Monopoly rights: A barrier to riches." *American Economic Review*, 89, 5, 1216–1233, 1999.

Parente, S. L., and E. C. Prescott. *Barriers to Riches*. The Walras-Pareto Lectures, École des hautes études commerciales, Université de Laussane. The MIT Press, 2000.

Perc, M. "The Matthew effect in empirical data." *Journal of the Royal Society*, 11, 2014. http://doi.org/10.1098/rsif.2014.0378.

Pérez-Castrillo, D., and T. Verdier. "A general analysis of rent-seeking games." *Public Choice*, 71, 3, 335–350, 1992.

van der Ploeg, F. "Natural resources: Curse or blessing." *Journal of Economic Literature*, 49, 2, 366–420, 2011.

Polishchuk, L. I., and A. Tonis. "Endogenous contest success functions: A mechanism design approach." *Economic Theory*, 52, 1, 271–297, 2013.

Prados de la Escosura, L., and C. V. Rodríguez-Caballero. "War, pandemics, and modern economic growth in Europe." *Explorations in Economic History,* 86, 2022. https://doi.org/10.1016/j.eeh.2022.101467.

Protopappas, K. "Manipulation of moves in sequential contests." *Social Choice and Welfare*, https://doi.org/10.1007/s00355-023-01461-7, 2023.

Reinganum, J. "The timing of innovation: Research, development and diffusion." In R. Willig and R. Schmalensee (eds.),. North-Holland, 49–908, 1989.

Reny, P. J. "Nash equilibrium in discontinuous games." *Economic Theory*, 61, 553–569, 2016.

Roberson, B. "The Colonel Blotto game." *Economic Theory*, 29, 1, 1–24, 2006.

Roemer, J. E. *Theories of Distributive Justice.* Harvard University Press, 1996.

Rosen, S. "Prizes and incentives in elimination tournaments." *American Economic Review*, 76, 4, 701–715, 1986.

Rosenberg, M. "External players in the political economy of natural resources." Mimeo, 2020.

Ryvkin, D. "Contests with doping." *Journal of Sports Economics*, 14, 3, 253–275, 2013.

Sanchez-Pages, S. "On the social efficiency of conflict." *Economics Letters*, 90, 1, 96–101, 2006.

Schaffer, M. E. "Are profit maximizers the best survivors? A Darwinian model of economic natural selection." *Journal of Economic Behavior and Organization*, 12, 1, 29–45, 1989.

Schaller, Z., and S. Skaperdas. "Bargaining and conflict with up-front investments: How power asymmetries matter." *Journal of Economic Behavior and Organization,* 176, 212–225, 2020.

Scharfstein, D. "Product-market competition and managerial slack." *Rand Journal of Economics*, 19, 1, 147–155, 1988.

Scharfstein, D., and J. Stein. "The dark side of internal capital markets: Divisional rent-seeking and inefficient investment." *Journal of Finance*, 55, 6, 2537–2564, 2000.

Sela, A. "Best-of-three all-pay auctions." *Economics Letters*, 112, 1, 67–70, 2011.

Sela, A. "Optimal allocations of prizes and punishments in Tullock contests." *International Journal of Game Theory*, 49, 3, 749–771, 2020.

Sen, A. "Labour allocation in a cooperative enterprise." *Review of Economic Studies*, 33, 4, 361–371, 1966.

Serena, M. "Quality contests." *European Journal of Political Economy*, 46, 15–25, 2017.

Serena, M. "Harnessing beliefs to optimally disclose contestants' types." *Economic Theory*, 74, 763–792, 2022.

Serrano, R. "Sixty-seven years of the Nash program: Time for retirement?" *SERIEs*, 12, 1, 35–48, 2021.

Shaffer, S., and J. Shogren. "Infinitely repeated contests: How strategic interaction affects the efficiency of governance." *Regulation & Governance*, 2, 2, 234–252, 2008.

Shapiro, C., and H. Varian. *Information Rules.* Harvard Business School Press, 1999.

Sheremeta, R. S. "Behavior in group contests: A review of experimental research." *Journal of Economic Surveys*, 32, 3, 683–704, 2018.

Shubik, M. "Does the fittest necessarily survive?" In M. Shubik (ed.), *Readings in Game Theory and Political Behavior.* Doubleday. 1954.

Sisak, D. "Multiple-prize contests – The optimal allocation of prizes." *Journal of Economic Surveys*, 23, 1, 82–114, 2009.

Skaperdas, S. "Contest success functions." *Economic Theory*, 7, 2, 283–290, 1996.

Skaperdas, S., and B. Grofman. "Modeling negative campaigning." *American Political Science Review*, 89, 1, 49–61, 1995.

Skaperdas, S., and S. Vaidya. "Persuasion as a contest." *Economic Theory*, 51, 2, 465–486, 2012.

Snyder, J. "Election goals and the allocation of campaign resources." *Econometrica*, 57, 3, 637–660, 1989.

Stackelberg, H. *Markform und Gleichgewicht.* Verlag von Julius Springer, 1934.

Sun Tzu. *The Art of War.* https://sites.ualberta.ca/~enoch/Readings/The_Art_Of_War.pdf

Sydsæter, K., and P. Hammond. *Essential Mathematics for Economic Analysis*, 4th ed. Pearson, 2012.

Szidarovsky, F., and K. Okuguchi. "On the existence and uniqueness of pure Nash equilibrium in rent-seeking games." *Games and Economic Behavior*, 18, 1, 135–140, 1997.

Szymanski, S. "The economic design of sporting contests." *Journal of Economic Literature*, 41, 4, 1137–1187, 2003.

Tirole, J. *The Theory of Industrial Organization*. The MIT Press, 1988.

Torvik, R. "Natural resources, rent-seeking and welfare." *Journal of Development Economics*, 67, 2, 455–470, 2002.

Tullock, G. "The welfare cost of tariffs, monopolies and theft." *Western Economic Journal*, 5, 3, 224–232, 1967.

Tullock, G. "Efficient rent-seeking." In J. M. Buchanan, R. D. Tollison, and G. Tullock (eds.), *Towards a Theory of a Rent-Seeking Society*, Texas A&M University Press, 97–112, 1980.

Tullock, G. "Why did the Industrial Revolution occur in England?" In C. K. Rowley, R. D. Tollison, and G. Tullock (eds.), *The Political Economy of Rent-Seeking*. Topics in Regulatory Economics and Policy, vol. 1. Springer, 1988.

Tullock, G. "The origin rent-seeking concept." *International Journal of Business and Economics*, 2, 1, 1–8, 2003.

Ueda, K. "Oligopolization in collective rent seeking." *Social Choice and Welfare*, 19, 3, 613–626, 2002.

Usher, D. "The dynastic cycle and the stationary state." *The American Economic Review* , 79, 5, 1031–1044, 1989.

Vázquez-Sedano, A. "Sharing the effort costs in collective contests." *The B.E. Journal of Theoretical Economics*, 18, 1, 2018.

Vela Tejada, J. "Warfare, history and literature in the archaic and classical periods: The development of Greek military treatises." *Zeitschrift für Alte Geschichte*, Franz Steiner Verlag, 129–146, 2004.

Vesperoni, A., and A. Yildizparlak. "Contests with draws: Axiomatization and equilibrium." *Economic Inquiry*, 57, 3, 1597–1616, 2019.

Vickrey, W. "Counterspeculation, auctions, and competitive sealed tenders." *The Journal of Finance*, 16, 1, 8–37, 1961.

Vives, X. *Oligopoly Pricing: Old Ideas and New Tools*. The MIT Press, 2001.

Vojnovic, M. *Contest Theory: Incentive Mechanisms and Ranking Methods*. Cambridge University Press, 2015.

Ward, B. "The firm in Illyria: Market syndicalism." *American Economic Review*, 48, 4, 566–589, 1958.

Wärneryd, K. "Distributional conflict and jurisdictional organization." *Journal of Public Economics*, 69, 3, 435–450, 1998.

Wärneryd, K. "Replicating contests." *Economics Letters*, 71, 3, 323–327, 2001.

Wärneryd, K. "Information in conflicts." *Journal of Economic Theory*, 110, 1, 121–136, 2003.

Watts, A. "Contests with gender bias: Evidence from a culinary competition." *Applied Economics,* 54, 60, 6875–6886, 2022.

von Weizsäcker, C. C. "A welfare analysis of barriers to entry." *Bell Journal of Economics*, 11, 2, 399–420, 1980.

Xu, J., C. Zhang, and J. Zhang. "Three-player sequential contests with asymmetric valuations." *Operations Research Letters*, 48, 5, 635–640, 2020.

Yildizparlak, A. "An application of contest success functions for draws on European soccer." *Journal of Sports Economics*, 19, 8, 1191–1212, 2018.

The first draft of this book was finished in November, 30, 2021, in Alicante and Madrid. The last draft was completed in August, 23, 2023, in Alicante and Madrid.

Index

Printed in the United States
by Baker & Taylor Publisher Services